BETWEEN KITTYHAWK AND THE MOON

Memoirs of an Aviation Pioneer

Written by Russell F. Holderman
Compiled by Nancy Holderman Durante

BETWEEN KITTYHAWK AND THE MOON

Memoirs of an Aviation Pioneer

Written by Russell F. Holderman

Compiled by Nancy Holderman Durante

Hope you enjoy reading about my uncle's
contribution to the history of aviation.

Nancy Holderman Durante

First Published 2009
Copyright © 2009 by Nancy Holderman Durante

ISBN: 1-4392-2812-4
ISBN-13: 9781439228128
Visit www.booksurge.com to order additional copies.

For information contact Nancy Holderman Durante.
Printed in the United States of America

PREFACE

This book is the story of the early years of Russell Holderman's contribution to aviation as a true pioneer of aviation. It spans the decades mainly from 1910 – 1940. This book was written by Russ and has been left in the format he used. He expressed many true feelings of the thrill of aviation and his sense of the "feeling of flying." The thrill of the first flight was as exciting as the thrill of flying with the Blue Angels some 40 years later.

Several decades have passed since the writing of this story. We can only imagine how Russ would feel today with the airline industry and space travel advances that continue to take place.

The pictures and other documents that are included in this book are all from Russ Holderman's private collection, and family albums, unless otherwise noted.

1950

MY SECOND GREATEST FLYING THRILL

by Past President Russ Holderman

Russell F. Holderman

After 47 years of active flying, I have just experienced my second greatest of many thrilling flying experiences—a supersonic flight with one of the famous Navy Blue Angels in a Grumman two-place Cougar jet. I say second, because I shall always remember my first thrill of being airborne in a power plane alone, nearly 47 years ago.

Last April, during the World Congress of Flight at Las Vegas, as president of the Early Birds, I was invited by Commander Knott, who is in charge of the Blue Angels, to take a flight in one of the Navy's F9F Cougar jets. As conditions were unfavorable on the scheduled day, the Commander called me at a latter date when the Angels were to fly a show at the Westchester County Airport at White Plains, N. Y. Of course I reported promptly.

After some delay, which seemed like hours, as this famous team prepared for their exhibition that afternoon, Lt. Don McKee said, "Russ, jump into this monkey suit and sign this release while I make out a flight plan. At last the time had come. I had a little difficulty zipping the flight suit past my expanding middle, but I made it.

Climbing into the rear cockpit of this sleek, beautiful plane, I sat among instruments much like those in the Gannett Lockheed, but as I looked out, I felt as though I were inside a missile. An aviation machinist's mate strapped me in and gave me instructions as to the ejection procedures 'just in case.' He said, "Feel this bar over your head. If the Lieutenant gives the word to bail out, pull this down. The canopy will blow off, the cannon shell under your seat will fire you and the seat free, then pull the parachute rip cord and enjoy your ride down." Just as simple as that!

The helmet was adjusted, the oxygen tube firmly snapped into place, the intercom and microphone were hooked up and we were ready to go.

Lt. McKee had obtained clearance from the control tower and we taxied past six one-place Grumman Tigers which would later show the crowd some real precision close-formation high-speed acrobatics by the world's finest precision team, the Blue Angels.

We were cleared for immediate take-off on runway 16, and as jet engines do not require warming up, we started down the runway. Being used to thousands of hours of piston engine take-offs, I was surprised at the smooth acceleration of the jet engine, slowly it seemed to me, but I guess that was because there is no noise. We took off, landing gear up and soon went into a steep climb and a left turn. My view changed rapidly from the confined space of the airport to the entire expanse of Long Island Sound,

the Island, and the ocean in the background.

Making a large circle, we passed over the Bronx where in 1911 I built and tried to fly a glider in the baseball field below us. It seemed like seconds and we were at 16,000 feet. In the pressurized, air-conditioned cockpit, it was very comfortable. In our conversation I stressed how I envied young men like Don who have the opportunity to fly such fine performing aircraft.

Soon Don said, "Russ, go ahead—take the controls." At first I realized I was over-controlling a little and used the rudder to coordinate my turns, as I had always done with the Lockheed, forgetting that there is no torque such as in a propeller aircraft. Don informed me that it was necessary to use the rudder but very little. Soon I felt like a kid again, wishing my wife could enjoy my latest thrill with me. Instead, she was sweating out my return, not realizing that this modern airplane is one of the safest of the hundreds I have flown.

Don told me to go where I wished. I maneuvered so that from 20,000 feet, in a slight dive, I was circling Roosevelt Field where Lindberg had taken off on his flight to Paris. During the First World War I had been an instructor there (then called Hazelhurst) and at the same field (known as Moisant Field) I had first soloed in 1913. At that time I flew less than 50 mph. Now over the same spot we were doing over 650 mph.

Don made turns and dives to give me the experience of 5 to 6 g's. At 5 g's you have pressure against the seat equal to five times the weight of your body, and I felt as though my head was going through my collar. Don then maneuvered so we were flying a few seconds weightless—a delightful feeling.

We then returned to the airport and Don explained that he would put on the speed brakes. I'm glad he warned me, for it was like it feels in a high-speed boat with the power suddenly shut off. This brought his speed down to 550 mph. He also warned me that he would fly across the field at this speed, making a sharp turn to the left which would cre-

ate about 4½ g's. Landing gear down, we made our approach, which looked to me as though we were coming in too high, but when the flaps were lowered, we sank rapidly. Don made a beautiful nose-high landing at about 140 mph, our speed decreased, the nose wheel touched and the thrill of a lifetime was over.

How important I felt as we taxied past the large crowd which was soon to be entertained by boys whom I envy but admire for their courage and ability. I felt that indeed I was born forty years too soon.

DEDICATION

This book is dedicated to my wonderful and loving father John Wilbur Holderman. Dad was Russ Holderman's younger brother by 18 years, and thus when Dad was born, Russ influenced the choice of name so he would be named after Wilbur Wright. (See chapter 21.)

Dad worked with Russ on this book in the fifties, but was unable to complete the process due to illness. Dad passed away at an early age.

I will pass this book on to my niece and nephew so their children can experience the thrills that "Uncle Russ" once felt during this amazing period of aviation history.

One of my favorite stories that Dad would tell goes like this:

In the early days of aviation, Russ would try to interest people in an airplane ride. He would take a plane out to a field in Long Island (somewhere near where Roosevelt Field is today) and his wife Dot, would sell hot dogs. No one was interested in a ride. But planted in the crowd was his young brother who was just waiting for a ride. So Russ would say to the crowd "who wants to go for a ride?" When no one responded, he would say "how about you, sonny?" The two would take off for a short spin over the field. After they landed, and the young brother (my Dad) was so happy, Russ would then say to the crowd, "OK folks, now who else would like to go for a ride?" And then he would finally get someone to take a ride. And so Russ was able to share his enthusiasm and love of flying.

ACKNOWLEDGEMENTS

Thank you to all who have helped in any way to finish this project:

My Dad, John Wilbur Holderman who encouraged this project in the fifties and sixties.

Brian J. Duddy, a native and resident of LeRoy, N.Y. He graduated from LeRoy High School, earning his private pilot's license at the new LeRoy airport while still in high school. He attended Embry Riddle Aeronautical University earning a BS in Aeronautical Engineering. He has an MA in History from Wright State University and an MS in Management from St. Mary's University. He served 24 years in the United States Air Force, retiring in 2007 as a Lieutenant Colonel. He has previously written articles for *Flying Safety, Defense Acquisition, Technology & Logistics*, and *Military Modeling* magazines. In the summer of 2008, he published the book *Wings Over LeRoy*. Brian has provided ongoing advice and encouragement throughout this project.

Mary Jane and Ernest J. Feleppa, Ph.D., my husband's sister and her husband. Ernie provided assistance in putting the manuscript into publishable form and Mary Jane provided essential sustenance to keep us going during the production phases.

My brother, William Russell Holderman, for finding another box of family photos in his basement, at the last minute.

And my husband Paul J. Durante who provided continual encouragement and support.

HISTORICAL INFORMATION
RUSSELL HOLDERMAN

1913   First Solo Flight, Mineola, NY
1917-1918 World War I Flight Instructor, U.S. Army Air Service
1918-1920 U.S. Post Office Flying Service – Mechanic, Pilot, Manager of the
      Eastern Division
1920-1928 Own Flight Service, Airplane Sales
1928-1936 D.W. Flying Service, Manager and President
1934-1972 Holderman Air Service, President and Owner
1936-1964 Chief Pilot, Gannett Newspapers
1960-1972 Consultant for Page Airways
Retired in 1972 (28,000 hours flying time)

LICENSES

C.A.A. License	#227	1927
C.A.A. License	#213	Airplane and Engine
F.A.A. License	#227	Air Transport Rated
Glider License	#166	
Glider License	# 80	
F.A.I	# 33	Signed by Orville Wright
R.M.A. (Military)	W.W.I	Instructor Rating 1918

MILITARY SERVICE

World War I 1917-1918
Flight Instructor U.S. Army Air Service, Mineola, NY

World War II 1942-1946
Lieutenant Commander, U.S. Naval Reserves
C.A.A. Contractor
C.P.T. (Civil Pilot Training)
Civil Air Patrol
Submarine Patrol

AWARDS & TROPHIES

Rogot Trophy – Airplane Model Contest – 1911
Winner of numerous Air Races, including Curtiss Trophy Race (main event) at Miami, FL – 1939

Runner-up Trophy – New York to Miami Air Race (lost by 36 seconds)
Air Force Association Citation – Air Pioneer
World's Loop Record – Glider – 50 consecutive loops from 7,200 feet
Award of Distinction – Women's Committee of 100 for Birmingham
U.S. Post Office Dept. Public Service Award – 50th Anniversary of the Airmail – 1968
Early Bird Plaque – Commemorating 50 years as Pilot – 1962
C.A.A. No. 1 Honor Award – Completion of 40 years as a Pilot – 1953
Legion of Merit – OX-5 Aviation Pioneers – 1964
Aviation Hall of Fame – OX-5 Aviation Pioneers – 1972

MEMBERSHIPS

National Aeronautics Association
Aviators Post #743 (American Legion)
Early Birds of Aviation – Past President and Trustee
OX-5 Aviation Pioneers – Governor
Airmail Pioneers
National Aviation Club
U.S. Naval Academy Foundation
Air Force Association
Aeronautics Fellow – Rochester Museum of Arts and Sciences 1943
Honorary Member Blue Angels
Wings Club
Silver Wings
Retired Officers Club
Quiet Birdman
Vieilles Tiges (Early Birds of France)

Russell Holderman, 1941

Russell Holderman, LT Commander, USNR

Russell Holderman with Gannett Newspapers plane

Rochester Museum of Arts and Sciences

CITATION

of

RUSSELL F. HOLDERMAN

in the field of aeronautics

Fellow of Rochester Museum of Arts and Sciences
(F.R.M.

Citation of Russell F. Holderman

LIEUTENANT COMMANDER, USNR, and Rochester's man of the skies, we salute you for your achievements of first magnitude in the field of aviation, with an approaching two million miles to your credit without accident.

You have piloted scores of America's most distinguished citizens from airport to airport, across the expanse of this republic. Today you are the master pilot of the Gannett Newspaper planes and leading officer and manager of important air fields. All this makes you as much at home in Miami as it does in Mitchell Field or Rochester.

Aviation was a choice you made while yet a youth inspired by accounts of the Wright Brothers. No mere novice were you at the age of fourteen, when with your colleagues you constructed a glider which unfortunately didn't soar, but fortunately challenged you to achieve the mastery which is now yours.

Rochester numbers you as its most accomplished airman and is proud to claim you as its own. Your prizes and trophies have served to mark you with the seal of wide approval.

Your government has not ignored your acumen, for it has chosen you as an Associate Member of the Naval Aviation Candidate Selection Board, but more than appointments and prizes is the affection of your fellow citizens. It would take a lengthy article and even an inspiring book, which we invite you to write, to record all of your experiences and achievements.

Because this Academic Council recognizes the true worth of your contributions to the field of aviation, and because of your long record of safe flying which inspires confidence in air travel, we hail you as Fellow of Rochester Museum of Arts and Sciences, and gladly present you with this certificate in testimony thereof.

FÉDÉRATION AÉRONAUTIQUE

INTERNATIONALE

AERO CLUB OF AMERICA

No 3263.

The above-named Club, recognized by the Fédération Aéronautique Internationale, as the governing authority for the United States of America, certifies that *Russell F. Holderman*

born 26 day of *Feb 1895*, has fulfilled all the conditions required by the Fédération Aéronautique Internationale, for an aviator pilot, and is brevetted as such.

Dated *Nov 27* 1918

Alan R. Hawley
President.

Augustus Post
Secretary.

[SEAL]

Signature of pilot:

Russell F. Holderman

REGISTRATION CERTIFICATE

This is to certify that in accordance with the
Selective Service Proclamation of the President of the United States

Russell Frederick Holderman
(First name) (Middle name) (Last name)

49 Brookside Drive Brighton Mon Co. N.Y
(Place of residence)
(This will be identical with line 2 of the Registration Card)

has been duly registered this 27 day of April 1942

Ray Draper
(Signature of registrar)

Registrar for Local Board 560 Brighton N.Y
(Number) (City or county) (State)

THE LAW REQUIRES YOU TO HAVE THIS CARD IN YOUR
PERSONAL POSSESSION AT ALL TIMES

D. S. S. Form 2
(Revised 6/9/41) 2897   16—21631

1903 1916

MEMBER - 1959

This is to certify that

RUSSELL HOLDERMAN

is a member of the EARLY BIRDS in good standing
with dues paid in full

Russell Holderman

President

Past President

Early Birds

Office—49 BROOKSIDE DR.
ROCHESTER 18, N. Y.

Holderman Air Service Inc.
ROCHESTER, NEW YORK
AVIATION CONSULTANT • AIRPLANE SALES

1912

1962

Phone DUDLEY 1-3141

RUSSELL HOLDERMAN—president
A.T.R. 227

Echoes of the 1972 Induction Ceremony

OX5 CLUB OF AMERICA AVIATION HALL OF FAME

Visis Gentry and Méeard wil the name of Amelia Earhart on the Hall of Fame as l/oetleoks on.

WALTER BEECH †
Wichita, Kansas
Pioneer, aviator and aircraft manufacturer. First flight in a Pusher in 1914. Test pilot, Swallow Airplane Co., Wichita. Founded and developed the Travelair Co., later known as Beech Aircraft Co. A life dedicated to the creation of the aviation industry to serve the world.

WALTER R. BULLOCK
Lakeville, Minnesota
1916—Soloed in a Jenny. Early barnstormer, instructor and veteran airline pilot with enviable record of flying hours. Built first airport and hangar in Minnesota. Senior Captain Northwest Airlines until retirement in 1961.

ARTHUR J. DAVIS
2121 Abbott Rd., E. Lansing, Mich.
Began career in 1918, Army Signal Corps. In a Jenny. Stunt and racing pilot, mechanic, instructor, airport owner and skywriter. Winner of many races; high point winner for 12 straight years in shows all over Florida. Served in Ferry Command, World War II, to all bases in the Pacific.

DOUGLAS H. DAVIS †
Griffin, Georgia
1934—First civilian to win over Army and Navy in racing. Won Barber & Baldwin Trophy for most meritorious flying. 1934—Winner Bendix Trophy. Contributed more to aviation in his career than others than any other individual.

WILLIAM C. DIEHL
7604 Park Ave., N. Bergen, N.J.
A pioneer in "home builts" starting in 1913. Civilian instructor prior to World War I, then military instructor, U.S. Signal Corps. Barnstormer, flight school operator, test pilot Curtiss-Wright. First to land at Teterboro Airport, was lifetime pilot beyond age of 70.

JAMES H. DOOLITTLE
233 Marguerita, Santa Monica, Cal.
A symbol of flight, reaching great heights in both civil and military aviation. A racing pilot of renown. An aeronautical and scientific pioneer; navigation and instrument flights. Greatest achievement was leadership in the Tokyo Air Raid, World War II.

AMELIA EARHART †
Atchison, Kansas
1918—Soloed after ten hours instruction. Holds international License No. 17. Set Women's Altitude Record of 14,000 feet. Broke Women's Transcontinental Record in 1932. First woman to fly across continent and ocean non-stop. Holds distinguished flying cross—only Woman Chevalier in French Legion of Honor.

JOHN J. FRISBIE †
Mineola, N.Y.
Hot air balloonist and parachute jumper 1888. Pilot—commenced aviation career and built first plane 1910, Mineola, N.Y. Made first airplane flight over Rochester in 1911. Exhibition Tour through U.S., Mexico and Cuba, 1910-11. F.A.I. License Number 24.

RUSSELL F. HOLDERMAN
49 Brookside Dr., Rochester, N.Y.
Lifetime career in aviation began in 1913. Military instructor World War I, Air Mail Pilot and Manager, Eastern Division, U.S. Air Mail early 20's. World War II, operated flight school for Naval Cadets. Achieved fame as a promoter of commercial aircraft for business and pleasure.

GROVER LOENING
20 Harbor Pt., Key Biscayne, Fla.
Engineer—Pilot—Designer—Industry Executive—Author. 1913—Assistant to Orville Wright. 1921—Recipient Collier Trophy. Pioneered and developed first retractable landing gear; first amphibian. 1926—Organizer Pan American Goodwill Flight.

A.B. McMULLEN
6103 Woodmont Rd., Alexandria, Va.
Began career 1917 as flight instructor flying OX5 powered Jenny. Barnstormer, aircraft dealer, builder, owner of several flight schools, one of nation's first flying farmers. Florida's Director of Aviation 1933; Chief Airports Section, Bureau Air Commerce 1936; Executive Vice President, Secretary and Manager, National Association State Aviation Officials. World War II, commanded four largest Transatlantic Air Transport Command Bases; Deputy Commander North African Division ATC.

EDWARD V. RICKENBACKER
45 Rockefeller Plaza, New York, N.Y.
America's "Ace of Aces," shot down 26 German Air Planes World War I. One of the world's most famous auto racing champions. Recognized and managed Eastern Air Lines on large expansion program. Survived a crash in the South Pacific, World War II, that generated an organization with humanitarian and patriotic objectives.

MAJOR WILLIAM B. ROBERTSON †
St. Louis, Mo.
One of first to enlist in Aviation Section, U.S. Signal Corps, 1917. 1920—Organized Robertson Aircraft Co., St. Louis, holder of Contract Air Mail No. 2. Established Lambert-St. Louis Flying Field. Employed and sponsored Charles A. Lindbergh. Creator of famous Robin monoplane 1918-27—Largest dealer in war surplus airplanes.

BASIL L. ROWE
743 Alhambra Circle, Coral Gables, Fla.
Career began in 1916, U.S. Army Signal Corps. Barnstormer, racing pilot, and one of the first fixed base operators. A career pilot with Pan American and recognized as their "Pathfinder," for their military airlifts from Miami to Africa during World War II—and Korean Airlifts.

ELLIOTT WHITE SPRINGS †
Fort Mill, S.C.
Ace World War I. Test pilot for Loening-Willard-Fowler Airplane Co. Flew in first international air races. A lifetime interest in the field of general aviation.

CHARLES I. STANTON
1709 N. Harvard St., Arlington, Va.
1917—Lieutenant, U.S. Army Air Service. 1927—Aeronautics Branch, Dept. of Commerce in charge of design, construction and maintenance, Federal Airways System. 1942—Administrator C.A.A., responsible for all C.A.A. activities world-wide.

STANLEY VAUGHN †
Columbus, Ohio
1907—flew home-built glider. Professional career began in 1913 with flight training, followed by mechanical work, design, supervision, piloting. During World War II, he supervised 4,300 personnel, Curtiss-Wright Corp. His knowledge of air dynamics obtained through 58 years in aircraft design industry, led to the acquisition of many patents.

JAMES R. WEDELL †
Patterson, Louisiana
A designer, builder and pilot of racing as a civilian instructor World War I. Winner of Bendix, Thompson and Phillips trophies and Shell Speed Dash. The famous Wedell-Williams racer was his best-known product.

CHARLES F. WILLARD †
1860 Hillhurst Ave., Los Angeles, Cal.
Early Bird—Pilot—Designer—Manufacturer. Career began in 1908, New York, as student of Glenn Hammond Curtiss. Exhibition flying 1909-12 in Curtiss aircraft. Chief Engineer, Glenn L. Martin, 1912-14. Holds F.A.I. License No. 10 and California License No. 4. Through shows and exhibitions, he created the desire to fly.

LLOYD D. YOST
225 Skeleoch Dr. W., Dunedin, Fla.
Enlisted 1918 and served as military instructor. Barnstormed until 1921 to become fixed base operator. Winner Ford Reliability Tour with Waco 10. Pilot World Wars I and II; F.A.A. license No. 58.

GEORGE A. PAGE, Jr.
2551 Taylor Rd., Reynoldsburg, Ohio
Professional career began in 1913 with flight training, followed by mechanical work, design, supervision, piloting. During World War II, he supervised 4,300 personnel, Curtiss-Wright Corp. His knowledge of air dynamics obtained through 58 years in aircraft design industry, led to the acquisition of many patents.

† deceased

OUTLINE
BETWEEN KITTY HAWK AND THE MOON

CHAPTER I
THE TAKEOFF

Between Kitty Hawk and the Moon, the sky was full of people.

Between the Wrights and Neil Armstrong, the story was written in a thousand ways and a dozen tongues, sung to the tune of singing struts, painted with ice and dust, milky cloud, soupy fog and blood.

Frankie Cordova hit a mountain in Africa. He was ferrying a bomber to the British for Pan American Airways Ferry Service when death reached out and grabbed him. That was on April 12, 1942. Frankie was 38. He had flown many planes many times.

Not long afterward, Brigadier General James H. (Jimmy) Doolittle made a special trip to Washington to pin the Army Air Corps wings on his two sons. Then he went off to bomb Tokyo.

Sonny Harris of Jamaica, L.I., who as a boy in knee breeches had pestered me with questions about Curtiss biplanes and Liberty motors while I was trying to woo his sister 24 years before, was ferrying bombers out of Miami to unnamed stepping stones in the South Atlantic and thus across the ocean to Africa.

Unlike Frankie Cordova, Doolittle and Harris came back to fly, again and again.

Cordova would never get the Congressional Medal. Neither would Harris. The gallant Doolittle won his Congressional honor in the way he gained all his laurels….. the Distinguished Flying Cross for his first cross-country flight from Pablo Beach, FL to San Diego, CA in 1922; the Oak Leaf cluster for further spectacular feats, and countless other awards worn becomingly on an unassuming brow. These he won by making himself a master of his art…....the science of aeronautics combined with the business of taking a machine into the air and bending it to his will.

The wartime Doolittle, and to a lesser extent men like Cordova and Harris were symbols, the result of 24 years of development in American aviation which followed the first World War. Doolittle's feats were those of one who kept pace.

But this is not to be the story of the Doolittles, the Cordovas and the Harrises alone. It is one man's backstage notes on the drama of man's first great achievement in movement and motion in the 20th Century.......his freeing himself from the earth which had held him bound for countless ages, his taking wing at last, powered by an engine.

This is but a chapter in an unended tale which began with pistons, moved to jets and then to rocketry. It is a stop on the way from Dec. 17, 1903 at Kitty Hawk to July 20, 1969 on the Moon. What it will tell is a story of forward movement, higher altitude and greater speed in the early years of the Air Age to which the Wright Brothers gave birth and without which the Space Age would have remained only a dream in the dancing minds of visionaries.

The early way was fraught with tragedy and sorrow, destruction and misfortune, disappointment and discouragement. Brave men died heroic deaths unsung. Brilliant men were killed before their time; fortunes were made and lost; dreams were broken and hopes were obliterated.

Those who survived saw many things come to pass. Doolittle, Claire L. Chennault of the Flying Tigers, Canada's legendary Billy Bishop, America's Eddie Rickenbacker were among them and made many of these things happen.

This account comes from one man whose business for 57 years has been flying. It should serve to give the record chronology, if nothing else.

When I first soloed a power plane in 1913, my only instrument was a 12-inch piece of string. Today, the panel board of even a light trainer plane shines like a jeweler's show window with many dials and the faces of marvelous instruments.

My purpose is specific. It is to tell what happened in the years immediately following 1913.

The air may be bumpy and the plane may vibrate. There will be forced landings and crashes, fires in the sky, driving sleet, ice on the wings and cold fear in the heart. But there are a thousand stories to be told by any airman about the men he has lived and flown with, and about the fears which have beset him there also, miles above his Earth.

Each flyer in his time meets many men like himself, but some are more reckless, some more daring, some less fortunate, others more cautious. More perhaps than any other arena of our endeavor, flying has drawn the daring spirits of our time....... the Doolittles, the Chennaults, the Bert Acostas and the Clarence Chamberlins. Men now gone, great flying men like Bill Lindley, and Freddie Lund, racing demons like young

Dick Bennett, pioneers like Lyman Doty, Red McCloskey and Max Miller, who flew the first official airmail flight, soaring geniuses like Warren Eaton, Jack O'Meara and Dick duPont all wrote their tales in the sky.

It is left to one who remains to tell their tales along with his own.

CHAPTER 2
BRONX AIR FIELD

One vital statistic: I was born in Buffalo in 1895 and transplanted at an early age to the Bronx.

Aside from its many other distinctions, the Bronx is of particular significance to airmen for two reasons. One is that it produced Alford J. (Major Al) Williams, who chose a flying life and wrote his name in smoke and speed across the sky. Another is that it had the old Morris Park Race Track. The track had passed through its days of glory as a playground for horse followers when the Aeronautic Society of America took it over and made it New York's first aerodome.

And there on Election Day, Nov. 3, 1908, some 20,000 people, including me, assembled to watch the society's first aerial exhibition and tournament. And if the occasion provided a cruel anti-climax in that none of the power planes rose into the air, it was not without its thrills. We could see and inspect the power planes and see the gliders and tiny model airplanes constructed of bits of wood, paper, linen and glue by our Aero Science Club of New York. We called them aeroplanes then.

Thirteen is an age susceptible to hero worship, and to my contemporary fellow members of the model plane club and me, the men who had brought their full-sized airplanes to the meet were figures of heroic proportions endowed with magical powers, strange beings who had conquered the air and made it theirs.

It was a beautiful day, and the weather could in no way be blamed for the failure of the power planes to rise and fly. A wonderful sky seemed to beckon the airmen, and a bright sun caressed the curious thousands of spectators with a summerlike warmth. New York has always been a city of crowds, but none perhaps was ever so patient as that one. This may have been because almost everyone came through the fences instead of the gates.

It may have been also that perhaps none of those thousands had ever seen an airplane in flight. And before that day, most of them had never seen a plane on the ground. And among them must have been hundreds who still believed that the Wright Brothers were myths and that Glenn Curtiss was only another jinx conjured up by the newspapers.

The curiosity that brought them there was the same brand of curiosity that had brought people to the banks of the Hudson to watch Robert Fulton's steamboat a hundred years before, the kind that brought people boiling from their houses to see the early horseless carriages.

This crowd was curious and in its patience exhibited a forbearance uncommon in American bleacherites. But there were many times when its patience was tried sorely, for everything happened to delay the meet.

Plane designers and pilots, each with his own mechanic, spent long hours puttering, attempting to tune motors which when turning over emitted only weak, intermittent gasps.

These pioneers of the singing strut and the soaring wing worked like ants around their individual anthills, oiling this, tightening that, twisting wires, bolts and screws, testing controls, listening, pulling, hauling, sweating.

The groups around each plane were like surgeons around a patient. At frequent intervals, the motionless mechanical invalids coughed, sputtered, spewed smoke or an occasional gob of flame, then groaned and were ominously silent.

Little crowds gravitated to each plane as it was wheeled from its stable-hangar between the grandstand and the old race track proper. Above it all was a constant buzzing.....the buzzing of the crowd, warm in its seats, and the buzzing around each plane. This summery droning was split occasionally by a loud explosion or a brief series of sharp blasts, followed closely by a cloud of smoke from a stubborn motor.

The planes shook and trembled, but were held together by some miracle of design and execution, one wrought with wires, bamboo sticks, linen and pipes.

A mechanic who persuaded his motor to run for more than a few minutes was regarded by the others as either particularly ingenious or downright lucky.

Yet the audible struggles of each coughing engine were food for the patience of that grandstand crowd. As each motor took heart and entered the air with a few hearty explosions, one could almost hear the crowd thinking, "Ah, at least those contraptions have something to keep them up once they get into the air."

There may have never been another crowd quite like that one. It had no idea of what was coming on that afternoon or the years ahead. It could not look beyond the fence of the old race track. It could not dream of anything beyond the horizon, because that itself had not yet been attained.

But, perhaps almost prophetically, that crowd sat and waited in unusual patience. Yet excitement rose with the heat of the sun as the day wore on and, finally, one pilot coaxed his motor into running smoothly. It popped along with a merry sputter for several minutes. Watching this performance tenderly, the pilot announced to us, his helpers, that he believed conditions were satisfactory enough to attempt a flight.

Then, for the twentieth time since the motor had begun running without a fatal skip, he walked to an ice scale attached to a rope. One end of the rope was tied to a stake, the other to the vibrating plane. Reading the ice scale, the pilot calculated how much pull the motor was generating. (Today, we'd call it "thrust.")

The motor kept up its clatter, and he fed it more gasoline, then read the scale again, nodding his head to indicate that he felt he had power enough for takeoff. Yet all this preliminary fussing was conducted with strict formality.

Directed by the pilot, ground crewmen untied the plane and wheeled it to the race track. Through wires and poles, pipes and sticks, the pilot climbed to his place, distributed himself somehow in the middle of the maze, turned his cap around backward and grasped the controls. It was a thrilling moment when he yelled back through the din of the motor that at least six of us should hold the plane until he gave the release signal by raising his hand.

The pilot fed more gasoline into the motor and carefully adjusted his goggles. The crowd boomed up a roar of approval and anticipation. We in the ground crew held the out rigging of the ship, a tandem monoplane in which the motor and the pilot were centered in the middle of all the wires, wooden struts and pipes. Our grips were firm; our eyes were centered on the pilot's shaking right hand.

Suddenly, he opened up the motor, and through a blinding cloud of dust churned up by the propeller, we saw him give the signal to usher in the big moment. We let go, and ran to one side to watch the takeoff.

A silence of expectation had settled over the spectators. As the motor roared, its blasts cut the hot calm like gunshots, playing a staccato counterpoint to the heartbeats of those thousands who had come for the first time to see a man fly.

We ground crewmen walked beside the plane as it slowly gathered speed down the track. But even when we were forced to trot, we kept up with it.

The plane kept rolling ahead, but the motor was sputtering, and the ship's slowness was painful. It rolled around the track for about half a mile and then, just before it clattered into a fence, the pilot shut off the motor. Then the machine and the fence mingled, and all was silence.

The crowd sighed with the sound of escaping gas as the big moment of the afternoon collapsed like a punctured balloon. The pilot climbed from the machine, ruefully inspected some damage at its front and ran a hand over the silent motor, which at no point in the takeoff attempt had been able to roll the plane faster than ten miles an hour.

The crowd was disappointed, but it never turned sour. The fact that this had been the pilot's first takeoff attempt ever may have softened the onlookers. A disappointed novice, he helped us wheel his plane back to the starting point. There, with the doggedness of the true aviation pioneer, he began to tinker with his motor and to make hasty repairs.

In this discouraged, but not disheartened novice there burned the tenacity of the Wrights, the zeal of Glenn Curtiss and the daring of Charles A. Lindbergh, and to him, the crowd and the disappointment of the moment mattered nothing. He never did get the plane running that day, and darkness fell before he even got the motor to start a second time. Then it was too late to fly.

But before that second triumph, he and his stubborn motor were forgotten, for attention had shifted to the Kimball helicopter, a fantastic affair which bore a startling resemblance to a gigantic bedspring with a motor in its middle. By the time the crowd had switched its attention to him, Wilbur Kimball and his assistants had his motor running. That was about all.

The Kimball helicopter was about 25 feet square, with the motor in the lower part. The motor drove 20 small propellers which, turning in unison, were designed to lift the machine vertically. The motor chugged and the propellers turned, but not all of them turned at the same time. Their leather drive belts kept slipping. First one slipped loose and its propeller stopped. Then half a dozen other belts slipped with the same result. Keeping the belt on the propeller shafts occupied all the time Kimball and his mechanics could find.

As this struggle of men against bolts progressed, my friend Fred Shneider made gallant but futile attempts to perch his Wright biplane on a starting monorail at the end of the race track infield. The grandstand crowd, by that time turning fickle, with so much to watch was dividing its attention among Kimball's wrestling match with the belts, Shneider's balancing act, and the activities of Lawrence J. Lesh.

Lesh was 16, about the age of most of us who were the model plane builders in the Aero Science Club, but he was a figure apart. He had flown. Now he was about to fly again, or rather glide, in his Chanute hang-type glider. But he had to wait for attention. To stimulate the crowd and to key excitement to the proper pitch, the committee, chaired by Lee S. Burridge, president of the Aeronautic Society, staged five motorcycle races around the track.

There was good reason for this. The crowd had threatened to flow over onto the track, and police and special officers were having trouble keeping people in place, and there was, as a consequence, danger of a serious accident. So the races were held to keep the crowd in check and to satisfy its thirst for thrills.

After the contests were held, Lesh took over, preparing for his exhibition. He was no novice. At 16, he was a real showman and a real aeronaut. Born in the U.S., he was then living in Montreal. At the time of the Morris Park meet, he held the world record for a towed glider flight. This he had achieved in 1907, with his glider hitched to a motorboat, which pulled him six miles over the St. Lawrence River. And Lesh had chosen no ordinary vehicle to tow him at Morris Park. The automobile which now made ready to assist him was Montague Roberts' famous Thomas Flyer, which had shortly before won acclaim as the first touring car to travel around the world.

Lesh made two flights that afternoon. The first was eminently successful. Then he tried a second. He made final adjustments and stood behind the Thomas, his arms thrust through the arm brackets of the lower wing of his hang glider. Once again, silence settled over the grandstand crowd and additional thousands crowded on the track. Mechanics working on other aircraft stopped their tinkering to watch the man-without-a-motor.

The big Thomas touring car rolled slowly ahead. Lesh started to walk in its wake, then broke into a jog, then began to run. Then the glider's wings buoyed him and he took off. But the auto's speed was too slow and Lesh struck the ground in a series of bumps as the glider lost altitude, then regained it, then lost it again.

Montague Roberts saved the situation by giving the car more speed and, with an accompanying roar of approval from the crowd, Lesh climbed to 50 feet and glided straight across the infield. At that height, he cut the tow-rope. He did this to enable himself to go into a soaring glide. He knew that if he accomplished a glide of reasonable distance he would win the Brooklyn Daily Eagle's gold medal.

But it remained for the curious, docile, wondering crowd to ruin his chances. He was soaring nicely when masses of spectators crowded under him. His glider struck an air current. Rather than take a chance on hitting the crowd, he tried to right his glider and regain control. But it glided straight down, dropping from an altitude of 25 feet. Lesh broke the fall with his right foot. Dr. S.B. Battay, a member of the Aeronautic Society, administered first aid, and then sent Lesh off to Fordham Hospital. He recovered to go on to greater attainments in gliding.

Such was the nature of the great Morris Park air meet, that Dr. Battay, after attending Lesh, returned to the lists to participate in one of several kite-flying exhibitions. In these, Wilbur Kimball, whose helicopter was pronounced not yet ready for a flight attempt, turned his talents to demonstrating how to fly a kite with a dummy figure and a weight. When he cut the kite loose, the weight shifted and the kite descended smoothly toward him as if drawn by a magnet.

One of the highlights of that glorious afternoon was the releasing of some 1,500 pilot balloons under the joint sponsorship of the Aeronautic Society and John Wanamaker.

But the great hit of the day, aside from Lesh's two soaring slights, was Johnny Mack's performance. Johnny Mack was a Newark, N.J. aeronaut, a true daredevil of his time. Dusk had started to fall when he took off in a Montgolfier balloon and, at 2,000 feet, baled out and parachuted safely to earth. This ended New York's first great air meet, with Mack and the evening shadows descending at the same time.

To their homes that night marched a determined group of young New Yorkers, who had seen enough that day to convince them that building model airplanes would never be enough. Lesh's accident in no way discouraged them. Mack's balloon and parachute demonstration only served to feed their enthusiasm.

I was as badly bitten as the rest by the flying bug. I have never recovered from the infection.

Lawrence J. Lesh in Glider Flight at Morris Park

Lawrence J. Lesh in glider flight at Morris Park. Reprinted from the Bausch and Lomb Optical Company 1958 Commemoration of the 50th Anniversary of the First Exhibition of the Aeronautic Society of New York, Morris Park, New York, NY, November 3, 1908

CHAPTER 3
DEUS EX MACHINA

All winter long, we built and flew model planes. Our enthusiasm was undiminished and then, word got around that the determined genius of Hammondsport, Glenn Curtiss, was coming to town, and we boiled over with anticipation.

Curtiss's trip to New York was little more than a business visit. The Aeronautic Society, whose club rooms the model plane builders used for their regular Saturday night meetings, had contracted with Curtiss to build the society an airplane. Packed in boxes, the new plane arrived in New York from Hammondsport on June 13, 1909. It was assembled at Morris Park and on June 16, late in the day, it was flown. Of all the planes..... biplanes, monoplanes, helicopters hangared at the park, this was the first to fly there. Curtiss made it fly five or more times for demonstration purposes before June 26.

And that day was more than just a bright, hot summer's day. It was more than just a good day for picnicking or canoeing with your best girl. It was the day of the first successful air meet of its kind in the world, the grandfather of all the air meets since then. And we model builders were almost paralyzed with excitement.

The crowd was smaller than that which had attended Morris Park's first exhibition. The day was stifling, and heat poured from the sun and seemed to rise from the ground. But the true fans were there....the distinguished members of the Aeronautic Society, the ebullient members of the Aero Science Club, and several hundred New Yorkers who were just plain curious.

The day's schedule included model plane contests, wind-wagon exhibitions, kite demonstrations and a glider tow by William H. Martin of Canton, Ohio, whose monoplane glider was pulled along by a six-cylinder Kissel Kar. Martin's show ended in near disaster, for he cracked up over a fence, wrecking his machine but escaping with bruises himself. This only whetted the general enthusiasm.

Excitement reached a new and different pitch when Glenn Curtiss was ready to fly. This was to be more than just an exhibition for the crowd, and was to serve also as a demonstration for The Aeronautic Society, new owner of the Curtiss plane. The ship was a biplane, with outriggers in the rear to hold the elevator and rudder. The pilot's seat was in the front, ahead of the motor and nearly over the front wheel of a tricycle landing gear. The motor was one of Curtiss's own design, and it sang a little song of superiority over anything we heard that afternoon or had heard in the November meet.

This little gem of the genius emitted not a series of uncertain explosions, no succession of wheezes or gasps or clouds of smoke. It spoke in an even tone, with power and authority. We all knew that there was real power there when we heard it start with a bang, then level off in a solid roar.

The ship was untied and Curtiss walked in front of it. Before climbing aboard, he held his handkerchief in the wind to determine its direction and velocity. Then the plane was rolled back as far as possible on the field and headed into the wind. Curtiss, with a final look around, climbed aboard. The motor's tone deepened. Six men gripped the plane from the rear. Curtiss raised his hand and they released the ship. It jumped ahead and rolled over the field at an amazing rate of speed.

Even in our most fantastic dreams, none of us had imagined that an airplane could start with such speed, or that a motor would sing so sweetly. The crowd roared right with the motor as the Curtiss ship rolled faster, faster, then bounced a couple of times and, almost more quickly than our wondering eyes could follow it, rose gracefully into the air.

For sheer thrill, I have never experienced anything to match the moment to this day. The feeling came to me that most of the people there felt the same sensation; for most of us for the first time were seeing man in flight and a machine perform to perfection to enable him to break the fetters that bound him to earth. I was transfixed, open-mouthed. The grandstand crowd was more noisy and active in its enthusiasm. While its cheers bounded from the ancient rafters of the grandstand, the crowd jumped up and down and hurled straw hats into the air.

Curtiss circled the field twice, then cut his motor and with the propeller almost stopped, glided to a perfect landing despite the bumps in the infield. That was enough for the crowd. In surging masses, the excited onlookers broke through the guard lines and rushed toward the hero and his plane. Only great effort by the guards and mechanics kept the plane intact. For even in those days, the zeal of the souvenir hunter was strong; he wanted a piece of airplane to take home with him.

CHAPTER 4
THE LITTLE PLANES

In the immortal words of Samuel Goldwyn, one of the most unheard of things I have ever heard of was the man who discouraged his son from building a model airplane. For anyone who does that may be retarding the development of a great aviator. A model airplane is not necessarily a toy. It has its important uses, even in war.

Early in World War II, American high school boys and girls constructed some 500,000 model planes for the U.S. Navy. The Navy used these carved, glued and painted formations of wood to teach flying cadets how to distinguish one airplane from another, how to tell an enemy from a friend and a squadron mate from an ally.

Model plane building was our bag in the Bronx in the second decade of this century. The Aero Science Club of New York thrived on model construction. From its competitions and experiments emerged a number of youths who devoted the rest of their lives to flying, carrying with them always that early knowledge of aerodynamics their model plane building had taught them. The list was not undistinguished: There were Percy Pierce and Cecil Peoli, Ralph Barnaby, Frank Shrober, Louis F. Ragot, John Roche. There were George McLaughlin, once editor of Aero Digest; and Vincent Burnelli, who designed twin-motored cabin ships, sensations of their time. There were George Page, later chief designer for Curtiss in St. Louis, and Andy Serini, who became chief mechanic for New York Daily News planes, working out of LaGuardia Airport.

I joined the group when I was 19 years old, at a time when my scrapbook bulged with newspaper clippings describing the early exploits of the Wright Brothers and the story of Orville Wright's first successful flight from Kill Devil Hill, Kitty Hawk, N.C. on Dec. 17, 1903 seemed nearly as important to me as the signing of the Declaration of Independence. I could vaguely remember that the news of that flight, first described to a nation of people largely by skeptics, was almost too much for human credulity to bear. And among those who found credulity at the breaking point were my parents.

In the years immediately following the Wrights' early flights, when my father and mother found me collecting, cutting and pasting every item I could find on aeronautics, they were seized with alarm. This attitude was no fault of theirs. They had become adult in an age which was only just getting used to the telephone, which looked upon automobiles as smelly, noisy, and undependable, and which still considered the horse not only the noblest of beasts, but the only sure method of transportation. They, like everyone else, had no way of knowing that mastery of the air would change man's world for him.

But enthusiasm is infectious. I was an enthusiast, and I found encouragement in the company of my fellow model builders.....Pierce, McLaughlin, Peoli and the others.

On the scarred walls of the onetime stables of the old Morris Park race track were the names of many pioneer American flyers.....Curtiss, by then almost as famous as the Wrights themselves; Fred Shneider, Capt. Thomas Baldwin, Charles F. Willard, Augustus Post, who later wrote a life of Curtiss and whose New York apartment, a tiny place in the 1940s, still was crammed with relics of nearly half a century of aviation's growth.

I roller skated from our home on Crotona Avenue to the park, about a mile and a half away. When skating seemed to require too much time, I got a job in a bakery and from the proceeds bought a bicycle. My first close contact with an airplane came one afternoon when I had cycled to the park and found Fred Shneider in a shed, huddled over the motor of a Wright-type biplane. When he asked me to hold the propeller while he adjusted the chain drive, I went numb with excitement.

I came to regret it in later years, but school work then had no appeal. Most of my spare time was spent with other members of the model club either building models or flying them throughout the week at Morris Park.

The model club met Saturday nights in the rooms of the Aeronautical Society and on those occasions planned Sunday contests. Such meets were held at Van Cortlandt Park in good weather and in one of the state armories when the weather was sour. The club enjoyed the beneficence of a kind patron saint. He was usually present at meetings and fulfilled all the functions of a benevolent patron. His name was Edward Durand. He wore a closely clipped white beard. His manner was gentle, but he had a burning enthusiasm for boys and model airplanes. He directed our contests and was their sole judge. I seldom think of him now that I don't picture him scampering across the rolling grass of Van Cortlandt Park, pushing a long bamboo rod with an eight-inch wheel on one end. This device was his own. He designed it to measure the flights of model planes, and was seldom without it. There was no disputing his measurements for he had attached a bicycle cyclometer to the wheel on the rod. Even in those days, we were learning to trust the accuracy of instruments rather than to depend wholly on guesswork or our own eyesight.

One of my own first models was copied from an early Curtiss pusher plane. I had occasional good luck at the meetings, but most of us had to bow to one or two acknowledged champions who seemed to have assimilated best the real principles of model aeronautics.

Percy Pierce was 16 when he set the first great record in 1909 with a model that flew more than 200 feet. That stood as a national mark until George Page beat it a year later. Shortly afterward, Cecil Peoli eclipsed Page's mark with a record flight of 1,691 feet, during which his model stayed in the air 48 and 4/5 seconds. Peoli, later a fine flyer who crashed to his death, was the first model plane builder to have great success with twin-propelling. His record-breaker was a twin-propelled stick model, the propellers pushing the plane rather than pulling it.

There are many little things that go into a flying man's personal history.......brief associations, unimportant incidents, minor accidents, coincidences, experiments, lucky breaks, thankful moments and moments of deep fear, sorrowful moments and crushing disappointments.

In later years, for example, I have often yearned for some of those many old golf balls I once carved up so prodigally. In 1908, materials for building model planes were expensive and we made many makeshifts do the work. I took golf balls apart and used the rubber strands with which they were wound to power my model planes.

One of the many associations which have been left impressed on me like a tattoo was my friendship with Fred Shneider. Fred had taken over a vacant store on 178th Street near White Plains Avenue, about eight blocks away from our house at 179th Street and Crotona Avenue. My bicycle wore ruts in the streets from our house to Shneider's place, where I spent many hours in a confusion of sawdust and shavings, the smell of glue and varnish and the clean odor of newly planed and sanded spruce. Frequently I wheeled home at nightfall with one hand steering the bicycle and the other clutching a precious quantity of scrap spruce, an ideal wood for making model planes.

In 1908 and 1909, while I was suffering acutely from the flying virus, my school work took a nose dive. I did much reading, but to the extreme disappointment of my teachers and the even keener, more obvious disappointment of my parents, my nose followed not the lines of a Latin grammar or the hieroglyphics of elementary algebra, but every obtainable line then being written about airplanes. Sadly, I actually enjoyed this shameful neglect of school duties, for there was a fascination about flying which Caesar never showed me, an attraction about deeds of daring in the air which far overshadowed the practical usefulness of a quadratic equation.

But after more than half a century in the air, I can look back now and see how right my parents were. When I had reached my teens and the urge to fly was an obsession rather than a means to a career, I tried every conceivable way to convince them that I was on the right path and that their attitude was not only wrong but perhaps unreasonable. If they were alive today, it would perhaps come as no surprise to them to discover that I have finally come to my elderly senses and finally have come to appreciate not only how right they were, but how patient. They felt that their son was living a dangerous life, that the line between living and dying in the air is a very fine line indeed, and that life and death moved side by side in his sphere.

But enthusiasm for the air showed no signs of diminishing, and they predicted dire consequences from our foolish whims for my friend Robert Lieb and me. Rob was a derelict in his academic pursuits as I was. He lived on Oakland Place near us and shared with me every waking hour, the same deep obsession for the air.

After the big meet at Morris Park, we both built scores of model planes. We talked, read, thought, ate and slept models. We dreamed fantastic dreams of great sky fleets and cross-country transportation systems routed through the air. I doubt if either of us actually believed these things would come to pass as swiftly as they did, but we dreamed them, nevertheless.

On the day that Louis Paulhan, a famous French flyer, shipped his plane out to Jamaica Race Track on Long Island, to give an exhibition flight, Rob and I arose with the robins. We boarded a Third Avenue elevated, which was powered noisily by a steam locomotive, then climbed aboard a ferry at 34th Street, and then took a trolley car. After a half a dozen changes of cars, we arrived in Jamaica, three hours from home. Our arrival coincided with Paulhan's take-off.

Paulhan was one of the most active of the internationally known flyers. With Cockburn, Rissandier, Lefebvre, Farman, Bleriot and others, he had competed with the single American entrant, Glenn Curtiss, in the world's first air speed races at Rheims, France, in August, 1909. With the others, he had been beaten by Curtiss in the race for the Gordon Bennett Trophy, in the winning of which Curtiss established himself as an international favorite.

There were few flying meets then, but Paulhan was usually on hand whenever there was one. He participated in England's second flying meet at Blackpool, near Liverpool, in October, 1909. When an American team composed of Curtiss, Clifford B. Harmon, Charles K. Hamilton, Charles F. Willard and Frank Johnson was lined up to oppose a French team, it was Paulhan and two of his fellow French aviators who comprised the opposition. The meet was held at Los Angeles in January, 1910, and Curtiss broke both the quick-starting record and the speed record for flying with a passenger. Paulhan established a new altitude record of 4,165 feet, more than 700 feet higher than any other man had ever piloted an airplane.

Paulhan was a masterful flyer. At Jamaica on the afternoon that Rob Leib and I saw him, he kept his plane in the air for some time, circling gracefully well within sight of the crowd which had gathered to watch him. He was roundly cheered on landing. Rob and I stayed at the field as long as we dared. There was no mistaking the depth of our serious interest in model flying, and we tried to make good use of those rare occasions on which we could see a real airplane in the air.

The seriousness of our discussions never amazed us then, but in retrospect, they seem unusually technical for young boys. We talked at length and with authority on wing curves, propeller shapes and the properties of various materials. Pilots whose names were like shining stars to us came to talk to our club.

It was in the late summer of 1910 when we were hard at work on model planes that a workman struck a fence at Belmont Park, Long Island, with his hammer. This resounding blow was like applying a sledge to my imagination. For the workman and his mates began ripping down that fence and other obstructions around the park in preparation for what I was certain was the greatest single event ever conceived by the mind of man.

The announcement of it appeared simultaneously in many newspapers and magazines and, while workman prepared the park, every flying enthusiast glowed with anticipation of what was extravagantly billed as "the world's largest international air meet." If the Morris Park meet of 1908 had been big, this one was to be colossal. If we had thrilled at seeing Curtiss and Paulhan, we were to burst at the sight of all the European planes and pilots the international show would bring to August Belmont's race track. There were to be $80,000 in prizes.

For those flying machines from across the sea, fine trees were being leveled around the park. To see the birdmen of the world in action, thousands of people began making plans to be on hand. Workmen started to build additional seats atop the grandstand. Three decades and more later, they were still there.

CHAPTER 5
WINGS OVER BELMONT

Summer can drag and autumn may be late in coming. Never has a summer dragged or an autumn been guilty of such tardiness as the seasons of 1910. Each balmy day seemed a year long, each sundown a month in arriving. The big international air meet was scheduled for October 22 to 30. After August 1, when Allan A. Ryan, son of financier Thomas Fortune Ryan, stepped in to take over, the action began. Ryan, the famous balloonist J.C.McCoy and Burton R. Newton, who left his position as aeronautic editor of the New York Herald to help them, were organizers of the meet.

They publicized it internationally. They raised the prize money. They offered a special prize of $10,000 to the victor in a race from Belmont Park around the Statue of Liberty. A special prize of $5,000 was set up for the aviator who should reach or exceed an altitude of 10,000 feet. The committee made arrangements for handling 200,000 spectators, for parking between 4,000 and 5,000 automobiles, even in those days when horses were still holding their own.

The Pennsylvania Railroad was to provide special service from its new station in New York. Within a few weeks after the competition was announced, private parties in Boston, Baltimore, St. Louis and Chicago had reserved special trains to bring them to New York.

The story at that time was that Latham and the famous French Antoinette flying machine were developed more or less together. It's the story of an aviation pioneer, the kind of story that makes a man proud to be a flyer, happy to have been part of flying in the early days of its growth. The tale always impressed me. It starts with a Frenchman named Levavasseur, a man who had little money but was a masterful mechanical engineer who had invented what up to that time was not only the lightest but the strongest motor known.

Levavasseur wanted to try his motor in a flying machine, but hardly had courage enough to ask anyone to put money in such a project. He then took a long-range view of the possibilities. He insisted that his engine could power a motorboat faster than any other engine had ever powered one. The answer to this was that the firm of Gastembide and Mengin began to build the engine. It was installed in boats and won races. It also won automobile races.

When Santos-Dumont heard about the engine and ordered a lighter one built, Levavasseur saw his dream coming true. Santos-Dumont installed the new engine in an airplane and flew with it. Soon Farman, Delagrange and the famous Bleriot were using engines of the same design. While others were becoming famous with his motor in their airplanes, Levavasseur stood by. The successes of the others convinced Levavasseur that he should build his own airplane. He did. It appeared as the "Gastembide and Mengin" machine. And it seemed to have only one defect....no one could get it safely off the ground. Each time it took off at high speed, it cracked up.

There then appeared on the scene a young man who had lived his few years to the full, traveled widely and led the gay life, who had money, but extremely poor health. Medical experts had told him that he was a doomed young man, with a year at best to live. His name was Hubert Latham. Determined that he should live the last year of his life with his habitual recklessness, Latham insisted on flying the Gastembide and Mengin airplane. He told the motor makers that the prospect of death in a smashup meant nothing to him. All he wanted them to do was to promise to repair the machine every time he wrecked it.

Latham and the Gastembide and Mengin people sealed a bargain. And he began to fly and to smash the machines at an appalling rate. Early in this series of crack-ups, from which the reckless young birdman emerged miraculously unharmed, the Gastembide and Mengin ship was named the "Antoinette," after Mlle. Antoinette Gastembide. Latham had dozens of crackups. Fearless because of his contempt for death, he flew with abandon. But each crackup taught him something new about flying and about the machine to which he was devoting what he thought was left of his life. Soon his health began to return. From a stooped and broken partial invalid he developed into a husky, bronzed sportsman. As Latham's health improved, so did the Antoinette machines improve as airplanes. He lived out his "last" year of life and became perfectly healthy. His end came many years later, not in flying, but in hunting wild boar.

That was the kind of man, along with Moisant and all the others, that Ryan, McCoy and Newton had lined up for the big Belmont Park international meet. Again, I was consumed by interest, desire, and anticipation, an amalgamation of sensations which sent me into long hours of argument with my parents over whether I should be allowed to attend the meet. My contention was that the most important events in the world would take place there, events which no young American should be allowed to miss. There were, I told them, $80,000 in cash prizes. I think they doubted my word on this. I told them that the honor of American aviation was at stake, that America's foremost flyers were being pitted against birdmen from France and England.

I named the teams as I had memorized them:

American....John B. Moisant, Walter Brookins, Eugene Ely, Charles K. Hamilton, Ralph Johnstone, J. Armstrong Drexel, Archie Hoxsey, Clifford B. Harmon, J. Clifford Turpin, Charles F. Willard, J.A.D. McCurdy, Capt. Thomas S. Baldwin.

English...Alex Ogilvie, James Radley, Claude Graham-White.

French....C. Audemars, Rene Barrier, Alfred Leblanc, Emilie Aubrun, Rene Simon, Count Jacques de Lesseps, Hubert Latham, Roland Garros.

I pointed out that they were to compete for the International Aviation Trophy, emblematic of the world's speed championship, that officials confidently hoped that Glenn Curtiss would be a last minute entry, and that at his laboratory at Hammondsport on Keuka Lake, N.Y., he was said to be working on a marvelous machine, greater than any other of his earlier airplanes.

I have never been known for my forensic skills, but these particular arguments worked. I went to the meet, buoyed on air, arrived at the park, dashed around the great outer fence and arrived at the same time as a gigantic Farman biplane. Fifty feet above the earth, it glided around and around with consummate grace. Eyes skyward, mindless of the milling people around me, I dashed madly behind the grandstand, running blind to everything but that big ship. I ran between two sheds and found my path blocked by a high iron fence. Through it I could see all the planes.

The Farman had landed by then, and sitting nearby were other planes. Already a Wright biplane and a Bleriot monoplane were in the air. It was a marvelous scene, saturated with romance. I felt that no jousting tourney of the knights of old had ever been held in a setting more grand. No vast assemblage of noblemen and ladies was ever bedecked more gaily than the crowd at Belmont Park.

The grass green field seemed to stretch miles in the distance. Fourteen red and white pylons 35 feet high, each with a flagpole on top, marked the flying course. Banners fluttered in the breeze. Everywhere men in flying togs were scurrying back and forth. The air was electric. The wooden hangars, extending for a thousand feet in a strategic location in the park, crawled with flying men. A reminder that this was not a mild sporting event was provided by a shining automobile parked at the side, ready to go into service.

I circled the end of the field outside the fence, for I had only car fare in my pockets, no money for admission. I found a spot where the fence curved inward toward the hangars and, nearby, a tree which somehow had escaped the general razing of obstructions to safe flying. I perched in the tree. Walter Brookins, the famous young American protégé of the Wright brothers, walked so near the tree I could almost touch him. His fame had preceded him to Belmont, where he had been established as a great favorite for the altitude record. At Atlantic City, he had climbed to 6,175 feet.

From my leafy box seat in the tree that day, I saw such flying as I never hoped to see again. I went home that night with a buzzing head and arrived long after dark. I ate no dinner. All that week the flyers broke records. Planes of many types performed with distinction and pilots outdid themselves. It was most significant that some of the keenest observers at the meet, the most interested in the performances, particularly by the planes, were military men.

Assigned by the United States Army to attend was Lt. Benjamin D. Foulois of the Signal Corps, an officer who had experimented with a Wright biplane at Fort Myer, VA, and at San Antonio, TX. In those days there were men whose breadth of vision was so great, whose perception of the startling revolution was so keen that they saw over the horizon of the oncoming years the day when wars would be fought in the air, when the machine should become as important as the man when nations came to grips.

What secrets of airplane construction military observers carried away with them from Belmont Park I do not know, but I doubt that any of them memorized the designs of those planes more thoroughly than I did. All that week as I pined away in the schoolroom, my heart and mind were in the sky over Belmont Park, and every Latin verb had a propeller. When the weekend arrived and with it the grand finale of the meet, I persuaded my parents to let me stay the night at the park. Saturday came, and I set out from home with trolley fare and lunch for two days. It didn't matter to me after I reached the park and found my perch in the tree that a high wind that nearly toppled me from the tree kept the airplanes grounded most of the day.

It was nearly dusk when they wheeled one of John B. Moisant's Bleriot monoplanes out and prepared it for flight. They had to roll the Bleriot nearly under me to get it into position against the wind. Just as the mechanics passed by me, pushing the plane, the wind loosed a ferocious blast, lifted the ship and set it upside down. It was badly damaged.

But bad luck seldom discouraged those flyers. The Bleriot was being dragged from the field like a broken fly when a Farman biplane was wheeled into the starting position and Claude Grahame-White, the popular young Britisher who the preceding April had lost to Paulhan in the $50,000 Daily Mail race from London to Manchester, strapped himself into the pilot's seat. Grahame-White gave his signal to the helpers and took off into a mighty wind for the first flight of the day. The Farman rose like a balloon, its forward speed reduced by the wind to a scant 25 miles an hour, ground speed. It bobbed in the churning air like a newspaper caught in a gale. The strapped-in pilot rolled with the plane as it rose and dropped, climbed and dipped dizzily. Then the ship hit a terrific downdraft and fell like an apple from the tree, striking the ground no more than a thousand feet from the point of the take-off.

The crash jammed the landing gear through the papery wings; it broke wires and struts, bent tubes and spars, and ripped the linen. But out of the wreckage climbed Grahame-White, jarred but unhurt, a wiser pilot but an undiscouraged one. That he emerged whole from the wrecked plane bordered on the miraculous. Quite as wonderful was the fact that he seemed ready to fly again. I didn't know it then, but I know now that men learned by misadventure in those early days and often paid dearly for their knowledge. But they never gave up.

But on that windy afternoon in October, 1910, I was only a small boy, disappointed that the Farman's crackup, second of the afternoon, was sufficient to cause the officials to cancel any further take-off attempts that day.

Night came, and I tried to sleep on a racetrack bench, but I beat daylight back to my seat in the tree. A guard appeared on the inside of the fence near my tree after sun came up. He had been there the day before. On this second morning, we opened a cautious conversation. He knew the names of all the pilots and planes. Eventually, he told me, with one of those unforgettable gestures we meet so few times in a lifetime, that if he walked away and I jumped the fence, he probably wouldn't see me, and then I would be inside. He departed, and I jumped and ran across the field to the hangars, whereon were painted such magical names as Moisant, Leblanc, Radley, Ogilvie, Brookins.

There I saw the fabulous Wilbur of the famous Wright brothers, acting as starter for Brookins and his Wright biplane. I peeked into the hangars of deLesseps and Garros, Hamilton and Hoxsey. But I spent most of my time like the thousands of others who were there with my face tilted toward the sky, watching the birdmen break records and risk their necks.

Grahame-White, by now at the controls of a second, intact plane, won the $5,000 Gordon Bennett speed race, mostly through the ill fortune of Alfred Leblanc, the Frenchman. Gunning toward the finish in the race in which he had broken every world record for speed from 5 to 100 kilometers, Leblanc crashed, and Grahame-White won.

Ralph Johnstone, an American, pushed the world's altitude record to a height of 9,714 feet, a stupendous distance to climb in a plane of that day. Then came the great Statue of Liberty race, for which Thomas Fortune Ryan had put up the grand prize of $10,000. It was in this contest, which was sensational from start to finish, that Count de Lesseps avenged the bad fortune which had dogged his countryman, Leblanc, in the Gordon Bennett speed contest earlier. Grahame-White crossed the finish line first in the Statue of Liberty race, but was disqualified for fouling at the first pylon, and Count de Lesseps was declared the winner.

Those Frenchmen.....de Lesseps, Leblanc and the others, were fascinating airmen. Most of them flew Bleriot monoplanes with daring and imagination, and were easily the most romantic figures on the field.

In many ways, the Bleriot single-winged planes were far in advance of their time in design and appearance, looking very much like the high-winged models of the 1940s, when airplanes were finally admitted to have achieved a distinctive style. And the Antoinettes, flown so magnificently by Latham, were pictures of grace in the air.

CHAPTER 6
CRACKUP IN THE BRONX

It may not be good story telling to disclose that my first attempt at flight and my first crackup were simultaneous. But that's the way it was, in the winter of 1910, when Rob Leib and I decided to build a man-sized glider, something we could soar in.

We followed the design of the famous Chanute glider. Ours was to be of the hang-type, a biplane affair with braces under the bottom wing through which the pilot put his arms, his body and legs dangling underneath while in flight.

It was in this type of glider that Lawrence Lesh had been injured in the Morris Park exhibition, but this did not discourage us. Chanute gliders, developed by Dr. Octive Chanute, who brought American gliding on a par with the art that was developed in Germany and France, ranked with any gliders in the world. Rob and I saved our nickels and bought spruce at a wood mill. Fred Shneider gave us spruce scrap for the ribs. We built the skeleton in the Leibs' cellar.

My mother, by this time almost totally reconciled to the fate I had chosen for my-self, bought linen at a drygoods store and sewed the seams, and we tacked it to the skeleton of ribs. Then Rob and I mixed a mass of white glue and solvent and painted the wings with it. This made the linen air-proof and properly taut.

It was spring, 1911, by the time we completed our glider. We looked around the Bronx for a suitable place for our first flight. The nearest spot with any possibilities as a gliding field and hill was the Crotona park baseball diamond close by the Bronx Borough Hall at Tremont Avenue, 177th Street and Third Avenue. But its location was the first problem we had to overcome. It was nine blocks from the Leib cellar to the field, and we could hardly see ourselves carrying a 22-foot glider through the streets in the daytime, let alone getting it intact to the takeoff point. Therefore, we decided it was best to move it at night.

On the first likely evening, we started out at midnight. My mother was worried, after the fashion of mothers. Although she had helped us build the glider, she didn't trust it. But my father, consumed with curiosity and a little proud of us, elected to help Rob and me carry it to the baseball field. But all the way there, he kept insisting that the glider couldn't fly, even though he was carrying his share of the load. Mother went along in prayerful silence.

Despite the lateness of the hour, we collected the unexpected but inevitable crowd that always collects at late-hour fires and accidents. Before we had gotten half way to Crotona Park, about 50 people were jogging along with us. Some of them helped with our load. With this earnest midnight audience at hand, we arrived at the ball park and chose as a starting point an embankment about 20 feet high, which dropped sharply toward the diamond itself. In the background was the Bronx Borough Hall.

The Wright brothers had tossed a coin to see which should make the first attempt to fly at Kitty Hawk. Rob and I did likewise. We flipped a nickel and I won, and inside me, the fireworks of an indescribable excitement started to explode. With trembling hands, I helped Rob and a couple of men from our audience tie a rope on each side of the glider. Then Rob grasped the rope on one side and a young fellow from the audience grabbed the other and I took my place between the arm braces and slipped my arms through. The glider weighed 75 pounds and felt like a ton. With all the assurance of Glenn Curtiss taking off in a plane I yelled, "Let her go," and Rob, the stranger and I began to run simultaneously toward the embankment.

I was blind to the danger ahead. The night was dark and mysterious. But the experiment was glorious and little else mattered. I had an audience and I had confidence. But these were not enough. I had little knowledge of the art of gliding and what little I did have seemed to have deserted me.

Straight we rushed toward the embankment and, as Rob and the other let go of their ropes, I gave a mighty push with my feet and disappeared over the dark brink. The glider wings lifted me only slightly and I executed a series of ridiculous bounces. I struck the field at the base of the embankment, my nose in the dirt and the 75 pound glider on top of me. I hadn't known that to take off in a glider, one has to have a good breeze to start against. And the air that night was as still as death. I was bruised, but my confidence had taken a more painful bumping. I crawled from under the glider. We picked it up tenderly and started for home.

My midnight experience was not wasted. At the next meeting of the Aero Science Club, my gliding attempt was the chief topic of discussion. I left the meeting far wiser than before, stuffed with helpful suggestions from such experienced students as Ralph Barnaby, John Roche, Percy Pierce and Cecil Peoli.

CHAPTER 7
HANGAR HANGER-ON

I suppose that no nation in the world's history has been so lavish in its expenditures for sporting thrills as the United States of America. The money its citizens and promoters have spent on visiting athletes alone would build cities and universities, great dams and great factories in every state of the nation.

The American sporting instinct was active and the American purse was bulging in 1911, and the prize money offered to foreign birdmen for exhibition flights throughout the country was so generous that many of the most famous European flyers stayed here after the Belmont Park international meet. The stupendous success of that affair so impressed Americans and foreigners alike that in 1911 a meet was planned for Nassau Boulevard field about 10 miles east of Belmont Park on Long Island.

Without having quite the grandeur or scope of the Belmont Park meet, the Nassau affair nevertheless received a substantial build-up. Foremost among its most active publicists were Rob Leib and I, who talked it up so continuously that some of our interested contemporaries began to avoid us. Even this failed to discourage us. We were on hand at Belmont Park when they tore down the hangars there, and on hand at Nassau Boulevard Field when they erected the same hangars there.

Among the pilots who made Nassau Boulevard his headquarters was Fred Shneider, persistent and benevolent aero-enthusiast, who brought out his plane and assembled it on the field. The arrival of the Shneider plane at Nassau filled me with almost as much pride as it did Shneider, for throughout the preceding winter he had let me help him build it. I considered the plane mine as much as his. Long hours spent working on it had given me a sense of ownership.

Among the other American pilots who bee-lined for Nassau were George Beatty, with a Wright Model B; Beckwith Havens, who flew a Curtiss "pusher," and John B. Moisant and Earle Ovington, both of whom flew Bleriot monoplanes.

Havens, one of the few "Early Birds" who were still flying by World War II, later headed the New York State Civil Air Patrol and in the early 1940s reported for active duty as a Lieutenant Commander in the U.S. Navy after years as a reserve officer.

Beatty, undeniably one of the most progressive flyers in the second decade of the century, opened a flying school at Nassau some time in advance of the air meet and with his handful of pupils early gave the aerodome a reputation as a center of aeronautical activity.

Nassau had a strong rival as an attraction for the curious. This was a field on Hempstead Plains at Mineola, about six miles east of the Nassau field.

When Glenn Curtiss brought his plane to New York and demonstrated it for its purchasers, the Aeronautical Society, at Morris Park in June, 1909, members of the society had decided that Morris Park was the ideal spot for a flying field. But Curtiss, with his keen perception of everything that made for good flying, persuaded the society to choose the field at Mineola instead. So there it was that Dr. William W. Christmas, Louis Ragot, Capt. Thomas Baldwin, Dr. H. W. Walden, Frisbie, Blood, Hadley and others kept their ships and made Mineola flights.

The establishment of the fields at Nassau and Mineola posed something of a problem for both my parents and me. It was possible to reach the general vicinity of either field by trolley car, but the time consumed in trolley rides usually so cut down my leave of absence from home that half the joy of being at the air field was lost.

Although energetic, I had no intention of attempting a run to either field by bicycle. Our family had no automobile…few families did…..and if it had had a car, I would not have been allowed to drive it. Only one course seemed to remain…the purchase of a motorcycle.

My parents gave me enough money to buy my cousin Vernon Hankie's machine, perfectly convinced, I am sure, that once I got used to riding the motorcycle, I would forget all about flying airplanes. Like the motorcycle itself, their decision eventually backfired on them. I learned to ride and, having become handy enough with tools to repair the motorcycle, began to make a weekend habit of riding out to either Nassau or Mineola, sometimes both, with a reasonable assurance of getting back home.

And so it happened that I spent more of the summer of 1911 on Long Island than I did at my home in the Bronx.

I watched John B. Moisant supervise the construction of five concrete hangars at Hempstead Plains, just east of the field at Mineola. The hangars stood the test of time well and three decades later were still standing sturdily on what later became known as Roosevelt Field. Thirty-one years after they were built, they were being used to house motor test stands for the U.S Army's mechanics' school.

The Nassau Boulevard air meet took place early in the fall of 1911. It was a fine meet, distinguished by Earle Ovington's flying the first airmail ever flown in the United States. This was an especially significant achievement, particularly to those of us who later pioneered in flying the mail from city to city for Uncle Sam. Ovington's Bleriot monoplane was powered by a 70 horsepower Gnome motor.

To make the first airmail flight official, a temporary post office was established on the Nassau Field. Each day, beginning on September 23, 1911, Ovington flew mail from the Nassau Airdrome and dropped a sack in a field near the post office at Mineola. I sent a postcard to my mother by the first flight. Countless times afterward, I saw it with other small treasures in a box. Early in 1942, a collector who had heard about the postcard offered $200 for it. I hunted for it in vain. After all those years, it had disappeared.

Glen Curtis and Henry Ford, Hammondsport, 1911, signed photograph

CHAPTER 8
BENEVOLENT BEATTY

It was in that marvelous year of 1911......everything seemed to be happening...... that George W. Beatty offered a special price for rides in his Wright biplane at Nassau Boulevard field to members of the Aero Science Club of New York. When I heard of this, I bore the news home tenderly but impatiently and dangled it before my father.

The model club had scheduled an important plane building contest, of which he had been duly informed. He told me that if I won the competition, he would furnish me the money for my first airplane ride, since Beatty had made the special reduced price offer. But there was more to winning a model contest than building a neat, pretty little replica of an airplane, and I had a challenge ahead.

The contest was held on a Saturday night in one of the state armories, and my plane topped its competitors. The Ragot trophy I won that night still hangs in the living room of my home, and I would sooner part with the upper floor of the house than that embossed square of metal.

The Ragot trophy contest was a competition both of performance and weight lifting. Rules were strict. To qualify, a model plane had to rise from the floor under its own power, clear a barrier, remain in the air at least 30 seconds and land normally. My winner was a twin propeller pusher, equipped with a bamboo skid on front and two more in the rear to keep the propellers from dashing themselves to pieces on the floor. When I released the plane, it made a determined take-off, cleared the barrier nicely and circled the armory three times, before the propellers stopped and it glided to a perfect three-point landing.

My father kept his word like a gentleman and good parent and gave me the money to fly with Beatty. That night I could not sleep. The sun and I got up together. Nassau and George Beatty beckoned, and I was not to be denied. My father and I set out early on the great adventure, the beginning of which was made by elevated, ferry and, finally, the Long Island Railroad, which dropped us at the Nassau Boulevard station. We covered the remaining blocks to the field on foot to Beatty's big green hangar with his name in tall white letters on the front.

Countless times in later years, I have asked the uninitiated how they felt before they made their first airplane flights. I have asked them whether being in the air, with the motor pulsating noisily and the cabin jiggling and the wind rushing by was any different from the sensation they had expected. I have yet to receive a satisfactory answer. Yet I understand why none has been given to me.

On that bright Sunday at George Beatty's hangar, I experienced all sorts of sensations, and none was quite like the other. When my father and I entered the hangar by a side door and I saw the big white biplane, my breath stopped for an instant. I gaped.

My father's words yanked me out of this reverie and we walked toward a small office in a corner. From this aperture, a slim young man emerged and introduced himself as Beatty. Then the great white biplane was moved out and made a truly lovely picture, with the sun reflecting from the snow white wings and dancing on the silvery struts and wires.

Beatty was a flyer who believed that cleanliness was a necessity. The plane's 35 horsepower motor was as spotless as a Dutch housewife's cooking pot. The plane sat at ease on two pairs of wheels attached to a pair of skids, an arrangement which was an improvement over the plain skids on earlier models, which could only be started from a monorail. On the Beatty plane, a rope was attached to the rear of each skid and fastened to a post. The seats for pilot and passenger were situated beside the motor, flush with the leading edge of the lower wing.

Starting a plane then was a little ritual in itself.

Beatty opened the ceremony by pulling a loose wire midway between the two wings and saying to his mechanics, "Switch off." When Beatty pulled the wire, two mechanics started turning two large propellers, which were driven by heavy motorcycle chains. At the propeller end, the chains were fitted into the teeth of a large sprocket. A smaller sprocket was fixed to the crankshaft of the motor. The small sprocket moved the chain at that end.

When Beatty pulled the mysterious dangling wire, the pull on the wire raised the valves on the two-cycle motor. This released compression, allowing the motor to turn over easily. With compression released, gasoline was automatically sucked from the carburetor into the cylinders.

The mechanics then stopped their propeller turning; Beatty released the valves from their "up" position; the mechanics stood by for the "switch-on" signal. Beatty raised his hand, and each mechanic pulled down on his propeller with a jerky motion. The motor started up with a series of uneven explosions; the plane vibrated; wires shook, and the drive chains became alternately loose and tight as they traveled endlessly from motor to propellers and back again. Then the motor stopped, and the procedure had to be conducted once more.

These preliminaries sharpened my eagerness. I side-glanced at my father, who stood beside that linen and wooden monster with mingled doubts, extreme curiosity and interest, and a number of other feelings, mostly unidentifiable, on his countenance.

By then Beatty and his men had the motor running and the big plane was pulling at its ropes. Beatty then opened the throttle, let the motor ride at high speed for a moment, then closed the throttle, pulled the valve wire and stopped the motor. He nodded at me. The mechanics untied the ropes and pushed the plane further out on the field. Beatty climbed into the outside seat and motioned to me to take my place alongside the motor.

Hands clammy, heart pumping madly, I struggled up beside him and lowered myself into a small, hard, wooden seat, with my feet resting on a cross bar about three feet forward from the front of the leading edge of the lower wing. All hands set to and fastened a safety belt around me. My father turned up my coat collar and I turned my cap around, peak back. I grasped a wooden strut with right hand in a death grip. My father snapped my picture with my Brownie camera. People then took many pictures of people in airplanes, whether for the novelty of the setting or because they perhaps had sneaking fears that it offered a final opportunity to snap a likeness of a loved one. Our picture ended sadly. We had forgotten to turn the film and it came out double exposed.

How shall I describe that flight? It happened 59 years ago and still the sharply outlined memory clings to me....how Beatty gave the "switch on" signal, how the mechanics spun the propellers once more, how the motor started again and purely, sweetly and explosively 18 inches from my ear. The force of gravity held us down, but not for long. The plane was released and we rolled forward, bumping gently over the rough field. I waved to my father, who stood almost sadly, his eyes fixed on the linen and wood that were carrying me off.

What can I say now, and how can I arrange my thoughts to bring into proper focus that ride of nearly 60 years ago, that aerial initiation, that introduction to the upper realm, to the clear sky, where the air seems purer and space takes on new dimensions?

I remember clearly that as we bumped along, Beatty opened the throttle wide and our ground speed increased, and with it the wind pressure. There was no protection for the pilot and he faced open on-rushing air. It beat against his chest and stung his mouth and ears. We rolled along and the wind kept pushing my chest. I tightened my cap and saw Beatty's left hand ease the control lever back. Then the ground slipped away beneath us and we became part of the air and were no longer earthlings.

Beatty's grin was wide, but mine was wider. I smiled and the wind puffed out my cheeks. It made my eyes water, but I saw all there was to see. Beatty leveled the ship off at 500 feet and kept it there by manipulating the outside elevator lever. The center warping lever kept the dipping wings from getting out of control. On top of the warping lever was another one…. a six inch lever which controlled the rudder.

With our great white wings sliding through the air and the four cylinder motor puffing away at a merry and reassuring clip, we circled the countryside, over farmhouse and henhouse, barn and barnyard. Horses kicked, reared and galloped along their pasture fences, seeking a way out, an escape from the great white bird. Farm folk stopped their work and watched us. Chickens ran for cover. As much as a 16 year old can, I felt reborn, somehow recreated in a different world from the one I knew.

That is what makes flying so difficult to describe to anyone who has never flown. I don't mean to say that one need necessarily sense the mysticism of flight through space as Anne Morrow Lindbergh has written about it, but I do mean that man in the air is a different creature from man on the ground. For the brief moment of his flight, he has left his ancestral home, the clinging earth. He has, for the instant, broken the shackles that have always bound him. And, I learned that afternoon at Nassau, even a 16 year old can feel the wrench of that parting.

There is spaciousness about the air above the earth known only to astronomers, flyers, and astronauts. To astronomers, it is a matter of a telescope's focus, and of hard, inescapable figures and symbols. To flyers, it is clean, never-ending space, the freest of playgrounds, the broadest of highways. To astronauts, those latter-century inheritors of the Wrights and Curtiss and all the others of their time, such spaciousness stretches forever, there are no limits and infinity beckons.

Flight seemed so effortless that day that we might have been hanging motionless, with the earth spinning below. Beatty brought the plane to 1,000 feet and we swept over the railroad. A train crept under us, crawling like a black worm between the doll houses on either side of the track. We headed back toward the air field, glided to a lower altitude and circled.

Beatty pulled the wire over my head, the motor "free-wheeled," the forward motion keeping the propellers turning, and we glided toward the ground in silence broken only by the rush of the wind through the wires and struts. The arms of Mother Earth reached out to meet us and gathered us in with the tenderness of a perfect landing. We bumped solidly and rolled ahead. A dog ran from behind the hangar and barked at us. We rolled by the fence and slowed down until we were in front of the hangar. Then all motion ceased. The plane was still. My heart was still, and I was still holding my breath.

My father's thankful smile said, "Thank God, that's over." He was shaking hands with Beatty and trying to get me to climb out of my plane at the same time. Beatty told him I had never shown a moment of fright. I told myself there was no reason for fright. It is highly probable that I had anesthetized the fright cells of my brain with a powerful potion of excitement.

My admiration for Beatty and my gratitude were boundless. I tried to pour out both these and my enthusiasm for flying in a cataract of words that made no sense. I saw my father wink at Beatty and heard him say to me, "Let's get going or we'll miss our train." Only then did I know that I was back on earth.

CHAPTER 9
UNHAPPY IS THE LANDING

Rob Leib and I repaired our broken glider in the winter of 1911-1912. I had done a fine job of smashing it up in my midnight gliding attempt at Crotona ball park, and there was much to be done on it. But we got it into sound enough shape to exhibit it in the first airplane exhibit shown at the Grand Central Palace.

It was in the next spring, 1912, that C. & A. Wittemann, aeronautical engineers who had a factory at Ocean Terrace and Little Clove Road, Staten Island, in which they built a biplane bearing their firm's name and gliders after Chanute's design, offered the use of one of the gliders to the Aero Science Club.

The more daring of the club's members accepted the offer, and immediately arranged a Sunday afternoon gliding exhibition. About eight of us were in on it, including Ralph Barnaby, Rob Leib and our two best model builders, Percy Pierce and Cecil Peoli. We all set out for Staten Island by elevated train, ferry and trolley one Sunday morning and arrived at Oakwood Heights, which boasted a fairly good air field.

The Wittemanns had selected a good-sized hill some distance from the airport for our gliding trials. They instructed all of us in gliding and, one by one, the members of the Aero Science Club made short flights. Then came my turn. Because I weighed only 110 pounds, I decided that I should make an excellent flight. It was to be my first attempt since the sad try at Crotona Park and I was not too merry about it.

But apprehension faded quickly because before I realized what was happening; my companions had given me the signal to run and had gotten me off to a beautiful start. I was soaring. Instinctively, I suppose, I pitched my body forward and the glider leveled off at about 20 feet and sailed smoothly ahead, parallel with the slope of the hill. Then the ground came up gently to meet me. I dangled my feet, hopped a few times and landed safely, upright. This was an entirely new experience, and it filled me with the falsest kind of confidence. I drew my arms from the glider braces and emerged, as far as I was concerned, a full-fledged glider pilot endowed, after that brief flight of seconds, with all the knowledge necessary to pilot anything with wings.

How false faced is the vanity of youth, and how painful its recognition!

Barnaby said, "Nice flight, Russ." I nodded affably. I watched the others try again with just a hint of condescension. And again it came to be my turn. I asked to be given an extra long run by those who held the ropes powering the take-off. With 30 seconds in the air to my credit, I felt destined for great things. Ah, vanity! As this is being written, I have more than 25,000 hours in the air and I fly nearly every day. And each day I learn something new.

But I felt beyond learnings as I prepared for that second glider flight at Oakwood Heights. I instructed my companions to give me that extra long run, that extra power I wanted to distinguish my second flight, the power I needed to make the flight supreme. I was given such a good start that before I knew it, I was gliding at a 40-foot altitude and was so startled that I might as well have been leveling off at 1,000 feet.

Instinct played me dirty this time. I pushed my body forward. Immediately, the glider pointed earthward. Carrying me virtually helpless under its wing, it dropped like a wounded duck. I tried to level it off. It was far too late. Mother earth came to meet me and we collided.

It was, however, a perfect three-point landing: the leading edge of the lower wing struck first, my knees ploughed into the ground second, and then third, my nose bored into the dirt. I lay stunned and injured in body, mind and heart, in a wrecked glider. Numbed from shock, struggling for breath, I was pulled from the wreckage, painfully embarrassed because my wrecking the glider kept the others from further flights that day.

But my friends and Charles Wittemann seemed more concerned for my welfare than the condition of the glider. Wittemann assured me that the glider could be repaired easily. Then they ushered me to the airport, where Ruth Law gave me words of encouragement. By then, I knew I was damaged, and that I had broken my left collarbone. The feeling was painful and familiar. I had cracked the same bone a few years before in a bicycle mishap.

That indefinable, nerve-wracking, grinding feeling of a fractured bone was there again. My side hurt. My body was bruised. Then Rob and I started for home early. That last long trolley car ride was agony of screeching wheels on steel rails, of pushing, jostling, sweating, irritable Sunday night wayfarers returning home. I had to stand. I was bumped, pushed and roughed a score of times. Every unheavenly passenger body which bumped me made contact with my left arm. I was tossed dizzily between a desire to collapse in the aisle and a grim, if by then vague, determination to reach home on my own two feet.

I dared not tell even the more kindly of my fellow passengers that I was hurt for fear that some benevolent soul with Samaritan instincts would send me to a hospital. I was hemmed in by thoughtlessness, unknowing humanity, an agonized waif paying a painful price for a few glorious seconds in the air.

Supper was in progress when I reached home. My face was scratched. Torn, red streaks stood out like paint marks against my pallor. My mother looked at me with a "now, what's happened?" expression. I sat at the table, kept my left arm tight against my side and tried to eat with one hand. I wasn't hungry. I told them I had a touch of car sickness but that it would pass away and, please could I be excused?

I had a bad night and saw the family doctor the next day. With more science than gentleness, he manipulated my aching frame until he pronounced that not only my collarbone was broken, but two ribs as well. By then, I was convinced that he had broken the ribs himself. I wanted the doctor to strap me up so that no one would notice my condition. He was uncooperative. I went home trussed up like a man fresh from an explosion.

My father made some vague remarks about my failure as a glider pilot's being a pretty good indication that I should never try power flying as a career. But my mother seemed to be more concerned with the miraculous fact that I was alive after emerging from an air crash. This indeed was something of a rarity. Crashes even in gliders were more often fatal than otherwise, I was soon to learn.

My glider smashup turned out to be a lesson in experience. The wreck itself did my body up in a mass of black and blue bruises. Then, I had to attend the next meeting of the Aero Science Club, which I did on Saturday night with my arm in a sling and my self-confidence in splints.

Louis Ragot presided at the blackboard. Ragot took the lead in a discussion in which it was decided that the glider accident was not wholly my fault. It was the general belief that in my attempt to level the ship off, I had pushed my body back, which was only proper, but that the glider had begun to descend at such a sharp angle that no shifting of my weight could change its center of gravity. The result, my fellow clubmen told me, was that the glider kept going down. This was all new to me, and constituted my first lesson in aerodynamics.

The next week, with the glider prepared, the club members tried further experiments while I stood by, unable to participate. That was an even greater punishment than my injuries.

CHAPTER 10
FLEDGLING

In the summer of 1912, Fred Shneider built a Curtiss pusher with a four wheel Farman landing gear in his shop on 178th Street. Having developed into a fair mechanic, I was of some help to him. When I wasn't lending him a hand, I was spending my spare time either at Mineola or Nassau Boulevard air fields.

Captain Baldwin was flying his so-called "Red Devil" at Mineola, where Ragot had a monoplane. Hadley had a big biplane at the same field. Both Dr. Walden and Dr. Christmas kept their monoplanes there and made numerous flights.

On some weekends there was too much wind for flying. I liked these especially, for they gave me an excellent opportunity to stand around with the pilots and get in their way. I was only one of several youngsters who made Mineola a hangout and the older men treated us kindly and with tolerance, often remarking that it would probably be up to us to continue the flying game when they had to leave it.

Cecil Peoli was also a hanger-about at Mineola. He was a little older than I was, a personable youngster well liked by the pilots at the field. Captain Baldwin taught him to fly. Peoli was an apt and willing student and soon became a good pilot, the youngest in America. How I envied him! The summer had passed and I still had only the memory of my glorious first flight with Beatty and my two disastrous gliding attempts to my credit.

Autumn came and Rob Leib and I built our second glider in the basement of Fred Shneider's airplane shop. It was an ambitious project. We followed the Wright design, building a biplane glider with seat, controls and landing skids similar to those on a Wright power plane. It had double surface warping wings with built-up ribs. But we never flew it. The chief reward for effort and money put into construction of the glider was its beauty. We exhibited it at the second airplane show in Grand Central Palace in the spring of 1913.

Then, when Shneider shipped another completed biplane out to Mineola, my interest in gliders and gliding waned. The help I had given Shneider on his ship once more gave me a personal interest in it. I hoped he would let me stay on as a helper when he re-assembled the plane at Mineola. I knew how to cut out metal terminals, splice and solder wires and rig a plane. Anyone who used an airplane then had to be versed in those fundamentals of mechanics.

I spent most of that summer as I had hoped to do….on the field at Mineola and struck up a special friendship with a pilot-designer. His name was Giuseppe Bellanca. Bellanca's hangar was next to Shneider's. He had two monoplanes at the field. Even in 1913, his ships showed the soundness and advancement of design that have marked them in later years, that particular Bellanca technique which enabled him to build a monoplane which was to make a pioneer flight across the Atlantic Ocean.

This was the famous plane Columbia, in which Clarence Chamberlin and Bert Acosta broke the world's endurance record by remaining in the air for more than 50 hours, and which Chamberlin later piloted non-stop to Germany to make the first United States to Europe crossing after Lindbergh's flight to Paris.

In those Mineola days, Bellanca's hangar was near one housing a plane owned by William Piceller. Piceller was a member of the Aero Science Club and the third model plane builder from that group to fly a power plane.

In the dim and distant past which every man likes to call the dark recesses of his memory, there stand solitary figures which have a special significance to us in later years. Piceller to me is one of these….a slim, dark, charming aero-enthusiast who was obsessed with flying.

Piceller had learned to fly in the seat next to the motor. To be flown, his ship had to have one of two things….a passenger or a lead weighted strut to give it even balance in that extra seat. Inasmuch as the lead strut was a long time in being shipped from the factory that summer and Piceller was not to be denied his regular flights, he needed someone to fly with him while he practiced. His practice flights were little more than short hops around and over the field, but on these frequent occasions I sat in his plane and took the place of the lead weighted strut.

I think the only day on which I did not fly with him was the day the strut arrived and he installed it. I was there, a little disappointed. Piceller fixed the strut in what I had come to regard as my place in the plane. Then he announced to the other pilots that he was going to attempt a cross-country flight to see how much altitude he could gain.

I had a curious, lonesome feeling when I watched him take off for Hempstead Plains. While I helped him tune up his motor, he told me he planned to fly there and back, a distance of about eight miles. It was to be his first cross-country flight. I snapped a picture of him just before he started. He took off smoothly, attained a good altitude, and faded from our sights in the direction of Hempstead.

After a few minutes, we heard his motor again and soon saw his graceful biplane winging toward the field. He approached in the orthodox manner, about to make a landing. We had already started to run out to greet him when his plane lurched suddenly and with no warning plummeted with terrifying speed and crashed only a few hundred feet away. Piceller breathed his last just as we reached him. His hands still clutched the controls.

When his broken body was tenderly carried out of the wreckage, pilots examined the ship. They discovered that one of the warping chains had broken and sent the plane completely out of control. Brave Piceller never had a chance of bringing the plane in safely, but he had died trying.

Many a brave man died trying then. My family had told me that. I had read about it in the newspapers. I remembered reading with a sinking heart five years before of the death of Lieut. Thomas E. Selfridge of the U.S. Army, first man to die in a power plane crash. Selfridge was killed on Sept. 17, 1908 while flying with Orville Wright. Wright was badly hurt. I felt almost as if I had seen the crash. Years later, the Army named its great Michigan field for Selfridge.

Now Piceller was dead, and death in the air was brought straight home to me and I knew that if he hadn't installed his new strut that day, I might have made the endless journey with him.

It has been aviation's salvation that the cruel ends of men like Lieut. Selfridge, Piceller and others have inspired rather than discouraged birdmen. Only death has made most of them quit. I have seen men battered in face and frame, time after time, still making flights. I have seen death written on their faces before they took off on fatal flights and yet have known that nothing would stop them. For most of them, in their hearts, are fatalists. They have entered careers in which no other attitude toward life and its inevitable end would be suitable.

In the summer of Piceller's death, Fred Shneider started an air school at Mineola. Each morning, we rolled out his two planes....one with a 35 horsepower Elbridge motor and the other with a 50 horsepower Roberts engine.

Shneider was a rare soul...a designer and builder and pilot. But he flew very little. He was an unlucky flyer, a kind of American counterpart of Hubert Latham. He cracked up frequently, not so much from lack of skill but through a streak of ill luck which dogged him throughout most of his flying career.

Because of his unfortunate penchant for cracking up, Shneider hired an instructor for his school, a pilot named Richter. Among Richter's first students were Lieutenant Walb of the German Army and a young New Yorker named Herman Ecker. Walb later returned to his fatherland, carrying with him a wealth of flying education. Ecker remained true to the business. He later dealt in airplanes in Syracuse, N.Y.

The field at Mineola had a long, level grass runway on which planes taxied back and forth in a maneuver then known as "grass-cutting."

The wind whipped over Long Island with a chilly blast those early summer mornings and cool motors were stubborn about starting. We spent most of our time waiting for the wind to die down and the sun to come up, meanwhile priming cylinders, cranking the motors, priming again, cranking again for hours. There was more solid drudgery in getting an engine started in those days than there is in a week of endurance flying in a modern ship. Whenever the wind stayed frisky after the sun rose, we had no alternative but to roll the ships back into their hangars and wait for another, calmer day.

Many of the nights were lonely, for Long Island was truly rural. After I had slept alone in Shneider's barn-like hangar a few times, Giuseppe Bellanca took pity on me and invited me to stay with him. Bellanca had partitioned off a corner of his hangar, installed a couple of cots, a stove and a huge supply of coffee. As soon as day started to break, he brewed a big pot of the steaming coffee, and we rarely started off a cold day without drinking it all.

When Shneider stayed in the city, I helped Bellanca warm up his monoplanes. Bellanca was giving lessons to a number of flying students. Among the best of whom was a New York policeman with the not inappropriate name of Murphy. Murphy was a demon for speed. He rejoiced in the handsome, racy title of "Mile-a-Minute-Murphy," an appellation he had won along with great but transient fame for a single bicycle ride.

Murphy's bicycle ride was one of the strangest of all time, and it made him probably the first man ever to ride a bicycle at the rate of a mile a minute. He attained this amazing speed behind a Long Island Railroad train which was rigged with a special funnel-like arrangement in the rear. The funnel created a suction. In the suction, directly behind the train, almost a part of it, Murphy had ridden his bicycle, pulled along by suction at 60 miles an hour.

Murphy had all the qualifications that make a good pilot, with the possible exception of a leavening amount of caution. But he learned rapidly and in Bellanca's hands became a creditable airman.

Bellanca's planes were easier to handle than most. His monoplane, by ordinary standards, was a relatively small ship, one of the first with a fuselage. The fuselage was built like a fence, with the wings fastened to the top rails. The plane was driven by a three-cylinder Anzani motor installed in front of the fuselage. The pilot's seat was fastened to the lower rail of the fuselage. Two small wheels on the bottom front and a third in the rear were used to take off and land. It was an efficient plane, as all Bellanca's have been, and flew well. The strong little Anzani motor was lubricated with castor oil. No pilot could keep the plane in the air for more than 20 minutes without being doused with the lubricant. Bellanca and his students generally landed swimming in oil.

But some pilots at Mineola never had even castor oil to show for successful flights. Some rarely got in the air at all. It was a great experimental era, and every sort of air-going contraption conceivable was hauled out to the field. Some of the planes were strange looking beyond all sense. Others were crudely constructed and unsafe. Wright-types and such soundly designed jobs as Bellanca's monoplanes and occasional Farmans, Antoinettes, and Bleriots were the most efficient and consequently the safest.

It was not unusual for an aero-enthusiast to sink a fortune in an airplane that never got off the ground. No one laughed and such men were rarely derided. For within the recent memories of all the pilots were the days when people snickered at the Wrights and could not be convinced of the genius of Curtiss. Men who flew and loved flying knew that there was so much to be learned, so many thousands of things to be discovered and tried in the limitless field of flight that few men were qualified to look upon a new contraption and say, "It'll never fly."

Yet even then, the most visionary and foresighted would have gazed with amazement on a 1942 Bell pursuit ship. A few would perhaps have said doubtfully, "It weighs too much," or "Where is the motor?" If you had told them, "This airplane carries a cannon, several machine guns, is as nearly bullet proof as a machine can be and can fly at more than 400 miles an hour and turn on a dime," they would have kept one eye on you with the other looking for the men in white coats with a straitjacket to come and take you away.

If, short years afterward, you had shown them a jet airplane, had told them that it didn't even need gasoline, had tried to convince them that its speed was faster than the speed of sound, that it had revolutionized flying and had shrunk the world, they might have walked away from you.

Vision in aviation has always been a matter of perspective. The more success-fully man has flown, the greater have been his horizons, the broader the scope of his inventiveness, the more imaginative his dreams of things to come and things to be done with ships that fly.

Each of the designers and builders who assembled and flew, or tried to fly, his ship at Mineola or Nassau Boulevard airdromes in 1912 and 1913 contributed something to aviation.....a gadget here, an insignificant little device there, perhaps a new type of wing, a new control lever, a new idea for a landing gear. Each gave something, and many gave their lives.

Some men had fixed ideas. Among these was the helicopter enthusiast, who dreams of the day when man could take off and land airplanes vertically in a minimum of land-ing space, who devised thousands of ways to try to make those dreams of easy flight, realities. The helicopter school has always had its proponents since those times. No matter how swiftly planes of the conventional type were improved and advanced, the helicopterites kept working over their designs and spending their money.

For many years, the helicopter seemed impractical and none over those years could have been called successful. And then Igor Sikorsky demonstrated his eminently workable helicopter and a new phase of the air age was born. Airmen who saw the first workable Sikorskys perform knew that a new field had come to aviation. Thirty years later, the war in South Vietnam has demonstrated that whirly-birds have a wide variety of uses......as machines of rescue, for transportation of troops, supplies and medical teams, for observation and as gunships. They are vulnerable to attack and yet they have proven their worth beyond any point of dispute.

As 1913 advanced into summer, several flying schools blossomed on the Long Island fields. Besides Shneider and Bellanca, John B. Moisant, Heinrich, Sloan, Eye and several others were giving lessons regularly. By that time, I had so advanced under Shneider's tutelage that he let me take the "M. I." school plane from its hangar to the runway. After some days of careful observation, he told me that I handled the ship well enough to be allowed to do some grass cutting. He followed this soon afterward with the unexpected question, "Russ, how would you like to learn to fly?" He might as well have asked me if I liked apple pie and ice cream or a good night's sleep, or Christmas morning. My reply to him left him totally unsurprised. "All right," he said, "another week of grass cutting and I'll let you take the throttle."

The throttle on a 1913 airplane was controlled by the right foot. It was "wired" for "grass cutting" purposes so that the carburetor could not be fully opened and the plane could not get up enough power for anything more than a straight-ahead roll at about 25 miles an hour. Beginners had difficulty keeping planes straight even while grass-cutting. A ship could be kept on a straight line course, even on the ground, only by proper manipulation of the rudder controls. Since the rudder always worked far easier when the plane was in the air, getting the proper feel for controlling the rudder in movements on the ground was a task. I got that proper feel in taking Shneider's ship from the hangar to the runway in my grass-cutting apprenticeship.

Shneider's plane had wheels in the middle of the skids and had to be balanced on these. With Shneider looking on each morning and evening, I practiced grass cutting first east on the field, balancing the plane on its wheels and keeping its course straight, then west. Before I could complete the second half of the course and return the ship to the hangar, I had to stop it at the east end of the field, climb out, put my weight on the front part of the running skid, keep the plane in balance and swing it around to head it west. Then I climbed back in, buckled a strap over my shoulders, pressed the throttle and cut grass back to the hangar.

Shneider was a stickler for safety. After a few days of practice, I assured myself that I was ready for real flight. Each time I looked at my teacher expectantly, he gave me a benevolent stare and said, "Not quite, not quite."

Some days were too windy even for grass cutting, and I watched seasoned pilots like Harold Kantner and Art Heinrich take off into the teeth of gales, fly out of sight and then bump back again and land safely. At odd moments, I climbed into planes in the hangars, grasped the controls and pretended I was flying. I went through all the maneuvers, all the motions. I swooped and dived in imagination, climbed and turned and banked.

Yet all this time I wondered about my parents and what they would say if they knew that I was almost ready to make a solo flight in a power plane. My conscience occasionally came down with the twinges because I had not told them. The climax came so casually that it seemed to be almost routine.

One day, Shneider told me to take my place in the little wooden seat of the plane. He removed the governing wire from the throttle, gave me instructions in the use of the ailerons, which are the hinged tips of an airplane's wings. Control of the ailerons was a matter of proper body movement. It was one of those steps in piloting a plane which in the light of later construction seemed clumsy and uncertain.

The more I think of the complicated devices with which men rigged the early planes, the more marvelous it seems to me that any survived to improve on those devices after once getting into the air and depending on them for their lives.

F. E. Shneider's First Machine

Reprinted from the Bausch and Lomb Optical Company 1958 Commemoration of the 50th Anniversary of the First Exhibition of the Aeronautic Society of New York, Morris Park, New York, NY, November 3, 1908

The ailerons were controlled by tubing and wires. On either side of the pilot was a strip of tubing, fixed to uprights on either side of the seat. The tubing touched his shoulders. Attached to the tubing at each shoulder was a wire leading to the bottom of each aileron on the wing tips. The wires were so arranged that when the pilot moved his body to the right, the movement pulled the left wing aileron down. By such movements he controlled the lateral balance of the plane.

It was not easy to explain all this to a novice. But I had absorbed a good feeling for balance from my bicycle and motorcycle riding, had managed to keep the plane from tearing its wings off in my grass-cutting practice, and after a while told Shneider that I was reasonably certain about what he was getting at.

I think he was convinced that I knew enough about ailerons to try a flight, because he was the soul of caution. The great difficulty with instruction then was that most planes were single-seaters and the instructor had to drum the vital lessons into the student on the ground and then trust to the student's natural ability to put those lessons into practice once he got the plane in the air. This method of teaching was shaky on theoretical grounds, for many an instructor worked patiently for days on end, only to see his pupil take off gallantly and then crash almost immediately because he became flustered or forgot some important part of his lesson once he was in the air.

Any mistake usually meant a crackup. Young as I was, I had been around flying fields enough to realize that, and it was with a kind of solemnity that I went about the rite of making my first solo flight. My enthusiasm was still high, but a small fear tingled at the base of my spine, and I had an indefinable feeling that it was then or never that I should begin a flying career.

Shneider told me not to fly higher than 10 feet, to land at the far end of the field, turn the plane and fly back, still at 10 feet if possible. I buttoned my sweater, turned my peaked cap backward, waved automatically at Shneider, and pressed the throttle. Power took hold of the shaking plane and pulled it forward. Expectant as a baby who sees his bottle coming, I increased speed and eased back the wheel. I had every reason to expect the plane to climb gradually and to see the ground slip away.

But the ship hit a rise in the ground and darted up in air at a dizzy angle, so that instead of taking off and keeping it at a 10 foot altitude, I found myself several times that height before I realized what was happening. Somehow, I leveled off. Fear assailed me for brief seconds and suddenly released me. I felt like a swimmer who has plunged into the water to a great depth with insufficient air in his lungs, and for three or four terrifying seconds has fought his way to the surface, where the boundless air breaks the grip of his momentary fears. I felt free as the swimmer when the air fills his lungs.

I took the plane down to the specified 10 foot altitude and, aside from a little trouble I had keeping it on a perfectly even keel, seemed to be doing all right. My air speed was inconsequential, but my trouser legs kept slapping against my spindly shins like a line of washing in a wind. My eyes watered, my heart pumped rapidly, my hands perspired, my brain sang strange songs, thrilling songs, songs different from those of a man attached forever to the earth and unable to enjoy the infinite freedom of the sky.

I landed at the far end of the field, 3,000 feet from the starting point, and before turning the plane around for the return flight, sat motionless in bewilderment, totally unable to comprehend what had happened to me. It was like finding for the first time, after hours of discouragement, that you could swim; it was like discovering that deep in you is a sense of balance that makes it comparatively simple for you to stay upright on a bicycle once you have acquired the knack that brings that mysterious equilibrium into play.

The flight back to the hangar was not anticlimactic. It was a thrilling repetition of the nameless pleasure I had just then discovered. I was congratulated and patted on the back, and after a few minutes, was allowed to repeat the flights several times.

I slept at the field that night, an eager mass of wrought-up nerves. The next day was windy and there was no flying, so I mounted my motorcycle and sped home to break the news to my father and mother. I may not have been subtle or gentle in telling them my news. I might as well have said that I had joined a carnival as a target for a habitually drunken knife thrower. My mother was completely frightened. My father was half angry and half pleased. My father told my mother that he believed Shneider had too much sense to let me fly very much. "And anyway," he said, "he wasn't flying very high."

CHAPTER 11
TOO YOUNG TO STUNT

I had to learn to turn Shneider's plane safely in the air before I could claim the name of pilot. All I had to my credit were half a dozen straightaway flights the length of the field. I did all my turning around on the ground.

Shneider prepared me for turning in the air by giving me instructions in instrument reading. I say that with reservations. The only instrument available to read was a 12-inch piece of string. The string was attached to a crossbar directly in front of the pilot's seat. The crossbar supported the forward end of the front skids and was about five feet in front of the pilot's place.

Simplest of instruments, the string was effective. While the plane was in the air and the string stayed straight, it meant that the plane was flying a straight course. If the string went limp, it meant that the plane had lost speed and there was danger of a crash. If the string was at an angle, it meant that the plane was "slipping," rather than ploughing through the air. All these "instrument readings" were very important, especially on turns, for a loss of speed in making a turn was an invitation to disaster.

Of all the instruments I have ever read or upon which I have depended for my life and the lives of my passengers, that piece of string stands clearest in my memory. It was so flimsy in comparison with the amazingly accurate precision instruments of today, so simple beside the dozens of instruments glittering on the panels of modern aircraft.

But back to the basics of stringed flying: after instructions pertaining to the properties of common wrapping string and its uses on an airplane, Shneider told me to take off for my first turns in the air. This meant taking the plane to a higher altitude than I had done before on my own. I took it up about 200 feet, flew it outside the boundaries of the field so that if the motor stopped, I would have the whole field to land on.

My circling debut was a success. As I approached the field for landing, I felt freer than I had ever felt before. I cut the ignition and prepared to let the plane down. I brought her in safely. Shneider and others told me I had done well. Shneider said I was probably the youngest pilot in America. I knew I was No. 1 in pride.

That night I went home by train, ferry, and elevated. I had decided on a flying career and I looked upon myself from a new perspective. I fear I looked upon other boys of my age with an air of conscious superiority and considered them much inferior because they were permanently attached to the earth. When I arrived home that night and unfolded my story of new adventures at Mineola, I learned that I was the only one in the house who was truly happy that I had become a flyer.

I made my first cross-country flight the next week, not with myself at the controls, but as a passenger with Art Heinrich. Heinrich and his brother had an airplane factory at Freeport, about 10 miles south of Mineola, and Heinrich made frequent trips from the Mineola field, where he maintained a hangar, to the factory. This time he asked me to go along with him. It was my first trip in a Heinrich plane. The ship was a big biplane of his own design, with a 75 horsepower Hall Scott motor, which we nicknamed the "Scald Hot."

Unlike the motors in pusher-type planes, this ship's motor was in front of the pilot and passenger. This arrangement was a decided safety factor. One of the great difficulties with pusher planes was that in the event of a forced landing, the motor was generally knocked loose and the first place it struck was the middle of the pilot's back.

Heinrich took me higher than I had ever been before. He followed the road over which I had ridden my motorcycle countless times, and kept the ship at a 2,000-foot level. We passed over the Hempstead reservoir and shortly afterward caught sight of the Bay and the ocean and soon saw the Heinrich factory. Heinrich swung the ship wide over the building, circled over marshland between Freeport and the flat, blue Atlantic. The marshland looked ragged and forbidding. Then the motor popped viciously two or three times and stopped dead. I went blue with fright but Heinrich's perfect confidence was an elixir. What a pilot he was! In a situation which might have meant death for both of us had he been less skillful, he brought the ship smoothly home to rest on a dry strip of land between two creeks in the middle of the marsh. There was hardly a bump. We might as well have landed on an acre of mattresses. Heinrich discovered that the motor had good reason for failing. The crankshaft had broken.

Shortly after we landed, a rowboat came up the creek, feverishly oared by an excited fisherman who fully expected, he told us later, to find our crushed and mangled bodies smashed into the marsh. He rowed us across one of the creeks, after which we hitched a ride on a farmer's wagon and were driven to the main road. We walked from there to the factory, where I left Heinrich who had work to do. I went by trolley to Hempstead, looked up a friend who operated a one cylinder automobile, and persuaded him to drive me to Mineola. There I hopped on my motorcycle and scooted home.

I give this recital principally to show that even in 1913, there were ways and means of getting places. That day I had been transported by airplane, rowboat, horse and wagon, trolley car, automobile and motorcycle.

I had made several flights on my own in June, 1913, when Fred Shneider proposed that I really begin to turn my skill into something concrete, to begin to realize on the hours I had spent and the dangers I had undergone to learn to fly. He said frankly that I was flying well enough to make exhibition flights at country fairs…an exciting and profitable pastime. He also told me the fact that I was the youngest pilot in America, being only 18, would show up well in publicity for such flights. I was carried away by the idea. I felt that once I got a reputation, I could earn good money. Not only that, exhibition flying was a great introduction to a lifetime career. All I wanted to do anyway was fly…..for either money or marbles.

I had toyed joyously with the idea for only a day or two when Shneider's lawyer threw the first of several monkey wrenches into the racing machinery of my dreams. He told Shneider that if he wanted to enter into a contract with me to do exhibition flights that my parents would have to sign a waiver because I was not yet 21 years old. Father and mother hurled the second monkey wrench with even greater force than the lawyer had thrown the first. They refused flatly to sign the waiver. My father said it would simply be signing my life away and he wanted no part of it. He admitted that he didn't mind my making a few flights in calm air for recreation, but that he could see no earthly reason for putting greater temptations in my way and inviting tragedy. He said he knew me well enough to know that I might be tempted to take off some day in a high wind and be brought home in a box. Exhibition pilots frequently came to such messy and tragic ends.

Shneider and I tried for hours to convince him that I could do exhibition flying safely. He refused to budge from his strong position of parental power. Of course he was right and sensible. But he made me very angry. I felt that he was nipping my flying career even before it had reached the bud stage. I felt that without flying, life would be lonely and empty. But father was firm, so Shneider went back to his planes and I dropped back into routine civilian life. I flew no more that summer and did not even go back to the field on Long Island.

CHAPTER 12
INTERLUDE ON TWO WHEELS

Having won his point on flying, my father bought me a new motorcycle. I was a little surprised when the new machine helped considerably to take my mind off my blighted hopes of aerial adventure. It was a fine Harley-Davidson. I rode it hell bent for leather all over Long Island and lower New York State. I joined the Crotona Motorcycle Club and went on long weekend trips with other members.

My previous motorcycling experience served me well. I entered endurance runs and those devilish contests known as hill climbs. I took every chance in the book. I developed a will to win that far outbalanced whatever good judgment I had. I went reckless with a will. I went into team racing with Ben Goldstein and Fred Christmas as my partners.

We tried to win our club a cup in a 12 hour endurance contest over country roads. If anyone remembers what country roads were like, he will know that they were hardly fit highways for horses, to say nothing of bouncing motorcycles. To win, our team had to maintain a 30 mile an hour average. Considering the fact that no turn could be taken safely at more than 10 miles an hour, this meant tough going on the straight-aways. One mile of the course lay through a rocky river bed.

When the prize run started, Goldstein took the lead, sending up thick clouds of dust in his wake. In the middle of this, I rode behind him. Christmas was behind me. Everything went smoothly until my machine struck a rut and I was hurled rudely from my seat and landed in a ditch, lost to the world. I woke up with Christmas pouring water over my face. I was shaken and bruised and my foot hurt.

Goldstein and Christmas wanted to end the run right there. I told them no. We finished the run after one of the most harrowing experiences of my lifetime. I needed two feet to ride, so I used the injured one, and through that mile of rocky river bed, I had to keep sticking it out as a prop to keep from falling. By two o'clock in the afternoon, the foot had swollen so badly that my shoelace burst. They poured black coffee into me. On we went again, checking in at each of the secret stations set up to get reports from the endurance contestants.

I was in agony by the time our team struck the state road leading to the ferry across the Hudson. Fortunately, on fairly smooth highway I didn't have to use my bad foot. But by then it was useless, anyway. We had a half hour wait for the ferry and I was getting groggy. I could barely wheel my motorcycle on the boat when it slipped into its pier. I felt faint by the time we reached the other side of the river. How I managed to mount and ride those remaining miles will be a mystery to me as long as I live.

We arrived at the finish between two cheering lines of spectators at 6:05 p.m., just 12 hours and 5 minutes from the time we had started. We won the cup for our club and medals and compensation for accessories for ourselves. We went into the club-house, where I promptly collapsed. I developed a fever and nausea. My foot was numb. My body was bruised and I was near exhaustion. They took me home to the kindly parents who had thought so much of my skin that they had refused to let me fly.

When the family doctor told them that I had broken my foot across the instep, I think they may have had doubts that raising a son was worth the trouble. I had broken the foot at 10 o'clock in the morning and finished the endurance run at 5 minutes past 6 p.m. What kept me riding I will never know. I doubt that it was courage. I think that it was sheer stubbornness.

In later years, I have seen that kind of foolishness pay off disastrously. Every time I do, my foot twinges. I like to think of it as a barometer of caution. The night after the motorcycle run, as I lay encased in my latest set of bandages, I heard my parents discussing a vital question, one close to their hearts: Had they done right in giving me a new motorcycle to keep me from flying?

Some time later, I met a young Westchester County athlete who went to school upstate. He told me his mother had forbidden him to play college football because it was so dangerous. However, she had told him that it would be alright to play ice hockey. She could see nothing unsafe in a harmless game on skates. Only when he returned home one Christmas recess with one eye bruised shut and a deep gash on his scalp did she revise her opinion of the ice game. My parents and that athlete's mother had much the same problem.

From 1914 to 1916, I went motorcycle wild. Kept grounded by parental orders, I still was determined to get into the air, even on a motorcycle. With a recklessness that has since appalled me in retrospect, I entered hill climbs, and endurance runs and races as a matter of course. I went in for trick riding. I won cups, medals, plaques and certificates. I set records, and was hurt. I built platforms and rode over them at high speeds to see how far my motorcycle would jump. Once it jumped 125 feet.

Whether these feats or the fact that the machine seemed to be holding up well through such a pounding impressed them I am not sure, but the Harley Davidson people selected me as a member of a three man team to represent the company in a 24 hour endurance run from Newark, N.J. around the edge of the state to Cape May and return. I was teamed with E.C. McDonald, Harley Davidson's ace professional rider, and Leon Mammini, another well known rider.

I covered far more territory than the run itself required. I rode from the Bronx to Newark before we started, completed the run and then rode back from Newark to the Bronx. At the end of this one cylinder odyssey, I had been 36 hours in the saddle and was a walking callous. The only thing I ate for 36 straight hours of bumping was chocolate bars. The endurance run was so rigorous that only 16 or so out of 40 starters finished. Our team was the only one representing a club that finished. For our bruising, we received the Splitdorf Trophy and medals.

I learned much from another Harley Davidson ace rider, Otto Walker. He taught me how to ride in mud and sand, how to ride a racing cycle, and how best to use my 110 pounds to advantage in competition with hardened veterans who weighed 180. Besides Walker, other well known riders of the day were William J. Ruhle, Art Harrington, L.G. Buckner, Orie Steele, J.N. Constant and Kendall Saunders.

It was only a matter of course that I should enter motorcycle racing. All my racing was done at the old Sheepshead Bay 2 mile board track where, on one occasion and accompanied all the way around by my old friend Lady Luck, I made a run averaging 90 miles an hour.

It was at Sheepshead Bay that Walker first tried out the 8 valve Harley, which attained a speed of 110 miles an hour. When he was killed putting that motorcycle through even more strenuous paces, the factory discontinued its manufacture.

Almost as if I were trying to prove that my parents had shown bad judgment, I pulled up enough minor injuries on my motorcycle to last a lifetime. I have scars today, mostly on my knees, which in my motorcycle days acquired several pounds of splinters, cinders and jagged pebbles.

It was at Sheepshead Bay that I first had a brief flash of insight into the science of streamlining. The idea came to me that if I could only eliminate the vacuum caused by my body in the rear of the motorcycle while it moved at a high speed, I could increase the speed. I built a large cone of stiff cardboard and fastened it at my rear. This eliminated the vacuum. The device caused much comment. I felt certain that it helped me ride faster, but was not able to prove it. But the tail designs of fast airplanes today have long since convinced me that my cardboard cone was sound in principle.

I was a dedicated motorcyclist. I liked the speed, the mechanical challenge, the thrill of competition, but by 1916, the longing to fly had come upon me once again and I sensed in my heart that I would never be rid of it. I rode out many times to watch new planes and new pilots take to the air over Long Island. I tried a couple of times to persuade my father to change his mind about my flying, too. But it took a war to do it.

CHAPTER 13
ARMY WINGS

1917.

Europe was a caldron. Her countryside was scarred, her cities and villages in ruin, her people bleeding, and the airplane had become one of the terrible instruments of a new kind of warfare. And now America had jumped into the caldron.

I was 22 and the Army was crying for pilots. I told my father so. My mother looked worried, as millions of mothers were looking. I think she must have known that the inevitable had closed in on her. My father said, "Go to it, my boy, and good luck. I wish I were young enough to go with you." Then he shook my hand and I went away.

I had been working with him for some time, and my leaving home left him without a helper in his construction business. I had been learning the trade at the bottom, laying out both bricks and works. I had little skill at bricklaying and told my father so. He told me there was no need to tell him. But by the time I decided to join the Air Corps, I think I had convinced both my parents that I would never be a builder of houses, schools and factories.

I rode my bicycle to enlist. I traveled a familiar route that day, a road which I knew by heart in every turn, every grade, every dip, for it led straight to Mineola and the field from which I had made my first solo flight in Fred Shneider's plane four years before. The Mineola field had been renamed Hazelhurst Field and was the site of a training center for soldiers and the home field for the First Aero Squadron.

I went through the routine of enlistment, but was told after the physical examination that I was far too much underweight. I tickled the scales at a mere 117 pounds. I argued with the medical officer. I told him of my flying experience and hoped this would add weight where my body lacked it. It was no use. I was rejected for service.

A few days after my first attempt, I returned to the field, weighted internally with a pound of peanuts, a good many bananas and a gallon of water, the same medical officer rejected me for the second time. I was still underweight despite the ballast. I rode away home to ponder my fate. The solution seemed to lie in my motorcycle.

Several members of my cycling club enlisted as dispatch riders. The commanding officer in charge of the 71st Regiment was a captain named McDonald, who knew me well and knew my qualifications. We had motorcycled together and he seemed anxious to have me in his outfit.

Ben Goldstein and I went down to enlist together. He passed easily. I was rejected again. The reason, not surprisingly, was "underweight." I went to the captain and pleaded my case. He put official pressure to bear, but the requirements held firm. It was some weeks later that I met Art Heinrich in Freeport one afternoon. I had seen little of him since our forced landing in his plane in the middle of the Freeport swamp. I told him my story of repeated rejections.

Heinrich was a good friend and he had a good friend who was the commanding officer at Hazelhurst, Major Kilner. Heinrich wrote to him and asked him to help me as a personal favor. He outlined my flying experience in detail.

Armed with Heinrich's letter to the Major, I went home. For days on end I drank a pint of heavy cream every day. Then I visited Hazelhurst for the third time, again loaded with peanuts, bananas and water. Small wonder I can't touch a banana today. Major Kilner read Heinrich's letter. Then he looked me up and down and called in the medical examiner. The medical examiner in turn read the letter, stared an instant at me and said, "You have been before me previously, haven't you?" I told him I had but that this time I was much heavier.

Whether the Major and the medical officer connived or whether Heinrich's recital of my brief experience was so impressive the Army men felt they could not afford to reject so promising an airman, I do not know. I only know that on the third attempt, I passed the physical examination, was sworn into the Army of the United States and ordered curtly to report for duty within 48 hours. I was a thoroughgoing romantic.

When I climbed on my motorcycle and rode home to break the news that I was at last a soldier, my thoughts were in the clouds above Hazelhurst with the circling training planes. I pictured myself at the stick of one of those tricky little Jennies, giving its 90 horsepower OX5 Curtiss motor, the gun. With my limited experience and ignorance of Army affairs, I had no way of knowing that many crushing disappointments were to come and that I was to come sadly close to not flying at all.

When I reported to Hazelhurst for active duty, I was assigned to the 15th Aero Squadron. The First Aero Squadron, which had been stationed there when I made my first attempt to enlist, was already overseas. The sergeant sent me to the quartermaster for my outfit and assigned me to a bunk in a low, wooden barracks, close by the spot where Giuseppe Bellanca's hangar had been.

When I heard my first bugle call, I just followed the others out of the barracks and from various corners of the field, and stood in line with them. I watched the man next to me and tried to do what he did. We stood at attention as the flag was lowered. A lieutenant gave a command to our sergeant. The bugle was blown again, this time for mess call. I followed close behind. In the mess hall I learned my first lesson in survival of the fittest.

That evening in the barracks the man in the next bunk showed me how to make up my bedding, and where to store my few belongings. I was in bed by the time "lights out" was blown at 9 o'clock.

My homesickness assailed me that first night. I had slept at Hazelhurst too many lonely nights in the old days when it had been Mineola field. Too many long, black hours I had heard the wind howling around Fred Shneider's hangar or the corner of Bellanca's long shed to be lonely in a barracks with a hundred others.

But the insulting earliness of the first bugle in the morning was a painful and surprising intrusion, although I swallowed my resentment, dressed with the rest and had breakfast. Then we returned to the barracks and made up our bunks. I watched the others change into blue denim work clothes. They filed out and I watched that too. Only three of us remained behind. The other two swept the place out. I sat in my bunk and watched them work. Then I came to the sudden realization that I not only didn't know what I was supposed to do, but that no one else seemed to know or care.

I was mistaken, of course, and the error of my ways was pointed out to me by a large sergeant with a voice to match his physique. He leaned in the doorway and screamed for Private Holderman. He demanded to know, in a large voice shaking with rage, shock and despair, why I wasn't in the kitchen doing K.P. I hastened to explain that not only was I ignorant of the meaning of K.P. but that I had no idea I was supposed to be in the kitchen. Then, with more firmness than violence, he gripped me by the arm and led me to a bulletin board where he pointed to my name on the kitchen police list.

Within a few minutes and baggy in oversized blue denims, I was peeling away with the best of them, puzzled to find a paring knife in my hand instead of the stick of a training plane. I told the peeler next to me that I couldn't understand it at all, having joined the Army to fly, not to indulge in a menial practice with which I had become thoroughly familiar at home. There was a certain heartlessness about that wretch next to me. I sat appalled as he repeated what I had said to him and heard the kitchen rock with laughter. But still I peeled and peeled while the planes whizzed and droned overhead.

If it hadn't been for William J. Ruhle, a pal of my motorcycle endurance run days, I might have peeled potatoes for the duration of the war. Ruhle was in camp that day talking about new motorcycles with the chief transportation officer. Ruhle was Harley Davidson agent in Jamaica, L.I. The officer told Ruhle that he had too many motorcycles that wouldn't run and that there was no one to repair them. Like a true friend, Ruhle put in a word for me. He told the transportation officer that I could fix his machines. The officer sent for me and told me to report to him the next morning.

Late that afternoon the top sergeant came up to me with an unlovely smirk on his homely face. He told me I had been assigned to "special duty" and he wanted to know, if he wasn't being too inquisitive, where I had gotten all the influence. I had no idea of what special duty meant aside from the fact that it released me from K.P. and guard duty.

But that night in barracks, the other men buttonholed me with less subtlety than envy. Many had been in camp for six months and had not been assigned to special duty. They were mired in routine. I had been given a break.

I reported to the transportation lieutenant the next morning. He took me to the garage, showed me a number of broken down motorcycles, told me to inspect them and report to him. It was rather like old home week in a grease pit. The machines were all Harley Davidsons, and I knew the make as well as I knew my own nose.

Temporarily, my disappointment at not being assigned to an airplane disappeared. I fixed up a shop in the corner of the garage, ordered the necessary motorcycle parts, acquired an assistant, and got all but two of the ailing machines back on their wheels and into use. The remaining two needed major repairs which we were not equipped to make.

Some of the machines had sidecars. One in particular was a good performer. I took it out on the field for a test run and went through some motorcycle gymnastics I had learned in three years of racing, running and hill climbing. I rode with the sidecar in the air. I rode on the handlebars. I rode sitting in the sidecar and at the same time lifted the sidecar. I showed off thoroughly before any who had time to stop and watch me.

All this probably did not advance the Army to any swifter victory, but it at least kept me out of K.P. and, in my capacity as motorcycle repairman, gave me a chance to visit the hangars. Those airplanes had me. I stayed close to them at every opportunity.

I was made a corporal and put in charge of all the motorcycles in camp. The captain looked in at the garage one day and complimented me on getting the motorcycle fleet into condition. I told him I was glad to have done it but that I'd be a much happier soldier if I could be transferred to one of the hangars. I explained that I had enlisted to fly, not to grease grounded motorcycles. Off he went, after assuring me that if he could find someone to take my place as motorcycle groom he would try to get me a transfer.

Then one day as I tested a motorcycle at a far end of the field, a straight soldier in captain's uniform hailed me for a lift to the main office. It was Capt. Frank Coffyn. His sudden appearance brought back a rush of memories of six years before when as a glider and model plane enthusiast I had watched him many times fly his Wright biplane from the Battery.

Coffyn was one of the bright stars of early American power aviation. He had flown in the Belmont Park meet of glittering memory as a member of the American team. He was one of the first six pupils of the famous Wright Brothers. He introduced to New York City for the first time, an airplane that could take off and land on water. His flights from the harbor near the Battery were famous.

Many times I had watched Coffyn drag his Wright biplane from the harbor police breakwater. His method of hauling it was ingenious. He simply had it lifted onto a large cake of ice, pulled the ice cake and the plane at the same time by ropes and slid the ship easily into the water.

His Wright ship was the first to be fitted with pontoons. The first time he took off from the water he did so at extreme danger, for the Hudson was full of floating ice. This never bothered Coffyn. On that historic first flight, he got into the air safely, flew to Grant's Tomb, turned back, sped out to the Statue of Liberty, circled that startled lady, and returned to land safely at the Battery. On Feb. 13, 1912, he flew under both the Brooklyn and Manhattan bridges, thereby startling a good fifth of the metropolitan population.

Coffyn was the first pilot to take a passenger down New York Bay to catch a transoceanic liner. He became a legend in his own time. When Wilbur Wright died of typhoid fever at the age of 45 on May 30, 1921, Coffyn received this simple telegram from Orville Wright:"Wilbur died this morning." That telegram, along with many other highly prized relics of the pioneer days of American aviation, became a priceless item in the Frank T. Coffyn Collection in later years.

Most of that was past history but fresh in my memory that day at Hazelhurst when Capt. Coffyn climbed into my sidecar and asked to be driven to the field office. I told him I had seen him fly from the Battery. It was typical of his modesty that he seemed surprised that anyone had seen him in one of those flights, to say nothing of remembering it. I told him that I had done a little flying myself, half hoping, I think, that he might be able to put in a good word for me at Hazelhurst. He was properly official and wished me luck in my attempts to fly again.

In far later years, Frank Coffyn and I were both members of the Early Birds and became fairly good friends. I never told him of our motorcycle meeting and I doubt that he would have remembered it anyway.

The weekend after I chauffeured Coffyn down the field, I was off duty. Not having been replaced as chief motorcycle boss, I made a beeline for the Crotona Motorcycle Club in the hope that one of the younger members could be persuaded to enlist, and somehow be steered into my position in the garage at Hazelhurst. Cobin, who was due to be drafted shortly, anyway, enlisted the next morning, was placed on special duty immediately and soon replaced me. Within a week, I was transferred to one of the hangars.

By that time I had had a bellyful of enlistment hardships. I realized bitterly that an enlisted man faced many obstacles before he could be assigned to the regular flying list. And for the first time in my life I regretted having neglected my school work. If I had been a college man, I could have enlisted as a cadet and would have been assigned at once to a flying class.

From my position as a member of the hangar crew, the obstacles in my way toward Army flying looked insurmountable. The only consolation I could find in a grim picture was that my work kept me near airplanes. My mechanic's experience stood me in good stead and I added to it immeasurably in those months at Hazelhurst. For some reason, I have kept my hand in and still hold Engine and Airplane Mechanics License No. 213.

After some weeks on the hangar assignment, I was promoted to sergeant and crew chief, with the commanding officer's own plane as my special responsibility. In this capacity as doctor to the boss's steed, I flew with him several times. His name was Major Rhinehart.

The Major was a distinctly human soul with exactly the right proportion of balance to make an ideal soldier's officer. He listened when it was proper for subordination to speak and he listened man to man, with no air of condescension and no sign of impatience. On one of those occasions I told him my story....how eager I was to fly, what difficulties had beset me, and how hopeless it all looked to me. The next time we went on a tune-up flight, he let me take the stick of the ship.

I hadn't flown a ship for three years. The plane was strange to me, but the knack of handling a plane came back swiftly, so swiftly that I was amazed. No less amazed was the Major. When we landed, the Major called for the officer in charge of flying. He told that officer that although it seemed to be an irregular procedure, what with my rating and lack of certain qualifications, he wanted me placed on the flying list. He also wanted to be informed how long it took me to solo.

I took my first lesson with an Army instructor the next day. One hour and 30 minutes after the lesson started, he turned me loose to solo once again. Of this Major Rhinehart was duly informed. Shortly afterward I was promoted to sergeant, first class, on flying status, which gave me an unparalleled boost in morale and a 50 per cent boost in pay, both of which were most happily received. Then I became an instructor, averaging four or five hours a day teaching cadet pilots, testing planes and doing patrol duty along the Atlantic Coast.

On those lonely flights in those Army Jennies along the coast in those dark days of the war, I had no way of knowing that history has a grim way of repeating itself or that 24 years later I would be a member of the Civil Air Patrol, whose sacred duty was to act as sky watchers along that same coast and be on guard against the same insidious enemy from across the broad ocean.

The flying sergeants at Hazelhurst were the envy of enlisted men and second lieutenants. Cy Young, Ray Willis, Clarence Combs and "Cracker" Woodward all were looked upon with downright jealousy by some of the non-flying men.

Along with the rest of them, I passed examinations for R.M.A. (Reserve Military Aviator) status. This brought us all in line for first lieutenancies and fat increases in pay, and we walked on air as well as rode through it until a ruling came through from Washington which set us back on our heels.

The new ruling specified that we had to pass ground school examinations before we could be commissioned. Woodward flunked and was demoted to the rank of sergeant without flying status. Woodward was the guinea pig. When the rest of us saw what happened to him, we all waived our rights to a commission and remained as instructors and flying sergeants.

Unhappily, this meant that when our 15th Aero Squadron was sent overseas, we were all detached from it and transferred to the 358th Squadron and kept on this side of the water. This official move kept us flying and kept us instructing, but it also kept us from getting first hand cracks at the Germans and their flying circuses.

Like many a specialist before and since, we knew then that we were fated to be Army men and not Army fighters. And so we flew and babied those frail Jennies, and taught college men how to fly them, and watched them catch on, get the knack and become first rate flying men almost overnight.

Pilots were in great demand, and this youngest active branch of the Army service was already bursting with romantic stories and tales of legendary feats over France, of Englishmen and Germans, Canadians and Americans who flew and fought like gentlemen, of Baron von Richtofen, the German aerial knight, fighting Billy Bishop of Canada and their fantastic duels over the flaming battlefields, Eddie Rickenbacker, America's greatest ace.

The great American drives for liberty loans were in full swing when Major Rhinehart told me he had been assigned to lead a formation of planes on a flight inland, to carry the liberty loan drive into the middle west by air. I was to fly his plane. Such an assignment was a great thrill. It meant a break in routine. It meant doing a spectacular job. It meant helping to whip up war enthusiasm. It also meant flying the Major's racy little Jenny, which had been painted pure white. A black skull and crossbones stood out like a symbol of fate on the white of the rudder.

The ship had a Hispanic-Suiza motor, one of the quickest and most powerful engines of its day. It purred like a million well fed kittens when we took off from our official starting point, Cincinnati, and it performed beautifully all the way to Indianapolis, our first stop. From Indianapolis, we were to have flown to St. Louis. I was warming up the plane when the Major called me out of the cockpit and told me that a flight medical officer wanted to make the St. Louis trip in a hurry and that he wanted his own pilot, Lieutenant Kelsey, to fly him.

I think the Major was as disappointed as I was, but he gave way to the medical officer and we both relinquished our places in the white Jenny and boarded a train for St. Louis. I met Ralph DePalma, the famous auto race driver, on the train. DePalma spent most of his time calculating the speed of the train by counting the telegraph and telephone poles alongside the track and timing the interval required to pass a certain number of them.

By the time our train arrived in St. Louis, we knew our white Jenny should have landed hours before. When we stepped off the train, newspaper headlines told a tragic story. The ship had crashed, killing both the medical officer and the pilot. That left the Major and me with no ship and the better part of the Liberty Loan junket still to go. But orders were orders, so we split up. I flew with a Lieutenant Welch. Our first stop was Kansas City. We followed the course of the Missouri River to Jefferson City, where we refueled.

At each of these stops, the Liberty Loan drive was in full swing, and from the bubbling spirit of enthusiasm shown by the citizenry, we knew that America was digging into its pocket with a will for money to finance the war.

We left Kansas City for Grant Park, Chicago, our next official stop. We landed and were roundly feted. At all stops we were wined and dined at special dinners by clubs and civic groups. Dances were given in our honor, and each locality turned out its most gala entertainment. By the time the trip was half over we were wearing silk stockings as helmets. These were the gifts of enthusiastic and generous ladies. We were given so many silk stockings that each man took a good supply back home.

We finished the trip after only one major mishap.....that in which the two men were killed in the wreck of Major Rhinehart's white Jenny.

A second Liberty Loan flight followed the first. Our course was set through New York and Pennsylvania. We landed at Scranton, Ithaca, Rochester, Buffalo, Syracuse, and Albany. These were my first flights over the territory I was eventually to know as well as my own backyard.

It was shortly after the second Liberty Loan drive that Grover Loening designed and built a special monoplane powered by a Hispano motor, and shipped it to Hazelhurst for testing. Ray Willis was assigned to the job as test pilot. Ray put the ship through remarkable paces and was well pleased with it. He chose me as a passenger for an altitude test and away we zipped, the motor screaming in powerful pain as the ship climbed and climbed. Long Island dropped into the distance below. Higher we went, and still higher. We touched 18,000 feet, remarkable in those days, and turned on the oxygen tanks. Before Willis nosed the ship down again, we reached a top altitude of 24,000 feet, which was almost unheard of in World War I times.

Days at Hazelhurst were full of such thrills, although the routine provided a dull contrast. Much of our life was enlivened by the officers who commanded us. Men like Maj. Rhinehart, Capt. Coffyn and Capt. Thomas Hitchcock are morale builders and character molders in any man's Army.

Capt. Hitchcock was a standout man and a first rate officer. He was commanding officer of the 15th Aero Squadron. Although he was 55 years old, he had learned to fly well. He was a marvel of physical condition. One of his great delights was in assembling us at reveille and marching us to the far end of the post and back at double time, then standing by the barracks to watch stragglers half his age come puffing along, well out of breath.

He instituted what he called an "extra prize" system. By this he put various platoons into competition with one another keeping their quarters clean, doing routine jobs and taking on extra tasks. The prizes were tickets to good theatricals, and he never failed to pay off. He treated men like members of his family, was strict but understanding, sympathetic and fair. He had a special affection for flying men. Much of this sprang from the fact that his son was a fighting flyer overseas. The captain kept us posted on his son's whereabouts and exploits from time to time as snatches of news came through from France.

I will never forget the look of restrained and gentle sorrow on his face when he told us one day that his son had been reported missing after a flight in France. There were tears in his eyes but his voice never wavered, and he gave us the news just as he had given us happier news on a dozen other occasions. We later learned that his son had been shot down behind the lines and was a prisoner of the Germans. He lived to become America's greatest polo player, and he lived also to give his life for his country in World War II. Few Americans ever gave more than Tommy Hitchcock, our captain's son.

Russell Holderman, WWI instructor, 1918

CHAPTER 14
ENTER THE CO-PILOT

Into the life of many young men there come periods of depressed calm before the storms of love set in. This happens in wartime as well as in peace. It happened to me at Hazelhurst, and provided me with the most fortunate meeting of my life.

Somewhat depressed in spirits, I was making one of those visits every young man has to make…calling on friends of my family in Jamaica…when it all started. These were the Archie Smiths, excellent people both, and hospitable as the day is long. Their next-door neighbors were people named Harris, one of whose daughters, Dorothy, wandered into the Smiths' while I was calling. She was young, friendly, pretty, cheerful and fascinated far more by my uniform and silver wings than by my sunburned and wind-reddened face.

We met under most suspicious circumstances in the home of those mutual friends and it wasn't long afterward that my flying Jenny got another name. I painted "Dorothy" in large letters on her nose.

More often than not while waiting for my lady at her home, I fell asleep in front of the fire, and was always properly embarrassed to have her wake me up. But a face reddened by motorcycle riding and flying open-cockpit planes was already ruddy enough to betray no further blushes. Dorothy was altogether wonderful.

She listened to my small talk about flying as if she enjoyed it. I'd talk until dinner, give it a decent interval, and then talk flying after dinner, a period in which I was usually beset by questions from her younger brother Frank, whom the family called Sonny. Years later, when he was ferrying bombers for Britain across the hazardous South Atlantic route to Africa, his fellow pilots still called him that.

But the future bomber ferry pilot's sister seldom appreciated his presence in the family library on those evenings in 1917 and 1918. He was unceremoniously dismissed from our presence more than once for asking so many questions that he threatened to turn each evening into an aerial quiz program.

Although she was to become one of our greatest women glider pilots, Dorothy was not air-conscious then. She was simply a charming and interested girl, with good sense and intelligence. That good sense and intelligence have been as beneficial to me as anything I can name. If she hadn't become my wife, I most probably would not have continued flying as a career. I have left some of the most difficult decisions of my dangerous business to her and she has never failed me. My mother had always told me that I needed someone to "take me by the hand," and over the decades, this is what Dorothy has done. Her decisions have saved me from having to depend too much on luck. He who does that in flying too frequently dies horribly in the process.

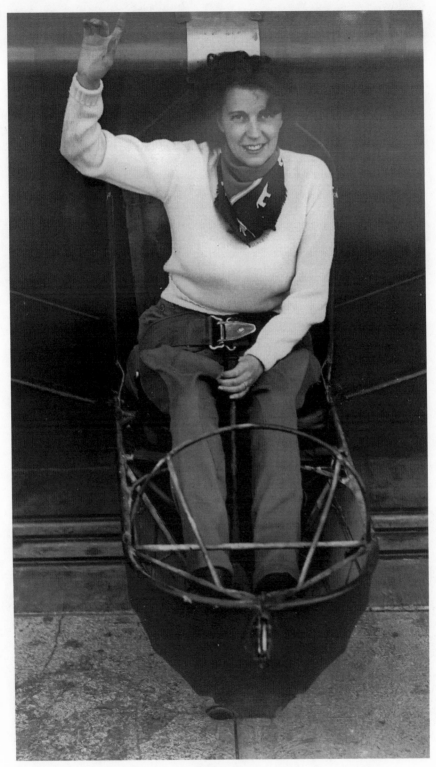

Dorothy

CHAPTER 15
BLINDMAN'S BLUFF

Before my personal age of reason set in, I did aerial acrobatics, more commonly known as stunt flying. I had a burst of this at Hazelhurst, somewhat in violation of regulations. I even gave stunting instructions, much to the joy of my pupils and the horror of my superiors. A favorite stunt was to approach over the field at about 2,000 feet, put the ship into a spin to about 200 feet, sideslip, then land. It was at about this time that I experienced a burst of conceit so large that it nearly cost me my life.

My friends in the Bronx had never seen me fly. So one day I telephoned my mother to tell her to expect me to fly over the house in about 30 minutes. Before she could form her startled words into a motherly protest, I hung up, after telling her to inform my friends that I would be coming straight over Crotona Avenue.

My Jenny, the name Dorothy lettered bravely on its nose, carried me off the field and across Long Island Sound to the Bronx. I first spotted Bronx Park, then I picked out 180th Street and followed it until I reached Crotona Avenue and recognized the red front of the Great Atlantic & Pacific Tea Company store in our neighborhood, half a block from our house.

By then I was able to pick out other familiar landmarks. There was plenty of open country in the Bronx then and spotting a familiar building was no great task. I followed Crotona Avenue south to Tremont Avenue, and west over Tremont to the Crotona Park baseball diamond near which years before I had tried my first glider flight and had my first crackup. I circled over the park and then flew back to Crotona Avenue, flying up and down its length until I could see people running from the houses. I dropped to a lower altitude and saw my mother, brother and sisters at our front gate.

I think that if I could have seen my mother's horrified face, I would not have attempted my next move. She was frozen with fear and I, although she did not know it, was dizzy with daring.

I sent the ship up to 1,500 feet and then pointed its nose straight down at the red A&P store front on 180th Street. Down dived the Jenny until the OX5 motor sang a shrill tune. At about 800 feet I gently pulled the stick back and went into a generous loop and then repeated it. The last time, the ship literally hung at the top of the loop, having lost too much speed. It was then that the fire extinguisher worked loose from its holder and smashed into the cowling in front of me.

A thousand fears rode rampant through my mind. Would the tail come off? Would I crash in my own back yard, right in front of my mother? Why had I left the post and gone on a personal pleasure flight in violation of regulations, without permission? Why had I ever taken up flying?

By then the ship began moving too fast to give me time for even the thoughts of fear. It dropped out of the loop upside down to within 400 feet of the street. Suddenly it nosed down. As it did so, I pulled back on the stick and cleared the top of my family's house by a scant 200 feet. Without further ado, I pointed the Jenny toward Mineola and wiped the cold perspiration from my brow.

I didn't know it at the moment, but I had finished only the first leg of a joyless and frightening journey.

I took stock of the situation just as I passed over what I thought was the shoreline of the Sound. The difficulty was that I couldn't see the further shore. This was puzzling. Over what should have been the middle of the Sound, I still could not see the other side. All I could see was water below, rolling, restless and beckoning with menace.

A thick haze had settled in and the horizon, by which I had learned to fly, was no longer in sight. There was nothing but a vast emptiness. The only way I could keep the plane level was by listening to the whistle of the wind in the wires, and keeping those wires playing their weird, familiar tune. A cold uneasiness gripped me. My hands and forehead were sweating freely. The stick all but slipped from me. It helped only a little to watch the water, and I really had no way of knowing how far below me it was. I was flying blind and I did not like it.

I have remembered that day repeatedly in later years. It has come back to me like a cold and terrifying image from the past. For many years now, flying blind with the greatest instruments of aviation science to guide me safely through bad weather has been routine. But how I could have used those instruments that murky day over the gray Sound!

I winged through the haze for 40 horrifying minutes before it came to me that the reason I had not reached the Long Island shore was that I was flying up the Sound, not across it. The sun had disappeared in the haze and I had to guess my direction and make a turn. It was a fearful decision, because to have turned the other way would perhaps have been fatal and one plane may not have reached home at Hazelhurst that night.

Within 20 minutes I saw the Long Island shoreline, standing gray and dim below me, but looking like a blessed land. The next thing I recognized was Oyster Bay. I followed the road to Hazelhurst and brought the ship down. There were barely three gallons of gasoline left in the tank when I taxied up to the hangar. I had learned my lesson about flying cross-country without permission. The greatest pleasure I knew at the moment was the solid feeling of firm earth under my feet.

When I next went home it was by motorcycle. But I discovered, to my surprise, that I had become a daring hero in the neighborhood. Everyone said I had put on a wonderful show. My mother told me that she thought my end had come when my plane dived for the house. I never told her how alike our thoughts had been at that moment.

Suddenly having to fly blind was a great fear of pilots in 1917 and 1918. I thought I had my proper dose that afternoon, trying to bring the ship from the Bronx to Hazelhurst, but apparently, I was billed for a series of treatments.

I took off one morning in a slight overcast and headed west. I was flying blind. In a few minutes, I found the sun directly in front of me and realized that I must have made a 180 degree turn unwittingly. I was flying out toward the ocean. I immediately descended in a dive and was glad to see the ground. I never tried blind flying again until I had the proper instruments. Few would fly blind successfully without them. In any conditions, it was a 50-50 gamble. It was either luck on your side or your body arriving in a box at the family doorstep. Flying on feeling and senses alone was not enough to assure success. The whistle of the wind in the struts and the wires, the memory of the last sight of earth and sky, often a faulty memory, were not enough.

Even for years after those war days, pilots had to fly by touch and feel when the going got murky. Too often they died in flames or were smashed to bits. They sacrificed their lives to a flying condition for which there seemed to be no solution. The roster of pioneer heroes who were killed flying blind was fat with fine names before instruments were designed which have made blind flying perhaps even more dependable and sure than flying by sight on a clear day today.

Our World War I Jenny planes were virtually devoid of instruments. Each one had a tachometer, which indicated the number of revolutions the motor was turning per minute. If the reading showed an increase and the throttle had not been pressed, then we knew the plane must be headed down. If, without pressure on the throttle, the reading was low, we knew the plane was climbing, in which case there was always the chance of a stall, followed by the horror of a spin. Aside from the tachometer, all the Jenny had was an oil pressure gauge, a water temperature gauge, an ignition switch and an altimeter. In all, these were little better as flying instruments than the 12 inch piece of string on Fred Shneider's old biplane back at Mineola.

One of the last flights I made from Hazelhurst was something in the nature of a personal triumph. It involved my father. Believing that I should perhaps not fly again after I got my discharge, I told my father on one occasion at home that I wanted to take him up before I had to stop flying for good. We set the date. Inasmuch as it was strictly against Army rules to take up a civilian passenger, I arranged with Sergeant O'Brien, a barracks mate, to bring my father by motorcycle to a field about five miles east of Hazelhurst.

I took off from camp and found them waiting at the field. Before my father had time to change his mind, O'Brien bundled him into the rear cockpit of the Jenny, strapped him in tight and stepped aside for our takeoff. We had flown for about 30 minutes before I looked back at my father and shut off the motor. We were flying at 5,000 feet. I shouted, "How about a loop?" He smiled, waved his hand and gripped the sides. I nosed over and made three loops, but he kept smiling. I gave him a chance to get his bearings and then did a couple of Immelmanns, a tailspin, made a steep side slip and then landed. O'Brien chugged alongside and helped my father out, saying doubtfully, "Boy, he sure gave you the works!" Said my father, "It was great."

I took off and circled around, picking them up going west toward Hazelhurst, with my father bumping along in the sidecar. I flew low and followed alongside the road as O'Brien opened up the motorcycle and kept pace with the plane. My father hung on for life….one hand gripping the sidecar, the other firmly planted on his derby hat.

At the Army field, he pointedly informed me that he had received a bigger thrill from the motorcycle ride back than from the comparatively mild airplane ride I had given him. He was a true sportsman. It had taken me years, successive step by step, to persuade him that flying was what I wanted to do. I considered it a victory well won that he would even fly with me, to say nothing of dismissing my stunting as a harmless form of amusement. He told my mother that night that she needn't worry about my flying. I told her I would take her up next. She gave me a hint of a smile, no more.

The day before I was to be discharged from the Army, I made a flight around New York City and Long Island. I did this at the dictates of an overpowering nostalgia. I thought I was making my farewell flight. I had talked myself into a fine case of gloom, one in which no light of cheer appeared, one in which the future never figured. My flying days were done, and I knew it with a dreadful finality. Gone, said I to myself, are the days of flying alone above all the other people in the cities and farms below. Gone is the solitude of glorious minutes and hours in the world of flight, so detached, so apart from the crawling world of business and commerce, domestic cares and labor in the fields that look like patchwork from the pilot's seat of a steady little ship. Gone, I said with a note of doom, is my career. I flew low over fields and brooks, and went high into the clouds. Then I pointed the ship toward Hazelhurst, brought her down, taxied to the hangar, stepped out and mumbled to no one in particular, "That's that."

The next day, I was no longer a soldier of Uncle Sam's. Neither were most of my flying mates. We were civilians again, cut loose from our routine, free to go home, to get jobs, to stay up late and sleep late, free from bugle calls and reveille, from orders. But most of all, we were freed from flying, and that was an unwanted freedom.

There should be much exhilaration in receiving an honorable discharge from the Army of the United States, in being told officially by your government that you have done your duty, that your nation has found your services acceptable and that they are no longer needed for the purposes of war. I must confess that I grasped my discharge papers with a shaking hand and that my throat was full of lumps. Hazelhurst had been more than an Army field to me.

At Mineola Field it had suckled me as an unweaned flying stripling. I learned to fly from it. I made lasting friendships with men and machines in its hangars. I was close to it and I loved it.

Hazelhurst Field gave me something I could not have gotten in any other way. The Army gave me something else. War is horrible, grim and tragic, but the Army is not. In peace or war, a young man who emerges from the Army or Navy flying service is a better man for it. He has won something that can never be taken away from him. And he has laid the groundwork for a career in the air if he wants to take that route.

Since that first great war I have seen thousands of our finest young men go into training in the air to help fight other wars. Many of them perhaps never intended to be pilots. But this is what wars do to young men. They change their lives. And those who go into flying may be somewhat different from the others....not more courageous, not more sacrificing, not necessarily more intelligent or dedicated. But one has only to stand on the flight deck of an American aircraft carrier and watch the jets take off in a screaming flood of noise and overwhelming speed and power to realize, perhaps, that here is a different breed of man and that the aerial defense of the nation is in very good hands.

CHAPTER 16
FLYING MAILMEN

A demobilized Army pilot is like a sailor on a raft....he drifts wherever the tides take him. I drifted back into the building business with my father, knowing all the time that our association would last only as long as there were no flying jobs open. I became an assistant superintendent, but the feel of blue prints in my hands only made them itch more to grasp the stick of a plane again.

Airmail was being flown daily from Belmont Park to Washington, D.C. I went out to get a flying job. None was open, but they needed a mechanic, so I became a mechanic and hoped to make the flying list at the first opening.

There were pioneers in the airmail business, too. Many of them gave their lives in the early days of developing a system, putting it on its course to becoming a great national asset. Those who lived to see the United States Airmail become the finest in the world experienced many hardships and suffered many heartaches.

It was a tough business, even for such skilled and dogged pilots as E. Hamilton Lee, now retired from United Air Lines, and who at the time of his retirement had more time in the air to his credit than any other pilot in the world. His is one of the most remarkable records in the history of power aviation. Late in his career, his own son became his co-pilot.

Color, character, eccentricities, vivid personalities characterized many of the early airmail pilots, men like Buddy Budwick and Max Miller, who made the first flight out of Belmont Park with mail aboard, and "Hammerhead" Smith. Smith was truly remarkable. He won the name of Hammerhead honestly, but strictly by accident. He was cranking a motor when it backfired. The propeller spun and hit Smitty on the head. The propeller broke but all Smith suffered was a slight bump. From that day forward, he was "Hammerhead" to his fellow pilots.

Then there was Turk Gardner, who was killed trying to make a good wager with another pilot, Charles I. Stanton, that he could spin a plane closer to the ground than Stanton could. Gardner crashed and died. Stanton, then superintendent of the eastern division of the airmail service, later held a key post with the Civil Aeronautics Authority.

There were Harold (Slim) Lewis, who could make a plane do everything but talk; Wesley L. Smith, who had more crackups than almost any other pilot and lived to tell vivid tales of them; P.W. Smith, Bill Lindley, Ira Biffle, who taught Charles A. Lindbergh how to fly; Bill Bishop, Red Reddick, Robie Robinson, Daddy DeHart, a great pilot named Hill, who later went down with Lloyd Berteaud in the old plane Old Glory in their attempt to fly to Rome; Dean Smith, an airways pioneer, and Big Boy Anglin.

There were Allen Adams, Major Ferron, who managed the New York airmail terminal, and Harry Powers, who succeeded him, as well as Bob Shank, Red McCloskey, Earl White and Lyman Doty.

Doty was a martyr to airmail and to the development of instrument flying. He was one of those who had to fly blind, without instruments, and, being in airmail, he flew whether death stared at him or not. Doty was everybody's friend, highly popular, skillful, courageous, and determined. He had only one fear and that was that if he crashed, he might burn to death.

One day on his airmail route, Doty had to fly in fog, and this meant, as we called it, flying by the seat of his pants. What happened to him can happen to anyone flying blind without instruments. His sense of touch and feeling gave him the wrong answers. It's a horrible feeling to realize, when you're flying blind in fog, that your senses have steered you wrong, that they too, have gone back on you. It's a feeling of utter helplessness.

All Doty could do was to descend and trust to luck in trying to get under the fog. He had no idea how high he was. He had no sensitive altimeter. Down, down he went. Luck was with him that first time. The plane broke out of the fog directly into a clearing. He might have hit hills, trees or a house, but he didn't. He broke out of that foggy 100 foot ceiling, spotted a field and set down his plane.

And there he was, having escaped death by inches, safe on the ground with death's cold breath still on his neck. But he had a load of United States mail aboard and he was loyal and faithful. The fog seemed to be lifting slightly, so he took a chance. He took off, and tried to stay under that murky ceiling. Obstacles loomed ahead, so he pulled up to try to avoid them. He had nothing to tell him what his air speed was .....no "turn and bank" indicator. No horizon shown ahead of him to guide him. He was flying blind again, and this time with too little air speed to make the ship respond to his touch. The plane stalled and carried Doty down and crashed and caught fire near Eatonville, MD.

The news of Doty's crash numbed us all at Belmont. When the word came in, no one said a thing for a while. But Doty hadn't burned to death and hadn't known the horror of what he had dreaded. Without regaining consciousness, he died from internal injuries three weeks after his crash. He was a great guy.

Red McClosky escaped burning too. Carrying mail out of Cleveland, McClosky's DeHavilland caught fire 10 miles from the city. The flames spread rapidly and soon enveloped the cockpit, all but trapping the pilot. The ship stayed level, a hurtling, fiery comet. McClosky climbed to the back of his seat to escape the licking, growing flames. Clinging precariously to the "turtle neck" behind his seat, he tried vainly to reach through the fire and grab the stick and somehow bring the blazing plane to earth. It was a heart rendering, uneven battle he waged in the sky, and the flames won the fight. Rather than crash in a flaming coffin of an airplane, McClosky jumped from 200 feet and was killed instantly. But the flames never got him.

Hardships were distributed evenly. Everyone had to be able to take the gaff. Had it not been for the good humored hardiness of many of the pioneer airmail workers, the system certainly would not have been developed so quickly to its eventual point of efficiency.

The chief mechanic at Belmont was Charles (Chuck) Freming, whose brother Herman was also on the mechanics' roster, along with me and a number of others who spent their days plastered with grease, and half their nights trying to wash it off. The Fremings eventually forsook their roles as physicians to ailing airplanes and went into the restaurant business in Olean, N.Y. where, years later, I visited them and spent half a day in the kind of reminiscing only airmen know. They are gone now, but even in their days in the restaurant they both expressed a wish to get back to flying, and I never would have been surprised to see them turn up again at a field, tools in hand and their old familiar grins on their old familiar faces.

In the airmail days, our mechanics crew boasted such motor magicians as Charlie King, Pep Smith and Fred Winzel. Winzel was the coffee king of the contingent. He must have made gallons, especially in cold weather, and could always be depended upon to produce a steaming pot when the going got coldest and the winds were most bitter. Besides having a way with a coffee pot, Winzel knew what was what with a camera. He was unofficial photographer of the airmail terminal. But over this part of his work there hung a kind of grimness. Foreboding filled the air whenever he took a picture of a new pilot, for many times the shot Winzel snapped was the last ever made of the man alive. Through Winzel, I acquired a good many photographs of early airmail days. They are now valued relics of an era now past, an era which took many of our best flyers with it.

The hardships those days brought were not relieved by the types of ships in service. These consisted mostly of several Curtiss Model R's with Liberty motors, converted Army DeHavillands, also powered by Liberties and called with birdmen's habitual morbidity, "flying coffins," a number of World War Jennies with Hispano motors, and several Hispano Standards. We also had an OX5 Curtiss Jenny of World War vintage which I used often to fly to disabled mail planes. We had two flying mechanics, me and Bill Lindley.

No one who worked in the early airmail service can deny that conditions were plenty bad. Actually, they were worse than that. The fog was so dense one day that we could not see across the field. Hamilton Lee's plane had been loaded with mail and was ready for takeoff, but to attempt to fly would have been suicidal. No one blamed Lee for not taking off. Conditions were impossible.

We had direct communication by telegraph between the Belmont Park terminal and the Washington office of Otto Preager, second assistant postmaster general and head of the airmail service. We were under orders to notify him by wire in the event of any delay in any of the flights. On that day of supreme fog, Preager was wired: "Mail delayed on account of fog." He replied immediately, with more attention to the creed of the Post Office Department than to the impossible flying conditions of the day: "The mail must go through. Have pilot fly by compass." A second wire went to Preager: "Pilot refuses." Preager wired again: "Pilot must go or resign."

U.S. AIR MAIL
1918~1921
Through sleet, rain, snow, wind and fog
The mail must go.

R. HOLDERMAN   "SANTA MARIA"

Lee again declined the opportunity of destroying himself in a hopeless flight. His reserve pilot, Hammerhead Smith of the sturdy skull, was ordered to take the ship up. Smith, too, declined the honor. Thus occurred America's first airmail strike.

Although the fog cleared later that day, none of the pilots would take off. They would only fly, they said, if Lee were reinstated. No reinstatement came through on the wire. No mail went out by plane that day. It was sent by train. On each succeeding day that week, the mail was loaded on a plane, and each day a pilot stood by, perfectly willing to fly it on the condition that Lee be returned to good standing. Each day, the mail had to go by train. Late in the week, Pilot Reddick made up his mind to fly and break the deadlock. He changed his mind when someone told him that a bomb might have been planted in a wing of the plane. The strike ended only after Lee was reinstated.

When Major Ferron was placed on the flying list, Harry Powers succeeded him as manager of the Belmont terminal, and one of the Major's first moves was to brush up on his flying. Ferron had never flown a DeHavilland, and much of the mail had to be carried in such a ship. He volunteered to test the next DeHavilland that could be made ready. Up he went, circled about for a time and prepared to land. He cut the speed of the ship too sharply and it stalled and crashed in front of the hangar and burst into flames. Before the ship hit, we had scattered in all directions, none of us being certain where it would strike. But when the flames roared out after the impact, there was nothing to do but run back. No one wants to see man cremated. I pounded back toward the flaming wreck. Someone yelled, "He's clear!" I grabbed a pyrene extinguisher from another plane and kept running towards the fire. I found Major Ferron rolling on the ground, his flying suit ablaze. He had been thrown out of his seat; his safety belt had broken. He had been burned cruelly. We beat out the flames, removed his smoking suit, his helmet and goggles. His face was a red, raw, pitiful sight, and he was in terrible pain.

I rushed up the government motorcycle from the hangar. The injured Major was lifted into the sidecar and someone covered his face with canvas and away we went. I opened the throttle wide and we roared off toward Jamaica, 10 miles away. I could see the Major's hands gripping the sides of the sidecar as we skimmed along. I kept the motorcycle horn blowing continuously to clear a right of way. I passed a motorcycle policeman. He immediately chased up and only caught us at the hospital, where he dashed up with a list of broken traffic laws tumbling from his lips. But he needed only one glance at the Major to forget all that, and helped me carry the burned man into the hospital.

Major Ferron lived, but he never flew again. His face, except where his helmet had covered it, was a mass of scars. He was another martyr to the cause of airmail in its early days, and another victim of a DeHavilland flying coffin.

FLYING MAILMEN

***

The operations building at Belmont terminal had a flag and flag pole. That little flag, symbol of freedom and liberty, banner of men who have pioneered to make this country what it is, was flown at half staff about half the time in tribute to some airmail pilot who paid the penalty of the brave and the price of pioneering. In one sorrowful stretch, the flag rested at half staff for seven days on end.

Seeing that flag at half staff never daunted those pilots. Each of the seven for whom it flew for seven straight days took off without a qualm; each died in the performance of what he liked to think was his duty. Somehow, although it was often delayed and sometimes damaged, the mail got through. That was the main idea. Men paid with their lives because they were doing something they knew should be done, and that they were risking their lives doing it in daily routine never seemed to affect them. They went ahead, living out each day with that philosophy and attitude toward death which is characteristic of their breed.

Pilots were killed at such as alarming rate that my name rapidly neared the top of the list from which replacements were being chosen. There was a relief in this, for I was finding the daily routine of the mechanic's duties monotonous. Changing spark plugs and cranking propellers for weeks on end has little appeal for one who has known the thrill of flight. Not only that , there was nearly as much danger in twirling a propeller as there was in flying the mail, and I felt I would rather die more or less gloriously at the stick of a plane than be decapitated unceremoniously by a propeller on the ground.

When Charles I. Stanton, our boss, next visited the Belmont field, I talked turkey to him, trying to convince him that I was ready even then to take a regular airmail trick, that he needed pilots faster than he could take them off the replacement list. He argued that I hadn't had enough experience. I told him that all he had to do was watch me for a few minutes to be convinced. Thereupon I jumped into the utility Jenny, greasy overalls and all, took her off and put on a show for him. I trotted out my full bag of tricks, showed him everything I had learned in the Army and a little more, and then landed to hear his verdict. He told me to report in Washington the next week.

About the time I signed on as a pilot, the Chicago airmail run was started. This time, instead of DeHavillands and deep fog, it was the mountains around Bellefonte, PA that took their toll from our pioneering band of aerial mail men.

Slim Lewis was the first to crash, or at least one of the first, but his plane sliced through a tea house and did not burn. He lived to fly again. Robie Robinson went next. Robie tried to fly under an overcast one day, following the winding Susquehanna River.

He made out all right until he failed to see a cable hung across the river north of Harrisburg. His ship ticked the cable and was spun into the river. Robie died of a broken neck.

I had made only a few flights between New York and Washington before our outfit was moved from Belmont terminal to Newark, to a field situated north of the city. The new terminal was called Heller Field, and a heller it was. Trees had been felled to make way for the airplanes, and all that was left for the landing field was a postage stamp surface. Tree stumps stood up like concrete posts in a hollow at one side. Along the opposite side a canal ran sluggishly. On still another side squatted one of the Tiffany Company's factories, a comparatively low building with tall smoke stacks. A railroad track ran beside the factory.

Of all the spots ever selected for a busy airway terminus, I suppose this was the worst. Accomplishing a successful landing there was something of an art. The pilot had to skim the Tiffany factory, making sure his wings were clear of the smoke stacks, pass over the railroad and set his wheels down just over the tops of the tree stumps. If he failed to do this, he more often than not, overshot the field and wound up in the canal. Occasionally, a plane came in too short, hooked a tree stump and turned over. Once in a while someone rolled straight into the canal after what looked like a perfect landing.

A pilot came in one day, straight toward the Tiffany building, and tried to shoot for the field between two chimneys, or what he thought were two chimneys. He struck the center one, sheared if off 10 feet from the top and dropped to his death in the wreckage of his plane. Down came our flag to half staff.

Not only was Heller Field laid out to the worst possible advantage for pilots, the hangar was built in as inconvenient a spot as any I have ever seen. A long low building, it was situated in the lowest part of the field, near the railroad tracks. Whenever it rained, the water quickly found its level on the hangar floor and soon covered it to a depth of several inches. One night it froze, and the morning came frigidly. When it did, we found the planes' wheels held fast in 12 inches of water and four inches of ice. We had to chop the ship loose to carry the mail. That was a dreary and discouraging day. The water system froze and we had no water for the motor radiators. Still, the mail had to go through.

Our problem was only solved when a freight train rumbled up the track near the hangar. We flagged it, explained to the engineer that we needed water, for the mail must go. Every pilot, mechanic and airdrome helper pitched in. We drew water from the locomotive's boiler into empty gasoline drums, rolled them across the field and filled the planes' radiators. Lubricating the motors was something of a problem that day too. We had a large pot-bellied stove in one corner of the hangar. We hung 5 gallon cans of oil around the stove and heated the oil until it could be poured. Despite such obstacles, the crew generally managed to get the mail through, even in the bitterest weather. On the day that we had to flag the train, we were happy to be able to report that the mail not only got off, it got off on time.

* * *

When Chuck Freming resigned as chief mechanic at the Newark terminal, I was asked to take over. Although I liked to fly the run, I knew I would be more valuable as a flying mechanic, able to boss the repairing of the machines and at the same time pilot if necessary. It turned out to be a tough trick and meant starting work at 6 a.m. and usually working through until midnight, servicing our pitifully small fleet of planes and keeping them airworthy so that the mail could go through.

Slim Lewis got the mail through one day by the seat of his pants and the skin of his teeth. He literally had a brush with death. The sky was heavily overcast when he took off for Bellefonte, and he flew the valleys. This meant staying inside the slopes and taking advantage of the generally clearer air in the troughs. As long as there was a valley, this was all right. But Slim came to the end of one valley and although the overcast was still heavy, he had to pull up into it to avoid striking a mountain slope. So he gave his machine the gun and pulled her up, flying blind until, after a few nerve-shattering minutes, he figured he was over the hump of the mountain. There were no radio beams, of course, and he was only following a dreaded and usually futile procedure.

Slim fully believed he was clear of danger, and he started to take the plane to a lower altitude. All at once, the ship shuddered as the left wing struck something. Slim cut the ignition immediately, thinking he was about to crash. Cutting the switch was the only way he knew to save himself from being burned to death when the ship struck. For several paralyzing seconds, he sat with his hands on the stick, waiting for a crash that never came. Suddenly the ship broke into the clear from out of the overcast, and he discovered at the same instant that instead of heading straight for a crash, he was zooming down the mountainside, parallel with the slope, clearing the tree tops only by inches. Luckily, the propeller was still turning, so Slim switched on the ignition, the motor caught and away he went, bringing the ship safely out of its mountain skim and landing it at Bellefonte.

Inspection showed that tree tops had torn away most of the underside of his left wing and that half the exhaust pipe had been ripped away. That was one of the days on which our flag remained at full staff.

But not all of Slim Lewis's close calls with death were accidental. He went to Hazelhurst Field at Mineola, L.I. one day to test a German Junker for our airmail fleet and asked me to fly from Heller Field to pick him up late in the day. When I landed, he jumped into the front seat and told me to keep the stick because he was tired and wanted to sleep. He leaned his head against one of the center section struts and slept until we were approaching Heller at an altitude of about 1,000 feet. I had just started to throttle for a landing when Slim woke up with a start, saw the field ahead and yelled to me, "Let me have it!" With some reluctance, I told him to go ahead, and grabbed both edges of the cowling. I knew something was coming, but knowing Slim Lewis, I had no idea what it would be.

Slim cut the throttle sharply, pulled the stick back with a jerk, gave the rudder a hard kick over, and in a split second we were spinning dizzily toward earth. I looked at the Tiffany factory. It seemed to be spinning, too. Of all the dizzy descents I have ever made, that was the dizziest. The ground spun nearer and nearer; the blood drained out of my head; my heart pumped jumpily. I had great respect for Slim's ability, but watching a man stunt from the ground and being at his mercy only a few hundred feet over a factory are two different things. I was as certain that we were about to crash as I was that death would be instantaneous. But the Tiffany building suddenly stopped spinning. And so did we. The ship slipped steeply over the stumpy hollow beyond the railroad tracks, and down we came in as perfect a three-point landing as anyone could wish. Slim grinned at me and never said a word. Neither did I. I was speechless. Only Slim Lewis knew how close we were to crashing.

The year 1927 was the beginning of the end of much of that kind of stunting. In that year, the Aeronautics Branch of the U.S. Department of Commerce stiffened the enforcement of regulations prohibiting low stunt flying. Later, no acrobatics were allowed under 1,500 feet excepting on special occasions. That was the altitude at which stunting usually started in the beginning, and many a good flyer died because he misjudged.

Heller Field bred accidents like flies. And facilities were so poor that the hardships of keeping ships in the air, getting them up and then landing them safely were so many that I recommended moving the terminal. Still another reason was that we had acquired several German Junkers and they needed more runway space than Heller field could offer.

The Post Office Department leased a large hangar at Roosevelt Field, formerly Hazelhurst Field, where I had been stationed during the war, and where I had first soloed. Roosevelt Field saw many strange sights in its tenure as an airmail terminal. One of these was Lawrence Sperry's small three-cylinder Sperry Messenger, a tiny single place biplane.

Sperry, who with his father was later responsible for the automatic pilot and all workable gyro instruments, was enthusiastic about his new ship and the ease with which it could be handled. He persuaded me to take the little thing up. I handled it so beautifully that I "wrung it out," that is to say, I hopped it around, looped it, spun it, and put it through every conceivable kind of flying pace. It was as nearly a perfect machine for a beginner as any I had ever seen. Sperry later took the ship to England for demonstrations and one day was rescued from the English Channel after the little plane's motor failed.

Motor failure was a common occurrence, but it became steadily less frequent as aeronautical engineers kept ironing out bug after bug in motor construction and design. Even before jet engines revolutionized flying, we rarely thought of a forced landing in terms of motor trouble.

* * *

Returning to Hazelhurst was like a home-coming to me. This time, it was as manager of the New York terminal of the airmail system.

The three Junkers which were shortly added to our fleet were a delight. They were faster and carried more mail than the other ships. All-metal, low-winged monoplanes, they had no struts or wires to reduce their speed. The pilots liked them and were relieved to be flying something even halfway modern in design and performance.

The one real fault in the Junkers was the design of their gasoline-line systems and this proved to be their downfall. Wes Smith was flying one at 8,000 feet near Chicago when the line clogged and the motor backfired. Flames shot through the carburetor and the air intake, which was fixed at the back of the motor, where raw gasoline collected. The raw fuel caught fire and flames darted back into the cockpit and licked Smith's feet and legs and those of his co-pilot. The co-pilot swung his legs over the side of the ship and dangled them there, a safe distance from the licking flames. But Smith had to keep the controls while his shoes and clothing caught fire.

One of the ways to stifle a blaze in flight is to sideslip the airplane. Smith tried it but was only partly successful. The fire on one side burned itself out. By that time, his hands, arms and face were singed, and the ship had gone into a sickening nosedive. Because the Junkers' wings were thick and the fuselage was short, the tremendous air current generated in the dive kept the elevator control from functioning and Smith couldn't stop the dive. He tried frantically to get the elevators to work as they plummeted toward destruction. He got control finally at about 2,000 feet. Looking for a field in which to set the plane down, with the motor dead and the propeller still, Smith ordered the co-pilot into the rear to put all the mail bags as far back as possible and stay there himself. Then Smith picked out a cornfield and set the ship down. All he did was blow out both tires.

Max Miller had worse luck. Max was flying a Junker over Morristown, N.J. when the gas line went wrong, the ship crashed in flames and both Max and his co-pilot were killed. This ended the life and career of America's first regular airmail pilot. What actually happened on the flight, no one will ever know. I had seen Max at the takeoff that morning at six o'clock and knew that he was anxious to make Chicago that night because he had a date.

The last of the Junkers were taken off the run soon after Max Miller's death. We saw no sense in flying such deadly ships until a better gasoline system could be designed for them. That left us with a single DeHavilland on the New York-Cleveland trip, making the flight each way, each day, for ten days on end. This made all night maintenance a necessity.

We were relieved from this plight only when a couple of converted DeHavillands came off the line at the L.W.F. factory at College Point, L.I. Shortly afterward, we acquired a few redesigned twin-motored DeHavillands. These had the same kind of fuselages and wings as the single-motored ships, but had enlarged center sections to bear the weight of their two 200-horsepower Hall Scott motors. Pilots looked upon these freaks as distinctly on the tricky side and not airworthy enough to be dependable or safe. And we were rid of one of them in a most peculiar way.

The honors fell on Mike Eversole, one of the pilots in the service who had ever made a parachute jump. Mike decided it was up to him to do away with one of the De-Havilland monstrosities, but he would tell no one what method he had devised for its destruction. One day Mike was ordered to ferry one of the two-motored D.H.'s from Roosevelt Field to Cleveland. Before setting out, he borrowed a parachute and collected a couple of handfuls of rejected spark plugs. The he took off. As Mike sped across country toward Cleveland, he began throwing spark plugs into one of the propellers. Every time a plug struck the whirling blade, it chopped a great chunk of wood out of it. Finally, its balance chipped away, the propeller began vibrating. It shook so badly that it pulled the motor loose. This loosened the wings. Then the ship started to fall apart.

Gleeful, Mike bailed out, feeling that in destroying the two-motored death trap he had only done a service to humanity. All it got him was his discharge from the airmail service, which was handed to him summarily after the authorities in Washington read him the riot act on willful destruction of government property, neglect of duty, etc., etc. I am inclined to think that Mike really did a service, in a way. He showed, beyond the shadow of a doubt, that even a good pilot could not be expected to take his life in his hands every time he took an airmail ship off the ground.

Those two-motored DeHavillands, the Junkers with the bad fuel lines, the made-over DeHavillands and the World War I Jennies were tricky and treacherous. The wonder is that any of them ever got through, and that the mail kept going through as steadily and regularly as it did. Keeping such ships in any kind of flying condition was an almost superhuman task. A week without a fatal crash was a week to mark well. A week without some kind of accident was rare.

Good pilots were killed or maimed flying unfit ships so that a system of air transportation could be developed. Those who paid with their lives or health are largely responsible for the great safety records established by our airlines today. Had the airmail pilots and the early transport flyers not shown the way with such courage, had they not died with such a will and taken chances with such good grace and grim determination, flying would be far less advanced than it is.

* * *

But not all was sorrow and tragedy. There were lighter sides of life in the airmail service. I remember one day when I noticed Red Reddick's unusual activity around the cockpit of a Curtiss R we had just serviced for the flight to Washington the next morning. Reddick had been assigned to the flight and when I first saw him buzzing around the ship, I thought he was merely checking the controls. But he kept at it and to satisfy my curiosity, I walked over to see what he was doing. He was tying a spark plug to the end of an 18-inch piece of string, the other end of which was fastened to the lower center of the instrument panel. "What on earth is that?" I asked him, not unreasonably. He explained that it was his own idea, that he was going to use the string and spark plug to fly through fog. "You see," he explained, "if the spark plug stays over that point on the floor, I'm flying level. If it points to any other spot, I'll control the plane accordingly."

The idea sounded silly, but anything seemed worth trying as a solution to totally blind flying. Reddick later claimed his device worked in smooth air but could not be trusted in bumpy weather. I still think he was flying by the seat of his pants all the time and not by the spark plug, even in smooth air. Furthermore, I think he was just plain lucky to get away with it.

Many years later, I saw Reddick again and asked him if he remembered his spark plug device. He smiled broadly and put his fingers to his lips in a hush-hush signal for fear I might tell the rest of the pilots about it. Whether Reddick's idea worked or not, he was not afraid to try it. In the barnstorming days after most of us left the airmail, Reddick, son of a U.S. Congressman, became known as the "flying hobo." He thought nothing of landing on a farm and trading a ride for anything from a few gallons of gasoline to a squealing pig. And he managed always to escape whole from his brush with death. So did Wes Smith. Smitty was flying the mail from Washington to Heller Field in a low ceiling one day when he struck trees and crashed. His head struck the cowling and he was knocked senseless for a few seconds. When he regained consciousness, the plane was in flames and he was in the middle. He crawled out barely in time to escape cremation. All the while we were anxiously waiting for him at Newark and feared the worst had happened. Then he walked into the office, like one returned from the dead. His first words were, "Look at my brand new leather coat!" He had torn the shoulder. That was all.

Airmail pilots, to whom forced landings were almost routine, had many encounters with farmers. One day Randy Page landed an airmail ship at the midway stop between Washington and New York. The terminal manager ran out to tell him that a farmer from nearby had complained. The farmer had told the manager that he didn't mind low flying planes scaring his cattle, but thought it was going too far when the planes flew so low the propeller blast knocked his hat off.

Airmail planes, early 1920s, Curtiss JN4, "Jenny"

CHAPTER 17
WEEKEND HOPPER

Daddy De Hart resigned from the airmail service in the spring of 1920 and bought a wartime Canadian Jenny. With this sturdy little ship as his sole stock in trade, he started a booming business, one of the first of many such enterprises which were to pop up all over the country in the years just after the war and which were to have a profound influence in making the people of the United States air-minded, getting them accustomed to the idea of casual flight.

De Hart started a passenger "hopping" business at a field in Queens, about two miles from Belmont Park. He did so well at the beginning that he soon bought a second plane and asked me to help him out by flying this ship on Sundays. He charged people $15 for a straight ride and $25 for a stunt ride, and business was excellent. It was so good that I decided to get a ship myself.

Late that summer, I bought a Jenny fuselage that had no covering, some tail surfaces and other odd parts. Bit by bit, I acquired wings, a motor that badly needed overhauling, and other parts until I had enough for a whole ship. I spent all my spare time working on it, hired Chuck Freming and Bill Ruggles, who were overhauling motors for the Army at Mitchel Field, to set up my motor in their spare time. We finished the ship that winter. She was a beauty, and made me homesick. She carried me right back to that flight as an Army pilot at Hazelhurst Field, for she was just such a ship as that Army Jenny I had flown the day I was certain I was flying for the last time.

I have been attached sentimentally to too many airplanes in my time, but that Jenny I rebuilt got a large chunk of my affection. It was the first ship that was all mine. I could fly it any time and anywhere I wanted to. There were no strings attached. Dorothy Harris shared my enthusiasm for the plane.

I was still flying for De Hart on Sundays, and Dorothy helped us out by tending the refreshment stand De Hart had set up at his Queens field. When De Hart left for California, I had high hopes that I might be able to lease his Queens field and start my own passenger hopping business. But Lieutenant Belvin Maynard, the famous "flying parson," who had set many records both overseas and in this country, and had won the Army's New York to San Francisco race, bought a house across the street from the field. His house was sold to him by the same real estate firm that owned the field, then called

Queens Village Airdrome, and he bought it with the understanding that he be allowed to use the field for his own plane.

When I heard of this arrangement, I started to look for a new location, fully believing that the lieutenant's taking over the field eliminated an outsider's chance of ever using it. And I was hunting for a new field for myself when Maynard, whom I had met while flying for De Hart, said he would like to see me.

Dorothy went with me when I went to see Maynard. He explained that he had bought his house because he wanted to build a hangar next to the house and use the field across the street for himself. He said he was paying $100 a month for the privilege, which was the same rent De Hart had paid. But he did not fly on Sunday. Consequently, he was willing to sub-let the field to me as long as he could use it for pleasure flying on weekdays. I closed the deal swiftly, and considered myself set up in business.

I resigned from the airmail service in the spring of 1921, just as the grass was growing green and the little field in Queens beckoned. By that time, Dorothy was a veteran air passenger, had been flown over her family's house in Jamaica, had survived her first loop and was a thoroughgoing enthusiast. She took over the Queens Field refreshment stand and opened it for business on the day I started hopping passengers for fees. We had been engaged to be married for more than a year and only the tiny size of my bank account kept us from getting married at once. I felt that I needed at least $1,000 before taking that step.

Our first Sunday at Queens Village Airdrome was a startling financial success. I charged $15 for stunt rides, $10 for regular rides, and both the refreshment stand and my trim little Jenny, her motor purring like a well-fed kitten, did a roaring business. We took in several hundred dollars that day. The Queens field was a good spot. Hillside Avenue, on which the field was situated, was the main thoroughfare from New York to many points on Long Island.

During the week, I taught students at $60 an hour, giving instructions at Roosevelt Field because the field at Queens was too small to be taking chances with novice flyers. Before we knew it, Dorothy and I had our $1,000 marriage money. She set the date for June 21. We had hoped that Lieutenant Maynard could perform the ceremony, but shortly before the day, he was called away. His family was to be represented by his daughters, Rosalind and Evelyn, as flower girls.

With married life in prospect, Dorothy and I decided that my motorcycle was not dignified enough, so we decided to buy an automobile. I bought one from Ernest Kothe, with whom I had built and flown model planes in the old Van Cortland Park days.

My first car was a Hupmobile with a Victoria top. In the eye of those used to getting places on a motorcycle with a sidecar, it was wonderful to behold. The car was to be delivered on June 20, the day before our wedding, and I sold my motorcycle and agreed to hand it over to its new owner that same day. I shall never forget our last ride in that machine. Neither will Dorothy.

We had dined at an inn on Jericho Turnpike in Queens, and in driving out of the place had to cross a set of trolley tracks. We were about to cross when a trolley screamed down on us. I applied the brake to stop. The brake rod was broken. There was no chance to stop. All I could do was turn quickly to the right. This pulled the sidecar up over my head, turned the whole motorcycle turtle and landed Dorothy in a mud puddle and me on the underside of the upset machine. The trolley stopped only a few feet short of crushing us. Dorothy has never ridden on a motorcycle since.

But we both recovered our composure in time for the wedding, which went off beautifully and smoothly, delayed only by my mislaying the marriage license and having to go hunt for it. This small incident failed to escape the eagle-eyed press. One newspaper next morning carried this headline: "Aviator bridegroom up in the air as marriage license is mislaid."

The press was on hand the next day, for our wedding trip was something of a novelty. We flew to Atlantic City on the first aerial honeymoon, and returned home in time to handle weekend business at Queens Village Airdrome. Dorothy still claims she has a honeymoon coming. We rented a room across from the Maynards and started married life right across the street from our place of business. At night, we tied the Jenny down right outside our window.

Those were ideal days. Business was excellent. We owned our own plane and the field was popular. On one weekend of Saturday, Sunday, and Monday (July 4th) business, the plane and refreshment stand took in more than $1,100.

One of my students was a well-known surgeon, Dr. Leo Greenbaum. He spent all his time at the field and brought me many customers. Business continued to grow with the generous and enthusiastic aid of such men as Dr. Greenbaum, and by the end of the summer, we had saved $10,000 and had paid all our bills. Not only that, we had acquired a new Packard touring car. The business of flying for a living was beginning to take on a golden tint.

We stayed at the Maynard's that winter, rested and made plans for the spring and summer of 1922. By the time the snow melted and the skies lost their winter grayness, our equipment was overhauled, the refreshment stand had a new coat of paint and the

Queens Village Airdrome was ready to do business again. We enjoyed a very successful season, but its end was clouded by tragedy.

The Maynards were most pleasant people and my wife and I thoroughly enjoyed being with them and their children, three small girls and a two-year-old boy, Belvin Maynard, Jr. I had great admiration for the elder Maynard, the famous "flying parson," and deep respect of his ability as a pilot. There were few better pilots, technically, and he had only the necessary fault of occasional carelessness. He did much of the necessary work on his planes himself, but even in this, he showed tragic neglect of some of the niceties of airplane maintenance.

Maynard visited a Coney Island photographic studio one day in 1922. A French Newport 28, the kind of plane he had flown with gallantry and distinction in the war, was being used as studio property background by the proprietor. Maynard formed an immediate sentimental attachment for the ship. It was just such a ship as the one in which he had once broken the world's loop-the-loop record. The flying parson walked up to the plane to inspect it. The ever-watchful photographer, sensing business, tried to sell him a picture. Soon they started talking at a great rate and the upshot was that instead of selling a picture to the flyer, the photographer sold him the old French airplane.

Maynard had the plane shipped home to Queens, where he worked on it in his spare time, repairing old parts, building new ones, replacing wires and other fixtures on the wings and motor. He soon had it in reasonable flying shape and took it up many times, despite the fact that the linen on the wings was loose and the turn-buckles and wires were a mixture of French and American manufacture.

When I heard Bert Acosta say one day that he wouldn't dare to fly the old Newport, I realized in what bad shape it really was. After that, every time Maynard took the ship up, I worried. Maynard came home one day in September, 1922 with the news that he had accepted an offer to do a week of exhibition flying at Rutland, VT. He planned to fly the old Newport to Rutland and there to take over a two-place English Avro to carry passengers in the exhibition flights. I tried so hard to discourage him that he finally tried to hire someone to fill the engagement for him, but without success. Unwilling to disappoint officials at the Rutland Fair, he started out in the Newport and we watched him take off.

It was with great relief that I learned a few hours later that Maynard had been forced down by motor trouble on Plum Island, just off Long Island. This put the Newport out of the picture, but he went on to Rutland by train. In Rutland, he found the Avro waiting for him, but there were so many passengers to be flown at the fair grounds that he took the rear seat out of the two-place ship and in its place built a double seat. This made a three-place plane of the Avro. Maynard tried the ship only once after that. He had two people with him on what was to have been a short flight over the fair grounds to test the ship with three people instead of its usual two. After a brief spin over the countryside, he brought the ship in at high altitude, ready to land. Then the gaping crowd below saw it happen.

Instead of coming down in the usual smooth glide, the Avro began spinning, came out of it and then spun again. It repeated this sickening maneuver several times and then, fully out of control, bore its three occupants, with gallant Maynard at the useless controls, to instant death.

Thus died a World War hero and a great gentleman, whose only fault as an aviator was carelessness. He had built the Avro's extra seat with inferior lumber. Investigators of the fatal crash agreed later that the wooden seat had collapsed and jammed the controls. And that is why hearts were heavy at the little Queens Village Airdrome in the rest of that season of 1922. A vast emptiness settled over the Maynard household, and we were a part of it. The death of Maynard left his wife, his four young children with little, and with the future staring unkindly at them all. Even a benefit meet staged at Roosevelt Field by Casey Jones, my pupil Milford Simmis, Bert Acosta, Lloyd Berteaud, Clarence Chamberlain and me netted Mrs. Maynard only enough for immediate expenses.

But Belvin Maynard's widow struggled bravely, and won the fight that many a bereaved aviator's wife has had to win. She later held a responsible and remunerative position. Her three daughters were happily married. And as for Belvin Maynard Jr., left fatherless at age two years old, there is more to be said.

Years later, I taught him how to fly. He entered the armed services and flew for his country in World War II, as his father had in the first Great War. It was the night after our benefit meet for Mrs. Maynard that Bert Acosta mystified New York City. Most of the pilots who had participated in the meet sat around talking pilot talk when Bert and Lloyd Berteaud announced that they were going to fly over the city. No one said much to them, but they left the room, warmed up their planes and took off in the pitch black.

Lloyd returned after reaching Jamaica, but a few minutes later, Bert was playing tag with the skyscrapers and giving pedestrians on the Great White Way something to gawk at. He flew the length and breadth of Broadway so low that there were buildings on either side of him. Having properly startled the populace and satisfied his craving for night flying, he came back to the field and landed.

The next day, New York newspapers all carried articles about the mysterious air-plane, with many wild conjectures as to from whence it had come and whither it had gone. No one ever tipped them off, even in later days when Bert Acosta made the lead of many of their aviation articles.

CHAPTER 18
WINGS OVER THE BEACH

It was Bill Lindley who persuaded us to go to Florida for the first time. The former airmail mechanic and pilot had since resigned from the service and was carrying passengers at Daytona Beach in a reconditioned Jenny. We drove down over winding, dusty, rutted roads which long since have given ways to straight, smooth, multi-laned ribbons of concrete.

Ted Kenyon rode to Florida with us. He had taken up flying at our Queens field the previous summer and was a natural pilot with an unusual mechanical knack, which he later used to great advantage for all pilots. It was he who developed the automatic pilot and worked with the Sperry Company designing and perfecting instruments for blind flying.

It took us six days to cover the ground between New York and Daytona, a journey I later made in a piston driven plane in about five hours and which now is a veritable breeze in a jet airplane. When we arrived in Daytona for the first time, we found Lindley winning auto races on the beach in a racing car fitted with an OX5 airplane motor, this left his Jenny idle, and he told me to use it as much as I wanted.

That was the "go" signal for enterprising Ted Kenyon. We rigged up a darkroom and went into the aerial photography business. With me at the controls of Lindley's peppy little Jenny, and Kenyon half-hanging out of the plane manipulating his camera, we got pictures of estates, boat yards, real-estate development and virtually everything the Daytona Beach area had to offer. Kenyon sold many of his air shots and soon had a booming business on his hands.

It was then that I bought my second Jenny and with it went into business at the beach in competition with a distinguished crew of flyers. Among them were Lindley, Eddie Balou, afterwards as ace pilot with Eastern Airlines; Slim Exstrum, later chief captain for Pan American Airways, and Stewart Chadwick. But like so many of our flying greats, Chadwick met a flyer's fate. One of the finest pilots I have ever seen, he had a knack for handling a ship which seemed to be true second nature. But he was killed testing a high-powered Navy plane built by Giuseppe Bellanca, my old friend of the old Mineola days.

We all kept our ships on Daytona Beach above the high water mark. Each day the tide, going out, left a wide, firmly packed stretch of sand, which swept gracefully down the coastline and was ideal for landing and taking off. As soon as the tide ebbed each day, we all moved our planes to this sandy runway and sold passenger rides to tourists. Business was good with all of us.

Once I reached the beach, all ready for a day's flying, hauled out my ship for business and stood by, waiting for passengers. After a time I realized that of the six ships operating out of that sector, mine was the only one ready to fly. The motors of the others were still covered with canvas. It was a beautiful looking day, with a fairly strong wind billowing out of the west. To me, it showed no flaws. But I wondered whether the other pilots had forsaken me out of sheer cussedness or by some odd coincidence had all decided to rest for the day and leave the field of business to me.

The first one I saw was Slim Exstrum. I was standing by my ship waiting for business when he ambled up, clad in a bathing suit. He looked surprised when he saw that I apparently intended to fly in such a wind. He inquired, "You're not going up in this blow, are you?" I replied with a condescending "certainly," thinking all the while that Exstrum and the others must have developed a strange softness to let a brisk breeze like that one keep them grounded on such an ideal day. "After all," I said, "I've flown in much stronger cross winds than this. Why stop flying on account of this one?"

Exstrum smiled and said," I think you'll find that the Florida west wind has a treachery all its own." Then, as he went off for a swim, my first passenger rolled up in an automobile. As I started south with my fare along the wide sand runway, which extended ten miles to the lighthouse, I gave the wind no more than a passing thought. It certainly did not worry me. It was only later that Exstrum told me he really enjoyed watching me take off, or try to.

Down the beach runway we scooted, going south. We were making good time but the ship wouldn't leave the ground. Finally it rose, then suddenly dropped like a rock and rolled on the sand again. Then I began to worry; for I knew that I had more than enough speed for a takeoff but still couldn't make the plane climb. When I finally did get off the ground without bouncing back, down drafts kept me from getting any higher than 50 feet. Then I was afraid to land because I felt that if I hit the beach too hard, I would crack up. All I could do was fight it out, and it was a rough ride. I passed the lighthouse, ten miles from the starting point, about at a level with its top. We bounced along like a cork on an ocean wave.

By that time, I was afraid to turn at such a low altitude and only when I reached the inlet and got the plane a little higher did I let it circle and head back north toward the beach. We landed with a bump I'll never forget. How the plane held together, much less rolling over the sand, I'll never know. I paused for a thankful instant, marveling at not only my good luck, but at the soundness of Slim Exstrum's advice. Then I stood up and looked at my passenger, fully expecting to see him white-faced and faint. But he was smiling. He said he had enjoyed the flight very much.

Wanting no more of the air that day, I taxied the plane for ten miles up the beach to its mooring spot, pulled it up on the soft sand and covered the engine, through for the day. I later learned that every pilot on the beach had learned about the Daytona Beach west wind in an equally rough lesson. Each had flown in it before being convinced. Next time a west wind blustered in, I left my Jenny covered and stayed home.

The afternoon after I jousted with the wind, I caught my first mess of fish off Daytona's Main Street pier. Flying had no appeal for me that day and for some reason, the wind didn't make the fish a bit shy.

That westerner blew steadily for three days, and on the fourth, the blow shifted to the northeast and finally, east, before I took my place alongside the other pilots at our sandy airdrome. I got more than my share of good-natured ribbing. It was all part of the initiation. All I could do was wait for a Yankee like myself to come along and try to outsmart the wind as I had tried.

Ted Kenyon and I tended pretty strictly to business after that. He took pictures while I flew the plane. When he wasn't with me, I took up passengers. Lindley won race after race in his OX5 special automobile. Sig Haugdoul, who was also using the beach as a speedway, set several consecutive world records there that winter, reaching a speed of 180 miles an hour in his Wisconsin Special.

I don't know if any of us quite realized it, but those were the beginning of the lush Florida boom days. Lindley, I think, was one of the first to catch on to what was coming. He had a good business head and was quick to seize an opportunity.

One of the new real estate developments mushrooming up all around the state was the Rio Vista sector north of Daytona on the west side of the Halifax River. Lindley sold the owner of the development on letting him paint "Rio Vista" on the side of his Jenny. With this flying advertisement, Bill did such a good job that Walter Hardesty, owner of Rio Vista, was convinced that the flyer could sell real estate as well as the next man and make more money in it than he could in flying.

So Lindley gave up the air, temporarily, turned his fairly new ship over to me while I arranged with a newly arrived pilot named "Bugs" McGowen to take over my plane.

We knew little about McGowen except that he could fly a plane. Our arrangement had proceeded for some time, with Bill selling real estate and racing his car on Sundays, and McGowen and I taking up passengers, when we learned one day that Bugs was not only a pilot but a wing-walker and a parachute jumper as well. We immediately arranged a series of Sunday exhibitions, charging admission and running the shows in cooperation with the American Legion. They clicked. Every pilot in our group shared in the programs, each doing his aerial specialty.

McGowen's wing-walking exhibitions were the best I have ever seen. I piloted for him and got a big kick out of watching him perform. He climbed around the ship like a monkey. First, he walked along the leading edge of the lower wing to the outside strut. Gripping the strut with one hand, he lowered himself over the edge of the wing and swung his legs through the loop of the wing skid. Hanging by his legs, he hung head down, then with one hand grasped the skid and dangled in space. After hanging thus, he climbed back, walked to the middle strut and hung from the flying wires by his toes, after which he climbed to the top of the wing and stood upright, his feet locked in the cabane struts.

Bugs achieved a spectacular grand finale by attaching a 20 foot rope to his ankles and tying the other end to the lower fitting of the outside strut. When he had tied the rope, it was my cue to fly over the crowd at a 50 foot altitude while he pitched head first like a diver, toward the people. Even the roar of the motor could hardly keep the gasps of those crowds from coming up to me at the controls.

The rope always caught Bugs up with a kind of thud and he swung dizzily over the heads of the spectators. While they were still sufficiently horrified, he untied the rope around his ankles and climbed hand over hand up it to the plane. Every time I landed I found him sitting on the landing gear, leaning on a wheel. As far as the crowd knew, he was doing this while the wheels were rolling, but in reality he lifted his arm just enough to keep it off the wheel. Bugs was the unquestioned star of our Sunday shows. After each of his performances, the rest of us took passengers aloft for spins. Then Bugs brought each show to a stirring climax with a parachute jump from my plane.

After a successful series of shows, Lindley, McGowen and I devised a new act to add to our repertoire....an automobile-plane change. This had been done before, with a rope ladder dangling from the plane to the car, and since on at least one occasion the ladder had caught on the car and the plane pilot had been dragged to destruction, I did not favor this method in our stunt.

Knowing Bugs' marvelous ability around the underside of a ship, I felt he could reach the wing skid if I flew low enough. Lindley, who was to drive Bugs in his racing car along the beach while I flew parallel to the racer, said it couldn't be done. He favored the rope ladder method, dangerous as it was. But Bugs persuaded him that he was equal to the challenge.

We tried it early on Sunday at low tide. There were few people on the beach as Lindley's racer came roaring down the stretch, with Bugs sitting alongside him, his cap peak turned to the back, wearing a white shirt, no coat, and a black necktie that stood straight out in the back, in the wind. The better to judge the distance, I flew in the front seat of the Jenny so the wing wouldn't keep Bugs out of my line of vision.

On the first attempt, I failed to get the wing skid within Bugs' reach. On the second, Bugs had to duck quickly and Bill had to swerve the auto to keep the wing from hitting the seat of the car.

After those two attempts, I was nervous, and about ready to concede that Lindley was right about our needing a rope ladder. Then came the third try. I brought the plane down until it was no more than six feet off the beach. I throttled as I approached the car and saw the tense faces of the others. Bill was crouched over the wheel. Bugs was motioning me to come even lower. I eased the stick to the right, and slowly, the right wing lowered and Bugs gripped the skid and shook it. This was a signal. As I felt the vibration, I eased the stick to the left and at the same time gave the motor full throttle, pulled the stick back and gave it left rudder. I felt the weight tugging on the right wing and I knew that Bugs was holding fast.

At about 100 feet, I saw a hand come up over the top of the lower wing, closely followed by its owner. Bugs pulled himself up, walked the wing to the cockpit, slapped me on the shoulder and said, "Nice work," as if I had done it all. After we got down, he said that after all, all he had done was "sit there, while Bill had to drive the car and you had to place the wing skid where I could reach it. All I had to do was to hold on."

That week, we advertised the auto-plane change, and on Sunday, thousands lined the beach to watch. Newspaper cameramen and newsreel men were on hand. It was Feb. 15 and there was no west wind. Before starting out, Bugs, Bill and I agreed to fake the first two attempts, and then make good on the third one, we hoped.

On the first trip down the beach, I put the wing skid right in Bugs' hand. He shook it and let go, smiled at me and thumbed his nose. We did it again. Then came the third and genuine attempt. The cameras were grinding and the newsmen were using up their plates fast, and I said to myself as I skimmed toward the auto, "This had better be good." After five attempts, three on the previous Sunday and our two fakes before the crowd, I had the knack of it. Bugs caught the skid and shook it so hard I thought he'd break it loose. I gave the plane the gun and it pulled him out of the car. He hung on with one hand and, true showman, waved to the wildly cheering crowd. Then he went right ahead with his wing-walking act and the people cheered themselves hoarse. The beach rocked with their applause when we landed. Thus continued a series of weekly thrill-shows with air fans. Then Bugs left our sky troop to fly exhibitions in Georgia.

One night in Georgia, he went up in an old Jenny, with the announced intention of setting fire to the plane and making a parachute jump to safety. He was roaring through the black night, pouring gasoline on the wings, when the fuel caught fire from the exhaust and Bugs was trapped. He died as we all had feared he might, trying to gamble once too often with his abundant good luck.

After Bugs went, a young man named Billy West drifted our way. He said he was a parachute jumper and could make the auto-plane change and had been doing these stunts with Mable Coty and the Flying Circus. He said he wanted to take Bugs McGowen's place in our show. We were skeptical. He didn't look like an aerial daredevil, and we were unimpressed by his recital of his exploits. But we needed a man and agreed to let him try to fill Bug's role, one of the toughest assignments ever handed to anyone.

West said he didn't want to practice the auto-plane change, so Bill Lindley and I explained it as well as we could and then set out to perform it, if possible, before one of the Sunday crowds. Three times I put the plane wing skid right in West's hand, and three times he let it go. I finally landed and waited for Lindley to bring West up in the racing car. I was ready for an explanation. West told me, before Bill's car had even stopped, that if I could get the wing skid lower, he could put his whole arm around it. He had no intention of just grabbing it with his hands and holding on while I pulled him up. Bill and I were angry and West, obviously nervous, asked if he couldn't do the parachute jump first, before trying the auto-plane change again. We agreed.

We went back, told the crowd that the auto-plane change would be done later, and then prepared for the parachute jump. West tied his old exhibition 'chute to the lower end of the middle strut on the left wing. It was the kind of parachute that hung in a bag that opened at the bottom. To release the parachute, the jumper had to cut the laces at the bottom of the bag. West strapped on his harness and climbed into the rear seat. I sat at the front controls and off we went toward the north. I had never flown him in a jump, but I thought he knew what he was doing.

Before I had turned the plane, he was out on the wing beside me. I motioned him to go back, but he made his way to the strut. By the time I made the first turn, he had lowered himself to the 'chute, fastened the hooks and was out of my sight, swinging and swaying in his harness. But I was certain that he would try no jump from that altitude, 500 feet, especially since we were flying down wind.

Expert jumpers of the early 1920s always jumped when the plane was throttled against the wind, so that the plane's forward speed was retarded when they let go. They also jumped from an altitude of at least 2,500 feet. But not Billy West. I could still feel him swaying in his harness as we flew back over the crowd and I tried to gain enough altitude for him to jump safely, thinking he would only cut the laces and release the parachute when we were high up and I had started to throttle the motor against the wind. But not Billy West.

We were just passing over the crowd when I realized with horror that he was no longer swaying from the underside of my wing. He had jumped. I turned the ship and landed at once, and as I climbed out, saw the crowd running toward a patch of white silk down the beach, I knew the worst had happened. I knew in my sinking heart that he was dead. But not Billy West. He was bloody and bruised, moaning, and groaning, battered and cut, but alive. They sped him to a hospital. People who had seen him plummet to earth told me the parachute opened just as he hit the ground.

That night I went to the hospital. He was conscious but in pain. But no bones were broken. He could neither talk nor smile, because when he struck the ground, his feet had landed first, then his knees had come up and hit his chin. His tongue was between his teeth and he had bitten it cruelly. He didn't bite it off because he had no middle front tooth. When he recovered, Billy told me he had taken the jump without any previous experience, that he had only tried to do it the way he had seen Bugs McGowen do it.

A year later, I saw him in another show. This time he held two automobiles driving in opposite directions, with an auto attached to either arm by a rope, and his hands clasped to keep him from being pulled apart. He told me some men might still try to be parachute jumpers, but not Billy West.

Russell Holderman, Daytona Beach, FL, 1921

CHAPTER 19
BIRD'S-EYE VIEW

We resumed flying at Queens Village Airdrome in the spring of 1923, with business continuing steadily and only two major changes evident.

The first was a reduction in passenger fares from $10 to $5. The second was the beginning of a series of flights for hire by newsreel film companies. The first of what were to be a great many flights for the sole purpose of getting film of something from the bird's eye view to satisfy the public's craving for pictorial presentation of news events.

It was shortly before the historic horse race between Zev and Papyrus at Belmont Park that Edmund Reek hired me to fly him over the park so that he could film the race from the air with his movie camera. Paramount had tied up all the picture rights on the track, with the result that no other newsreel company was to be allowed to film the race from the ground. That meant that Paramount had laid all the groundwork for a first class film news scoop, providing, of course, that some competitor failed to find a way to steal some shots of the race. Reek knew that the logical way to steal shots of the race was from the air. So he and I took off that beautiful Saturday afternoon about a half hour before its start, and arrived over the park to find five or six other planes, each with a cameraman circling and waiting.

It was then that a long acquaintance with jockeys and with all the routine business preliminary to a big horse race paid off. The other pilots and their camera men circled aimlessly, waiting for the big event between the two great champions. Reek and I circled with a purpose, our eyes fixed on the paddock, since it was evident from the aimless course being followed by the other planes that none of the other pilots knew what was taking place below.

We were flying at about 1,000 feet when I saw three horses come out of the paddock; the lead horse, then Zev, the American champion, and Papyrus, the English champion. The horses paraded in front of the crowd and then headed for the starting barrier. Since it was to be a two-horse race, I knew they would waste little time at the barrier. So I brought the plane into position and, as the horses were lined up at the barrier, put the ship into its dive.

Luckily, our timing was perfect. The plane was directly over the outside rail of the starting gate at exactly the second the horses were off. Flying at a 100-foot altitude, I throttled the motor and Reek began turning his camera crank furiously. He kept his lens on the horses throughout the whole race, with the result that his was the only newsreel company to get a perfect serial recording of the contest. In talking to the other pilots afterward, I learned that none of them had realized that the big race was going to start when it did, because none knew that the first horse out of the paddock was the lead horse. All had thought it was to be a three-horse race preliminary to the main event. Reek and I both received generous bonuses from his company for scoring that aerial beat.

The seasons changed and in December, we returned to Florida and there found Bill Lindley still hard at selling real estate at Daytona Beach. Lindley was so busy persuading people to buy Florida land that he was using his Jenny, the Rio Vista, only infrequently, so I made arrangements to take it over and with it, entered my second season of flying on the beach.

One day I tried to sell a ride to Walter Hardesty, owner of the Rio Vista real estate development. I gave him the best sales talk I knew. He listened attentively and after I had ended my spiel told me, "Young man, if you used the same sales talk selling lots for me, you could make a lot more money than you do flying. Why, look at Bill Lindley!" I told him I'd rather stick to flying. As he drove off, he said, "Think it over and I'll talk to you again some time."

It was only a few days later that a middle-aged woman in a chauffeured car drove up to the beach. I immediately tried to sell her an airplane ride. She declined politely but firmly and said, "What I would really like to know is…what does Rio Vista mean?" I explained that it was a subdivision of considerable beauty a few miles up the river. She continued to ply me with questions and finally, in order to see the development, agreed to ride with me in the plane. Off we went, up the river. I circled the real estate tract several times and then brought my question-firing passenger back to earth, where she immediately sought more information about the tract.

Finally, she asked me to ride to Rio Vista in her car. Hardesty wasn't there, but I gave her the same glowing descriptions I had often heard Lindley pass out to prospects, and then persuaded her to drive to Daytona, where we found Hardesty in his office. Before the woman left, Hardesty sold her a $3,500 lot. I went back to the beach to fly passengers at $5 a flight.

Late that day, Hardesty drove out to tell me he wanted to see me in his office the next day at 9 a.m. I kept the appointment. He greeted me with a handshake and congratulations and handed me a check for $350, commission on the sale of the Rio Vista lot to the woman with the chauffeur. He followed this immediately with, "Now, don't you think you'd better join our sales force?"

I became a bona fide real estate salesman the next morning, attended a sales meeting with Lindley and was teamed up with Jack Retaliatta, an ace at selling anything. With his experience and my enthusiasm, we clicked as a team and business came fast. For the rest of that winter, I confined my flying to taking prospects up to show them Rio Vista, becoming, I am told, the first real estate salesman to sell lots from the air.

When Lindley came to me one day with a proposition, I took a plunge and ended up as a real estate businessman. He needed $1,500 for a down payment on $10,000 worth of riverfront property flanking Rio Vista, and agreed to split the profits with me 50-50 if I would furnish the down payment. I turned over $1,500. A few weeks later, Lindley sold our tract for $20,000. That launched us. All over Florida, flourishing real estate businesses were growing simultaneously. The big Florida boom was on.

When Dorothy and I returned north in the spring of 1924, our little Queens Village Airdrome had disappeared under housing construction and we were forced to search for a new location for our little flying business. We found it on the road to Rockaway, near the Jamaica racetrack, which is now part of Kennedy International Airport.

The field was small, but I was accustomed to small fields. We built a new refreshment stand, took the bumps out of that portion of the field that was to be the runway, installed what little equipment we had, and opened for business. Luck continued to ride with us. There was no question but that flying for pleasure and flying to gain instruction had come to stay. There were no limits to public enthusiasm. Age was no bar to flying for fun or learning how to fly. I took up people of all ages, and taught them from 18 to 50.

We prospered that season and in the late fall put our car on a boat again and headed for Daytona Beach and a return to real estate. But instead of settling there, we joined Jack Retaliatta in Sarasota, where he had found new and promising fields to conquer. I joined the A.S. Skinner company as a salesman. Retaliatta was its sales manager.

Business went well, but through it all the longing to fly for my bread was strong and I finally talked to Skinner and Retaliatta about it, telling them we needed an airplane, or, better still, a flying boat, to sell real estate from the air, give the business a new and thrilling twist and play a spectacular yet practical angle.

Harry Rogers' air passenger business was booming in Miami. He used flying boats with great success. I had already flown one of the big ships in Miami, so I got in touch with him and he agreed to sell us one, a big Curtiss Seagull. Dorothy and I went down by train to take it over.

We had to wait for a week for it to be overhauled. In that week, I went through new and wondering experiences.......flying to Bimini, Nassau and Cuba, seeing for the first time from the air, the marvelously colored waters off the Florida coast and the hundreds of small islands that dot the sea south of Miami. Harry Rogers was an expert with the big flying boats, as were several of his pilots. With their help, I soon learned how to handle one.

Flying for Rogers were such aces as Ed Musick, who later became chief pilot for Pan American Airways and was killed blazing an aerial trail across the South Pacific, a sky route along which history was made in World War II by bomber and flying Army transport, a route on which many a civilian was successfully evacuated from the blazing war zones.

Another of Rogers' pilots was Bob Moore. Moore was once forced down in the Gulf Stream with a family of three aboard, a man, his wife and his child. All but Moore perished after one of the most harrowing experiences in the grim annals of aviation. When their flying boat struck the water, it capsized. Somehow, all four managed to climb on top of its turned up bottom.

One by one, the family of passengers slipped off and was lost. The child went first, then the mother. When it became evident that he could hold on no longer and that Moore, although weakened from hunger, exhaustion and exposure perhaps might out-live him for a few hours, the man handed Moore $2,000 and said weakly that where he was going he would have no use for it but that Moore could use it if he were saved.

Shortly afterward, the man slipped to a salty grave, with Moore powerless to help. Moore drifted helplessly, baking in the white-hot tropical sun for 10 days in all. At the end of the 10th day, he was rescued. He was found semi-conscious, burned black, cling-ing to the upturned hull of the flying boat.

Other pilots with Harry Rogers were George Cobb and George Rummel, both later with Pan American, and Eddie Nehmeyer. Rogers' brother, Russell, was also a member of his staff, but Harry kept Russell more or less grounded by insisting that he supervise all the mechanical work on the planes.

The rest of us, fanatically devoted to flying, were convinced that Harry's keeping his brother from being a pilot was unjust and unreasonable. The result was that whenever Russell rode with any of us, which he did frequently while checking motors; we turned over the controls to him. He got his first real piloting experience that way. It was apparent that he was a natural flyer and that nothing was going to stand in his way.

Russell Rogers more than fulfilled his early promise. He became chief test pilot for Consolidated Aircraft Company, whose long-range flying boats helped tip the balance of air power in favor of the United Nations in World War II. He became head of all the ferry pilots, a difficult and vital job he performed with distinction. He was in his day the nation's outstanding flying boat pilot and one of the best of all pilots of multi-motored airplanes. Much later, he was killed.

Shortly before the beginning of World War II, Russell Rogers showed his truly bright colors as a pilot by flying the big P.B.Y. Consolidated boat Cuba around the world, and in that trip flew new routes across the South Pacific and Indian oceans for the first time. His navigator was Lon Yancy, one of the best in the business.

Harry Rogers' pilot list contained the names of others who lived to use their vast experience and daring to help the United States and her Allies fight the Axis from the air. Two great pilots were among them....Eddie Stafford and Harry Smith.

* * *

At the end of our week in Miami, Rogers turned over our new flying boat to us and Dorothy and I took off in it, headed for Sarasota over strange and mysterious country. The Rogers gang had told us to stay over water all the way, so we headed south along the eastern shoreline of the state, keeping the placid waters of Biscayne Bay always in sight, always ready to use as a glass-smooth landing field in the event that we had to go down. We followed the shoreline as it bent west and soon were winging over Florida's southern tip, soaring over many islands, catching an occasional glimpse of the vast Everglades and the countless, lake-like bodies of water running through them.

Scattered showers, a typical southern Florida weather phenomenon, forced us to skirt clouds by flying south and then directly north in an effort to stay in clear weather. We then found ourselves traveling northwest and eventually pointed the ship's nose due north again, following the shoreline again, with the Gulf of Mexico stretching widely on our port side. We had sighted few signs of habitation since taking off from Miami and the only life within our view was tropical birds winging close to the sea and an occasional porpoise rolling in the warm waters.

By then, our gasoline was running low, so as soon as we sighted Punta Rassa, I put the ship down on the smooth bay and taxied to the first sizable dock I saw. We didn't get out. We were drifting in to make contact with the pier when Dorothy noticed that its sole occupant was a water moccasin of wicked proportions. Instead of tying up at the dock, we let the plane drift onto the beach. A native trotted up to assist us, swung one wing over the beach, and we climbed out just as a Florida shower generously dumped its doubtful, wet blessings on us.

Far more difficult than evading the rain, was getting gasoline. It took us two hours to get enough to take the plane up again safely, and all we found was automobile fuel. But it was good enough to take us on to Sarasota, where we landed later that afternoon on the bay. Skinner, Retaliatta and many of their friends insisted on being taken up for their first airplane rides that same day.

After that came our great experiment. With carpenters and other helpers, we built a ramp on the bay so that we could roll the big flying boat out of the water at night. It was completed within a few days and from then on, the A.S. Skinner Company began to sell real estate from the air. Skinner's became the only firm in the country using a plane for transportation and selling at the same time. The plane cut time amazingly and simplified many problems. Skinner had one tract which took two hours to reach by automobile and 15 minutes to reach in the Curtiss Seagull.

A prosperous looking northerner wandered into the real estate office show room one day and politely told me when I made salesman like overtures that he was only looking at the pictures of the real estate tracts to pass the time. The man had such as air of prosperity and I was so thoroughly imbued with the idea that everyone and anyone was a sales prospect that I offered to drive him around Sarasota in my car to help him pass more time. He finally accepted and we toured the city in my new Lincoln, in which all roads led to the flying boat. Having never been up, the stranger at first hesitated to accept my offer to fly him over the city he had just seen by automobile.

But the day was fine, the air was still, the water was calm and blue and the Curtiss flying boat looked so airworthy and sturdy that he finally consented to be shown.

Up we went, and toured Sarasota and its surrounding subdivisions by air. Up and down and across the shoreline we flew. I gave him a full afternoon of Sarasota from all the top views. When we landed, he admitted he liked the place. In fact, he liked it so much that within a short time he bought $150,000 worth of property from Skinner for a Lima, Ohio syndicate he represented. He admitted that the airplane ride had done the trick.

The world champion New York Giants trained in Sarasota in the winter of 1926, with rotund John J. McGraw in command. The champions were a friendly bunch... Frankie Frisch, Jack Bentley, Long George Kelly, Hank Gowdy, Travis Jackson, Roger Bresnahan and the others. I took many of them flying. Bentley particularly fell for aviation and became my first student in a flying boat. Kelly, Virgil Barnes and I occasionally broke our routine with a fishing trip.

It was not easy to sell John McGraw on the attractions of flight. Only his strong desire to see Sarasota from the air because he was interested in making some real estate investments made him change his mind about going up. I told him I was thrilled and honored to be able to take him on his first flight. With a slight smile, he returned the compliment, telling me that the honor was his in making the flight with such a well-known pilot. His flattery was of the finest.

McGraw, a friend of his named J.J. Powers, Retaliatta and I made up the flying party on a clear, calm day. We took off, circled the city and continued up the bay to Bradenton, then across the gulf and south landing along the white beach of Long Beach shores. McGraw's wide smile never left his face in forty minutes of scenic air ride. We made a smooth landing and taxied up to the ramp. His first audible words after the motor had stopped were "Now I am really sold. It gave me a bigger thrill than winning the World Series."

McGraw was then working with Skinner on a new subdivision called Pennant Park, with streets named for famous baseball players, and the main thoroughfare was called Mathewson Boulevard in honor of the incomparable Christy himself. After that first ride, McGraw asked me to take him up several times. On one occasion, I flew him to St. Petersburg, where he appeared on invitation of the city fathers with Miller Huggins of the New York Yankees, his great managerial rival.

Russell Holderman, pilot. Courtesy of A.S. Skinner, realtor, San Leon Studios, Sarasota, FL

Our flying real estate business soared along with the Curtiss Seagull. I even flew to Miami, armed with maps, literature and a whole series of strong Sarasota sales talks, and after making a connection with a Miami real estate office, sold $200,000 worth of lots in our Long Beach subdivision. Dreams of fortunes came thick and fast to many men then, and I dreamed right along with the rest. My 10 per cent interest in the Long Beach property figured to net me $125,000 when the whole subdivision was sold. In 10 days, $200,000 in sales netted me $10,000 in commissions. Money rolled in so fast our heads swam. Gone were the happy days when taking up passengers at $5 a head seemed like a prosperous existence.

Out of those golden dreams of fantastic financial success I retrieved one small, black thought, "How long will it last?" Somehow, sometime, I felt that the lush days would come to an end, with a lot of people holding the empty bags that money fills in boom times. I talked it over with Dorothy, who suggested that if I felt that way perhaps I had better put some money aside, "just in case." The next day, I cashed a check for $2,000 and put two $1,000 bank notes in my safe deposit box. More money came rolling in and I all but forgot that little nest egg.

By that time, other things were happening. Basil Rowe, later a chief pilot for Pan American, had appeared on the scene with a seaplane and was carrying passengers out of Sarasota. Pennant Park was fast developing. With hundreds of men grading streets, finishing the landscaping and smoothing a suburban residential section out of what had once been waste countryside, Skinner felt that the time was ripe for someone to go north and stage a whirlwind selling campaign directed at baseball fans. Both Skinner and McGraw, knowing their fans, felt that in the north there were many followers of baseball who would be more than eager to invest in the park, especially as a memorial to their athletic heroes.

Preceded by full page advertisements in New York newspapers, I was sent north to open the New York office, which we organized in McGraw's private quarters and the New York Giants' rooms at 104 West 42nd Street. The place hummed with applicants for selling positions, with prospective purchasers, would-be investors in the Pennant Park project, attracted to the idea by their love of baseball and its almighty men, confident because the honest name of John J. McGraw stood behind the development.

Many investors made deposits on pieces of Pennant Park. Days passed. Other people came in. The sales force was organized and beginning to get results. More people paid deposits. Other days passed, and I still received no contracts to give the people who were waiting so eagerly to buy their pieces of baseball's greatest memorial. Weeks went by and no contracts came. Telegrams were sent and telephone calls burned the wires from New York to Sarasota. The contracts did not come.

Then Skinner arrived in person and threw the thunderbolt that was to blast our dreams. He announced that the whole idea of Pennant Park was definitely and finally off. McGraw's backers had pulled out at the last minute without coming through with even the first payment on the property. That was the beginning of the end. The Florida boom was petering out. John J. McGraw was one of the blameless victims. The failure of his financial angels to go through with their deal on Pennant Park put the great manager in a cruel spot. Had McGraw been able to put his deal over a year or six months earlier, Pennant Park today would probably be the memorial to his game and to his time he had hoped it would be. Out of his own pocket, John McGraw took money to repay widows of baseball men who through his recommendation had made large deposits on Pennant Park lots. He paid them all, and took the beating, a great and generous personality victimized by one of the most colossal financial booms of our time.

* * *

The collapse of Pennant Park took us back to Florida. More things began to happen. Disaster piled on disaster. Hoping to save some part of our investments, we threw good money after bad, and spent that unhappy summer looking forward to the next season in the hope that we could weather the storm until then and that everyone would return to normalcy. The trouble was that what we came to believe was normal, was something far out of proportion to any way of business we had known, or most of the other real estate operators had known. We were struggling to hold finances together, to try to bolster our rickety investments with our weakened purse strings when inscrutable, indomitable nature stepped in and knocked our real estate house of cards flat.

Warnings had come through from Miami that high winds of hurricane force had struck the southern tip of the state and were headed north and could be expected to strike Sarasota within eight hours. We prepared for a hard blow, but not for what came. I tied the seaplane down with extra ropes and filled the hull with water to give it weight. Then the hurricane struck its first blows, and the city shook. The second blows were stronger, more forceful, with a mysterious and frightening authority. We looked out our window and saw an automobile rolled out of its parking space, with its owner running into the wind to try to stop it. Store signs and street signs crashed into the streets. The sky grew deathly dark. Then the rains came on the wings of great, howling gusts of wind strong enough to blow out a man's teeth and rip the clothing from his back.

It was early afternoon and almost pitch black, and growing blacker, with the mighty, invisible force of the hurricane viciously hurling torrents of rain against the pavements and battering the flimsy sides of houses and business buildings. I wondered how the seaplane was doing and drove over to see. The wind shook the car like a leaf, and the battle of the automobile motor to keep the car in forward motion was a frightening thing. I found the plane straining at its lurch like a mad mastiff on a leash. A rope broke. Dorothy started for a hardware store for more and stouter rope and I tried futilely to tighten those that still kept the ship down.

As the car moved away, its lights picked up something on the glistening pavement just ahead of it....a fallen tree, newly snatched from the earth and laid low by the wind. Dorothy stopped and put the car in reverse and tried another street. A policeman ran out and tried to send her home, but she was determined to get rope, and off she drove. She found the hardware store without any roof and the rain pouring into it in tubs full. No one was there. She helped herself to rope from the stock and made the perilous return journey and arrived as I was making a last attempt to save the plane.

Our efforts were futile and sad. Not only did the hurricane rip the ropes from our grasp, the waves rose in the bay, and the bay seemed to be moving in slowly and dreadfully on the land. We gave up when the waves tore the wings off the airplane, and made our way home through the wild wind. We lived in a howling, blowing hell for two straight days and emerged only to find that most of the city's gorgeous trees were crushed flat to earth, wires and poles were a tangled mass of wreckage, boats and boat houses, docks and piers were in splinters, and Sarasota, a city of beauty, was a scarred and tragic place of bitter, buffeted men.

After the hurricane, I had no plane and I had no business. Nobody bought real estate. My own holdings were foreclosed. By November, my cash was gone...or so I thought until I remembered the two $1,000 bank notes I had put in my safe deposit box and then all but forgotten, for just such an emergency.

Otis Hardin, who sold planes for the Waco Airplane Company, had a new Waco on the market for $2,200. He said he'd take $2,000 down and let me pay the rest later, so I placed my order for the ship, which arrived after several weeks. It was delivered at Sebring. Dorothy drove me over to get it. The Waco was a beautiful silver biplane powered by the famous, trusty OX5 Curtiss motor I knew so well. It handled like a dream as I brought it into the fairgrounds at Sarasota.

I went into business at once and by the end of December had established the Sarasota Airways, with permission from the city to use the fairground as a permanent landing field. Business came steadily, with messenger flights fairly numerous and a promising number of students to take flying lessons.

Stewart Chadwick, one of the old Daytona Beach flying gang, came in one day with his Waco, and went into business with me shortly afterward. Whenever trade slackened, we went barnstorming on weekends in towns around the Sarasota district. Barnstorming had its bright moments, particularly one Saturday afternoon and Sunday when we netted more than $700. It seemed like old times at the Queens Village Airdrome.

Two years later in January, the Sarasota fairground was formally dedicated as an airport. Otis Hardin, Fred Williams, George Haldeman, Chadwick and I put on a show. In that first winter of barnstorming around Sarasota, Chadwick and I were frequently joined by Haldeman, who lived at Lakeland, and we barnstormed as a three-plane flying circus. We did a lot of charter work.... a far different and more precarious business than it later became. Then there were few airports even in cities of considerable size and virtually none of the smaller towns had landing fields.

This meant that on taking up a charter fare the chief problem generally was to spot a decent field to land it, once you neared your destination. Good spots were the infield of a fairground or a level golf fairway. We had no weather reports to guide us, either. We simply picked out good weather to take off in and landed if it turned sour, taking off again when the sky cleared.

It was about that time that the United States Department of Commerce issued a set of regulations which was the first move toward government control of civil aviation in this country. The new rules made it compulsory to pass an examination before being granted a license to carry passengers. When Chadwick and I got this news one day in May, we were instructed to report at Sebring to an inspector who would give us our test and inspect our ships, which also had to be licensed. We both were passed, but balked futilely at having to paint black numbers and letters, the plane license numbers, on our beautiful silver planes.

It was shortly after this that Chadwick and I signed with the Mable Coty Flying Circus and toured Florida with the aerial troupe, stunting, making plane changes and carrying passengers. But summer was fast approaching and we foresaw a deadly lull in the flying business, so we decided to make for the north as rapidly as possible. We left Sarasota on Memorial Day making Sebring our first stop.

Chadwick and I flew from Sebring to Daytona Beach where Bill Lindley was still keeping shop. He had suffered heavily as a result of the real estate crash and had bought himself a Waco. He forthwith joined us on our flight north. Bad weather kept our little flight of three ships from doing any better than Jacksonville by the night of May 31. I picked Dorothy up at Jacksonville, Chadwick decided to stay there for the time being, and Dorothy, Lindley and I started out in the two remaining planes, hit bad weather and only made Savannah, GA.

The next day dawned clear and we struck Columbia, S.C. at noon, got gasoline at the fairgrounds, where we landed, and then took off again, following the railroad track straight north. We almost immediately ran into overcast and were forced lower and lower until at 50 feet I decided the better part of valor was to pick out a good field. I circled as a signal to Lindley and set the plane down in a postage-stamp meadow without mishap. Dorothy and I tied the ship to a fence, hitched a ride to town and put up at the only hotel McBee, S.C. had to offer. It wasn't long before news of Lindley was brought to us. He had landed three miles further north, but the field he picked was soft and he had turned over and snapped his propeller. The next problem was where to find a new propeller.

McBee residents told us that Elliott White Springs lived nearby at Fort Mill. By telephone, he told us he had a propeller we could have if we could use it. We rushed out, hired a car, drove to Fort Mill and discovered that the propeller was a relic of World War days and no good for Lindley's Waco. We finally found one in Charlotte.

Next day, we repaired Lindley's ship and on June 3 we both got off again, landing at Charlotte that night. We made Richmond the next day after stopping at Fayetteville,

N.C., site of Fort Bragg, for fuel. We stopped briefly at Philadelphia on June 5 and before nightfall made Curtiss Field, truly home, for Curtiss had once been Roosevelt and Roosevelt had once been Hazelhurst and Hazelhurst had once been Mineola, where I first had soloed, and I knew every blade of its grass. Across the road from Curtiss Field was Mitchel Field, U.S. Army airdrome named for a former mayor of New York City who had been killed in an air crash, and not, as many people believed, for Brig. Gen. William (Billy) Mitchel.

Preparations were made for a big air meet at Mitchel Field that July. The Curtiss Company had exclusive passenger-carrying rights, thus eliminating Bill Lindley and me as independent passenger carriers. But there was money to be made and we needed it and knew that somehow we could work out a profitable idea.

It was then that I got the idea of selling chances for rides at 25 cents a chance. I told Charles (Casey) Jones, Curtiss's chief pilot, about it and said that if he would give us the signal to go through with the idea my mechanic, Jimmy Mulcahy, would put on wing-walking exhibitions purely as an added attraction on the Mitchel Field program. Jones was agreeable, and I bought punchboards to use in selling chances on rides. The idea went so well that we did a good business all through the meet, and Jones told us afterward that we did almost as much business as the Curtiss Company.

It was shortly after the Mitchel Field meet that Lindley and I located a field at Wantagh, L.I. about eight miles due south of Curtiss Field, and once more plunged into the routine of teaching student flyers and carrying passengers on weekends, a steady and profitable pastime.

Two of my best students were Marion S. Burkhard and Lionel E. Herrmann. That August, Lindley and I both sold our Waco Nines and bought the company's new Waco Tens, ships powered with OX5 motors like the others, but more streamlined and with hydraulic shock struts on the landing gear instead of the old rubber shock cords.

We lived in a cottage by the sound, close by our landing field. One day a slim high school girl came to the place and asked to see "one of the pilots." She was Elinor Smith, daughter of Tom Smith, famous as a vaudeville actor. Tom Smith owned a Waco Nine, hangared at Curtiss Field. Elinor had been taking lessons in her father's plane with Sonny Harris, my brother-in-law, as instructor, but her progress was considerably retarded by her father's reluctance to let her fly. But she told me she had a little money of her own and wanted to learn to fly despite parental objections, and asked if she could continue her lessons with me. The only stipulation she made was that I teach her early in the morning before school began and while her father was asleep and wouldn't know what she was doing.

Thus it happened that Elinor Smith appeared every morning at daybreak or shortly afterward at our little field in Wantagh. We flew from Wantagh to Curtiss Field because Wantagh was too small for lessons. We finished each day in time for breakfast and in time for Elinor to reach school. Elinor was a great sport and more determined to be a good pilot than almost anyone else I have ever met in flying. She was naturally skillful, full of courage and the desire to do everything well. It is small wonder that she became one of the world's outstanding women pilots and broke record after record, both for distance and altitude in a high-powered Bellanca monoplane.

The day Elinor first soloed brought her father around to her way of thinking. He was so surprised and pleased that he turned his own plane over to her to use for practice flights. We saw Elinor only occasionally after that until on April 4, 1930 she dropped in at our airport in LeRoy, N.Y. on her way to the Detroit Aviation Show. She had come a long way since those early morning lesson days on Long Island. She was already world famous when she landed at LeRoy, a veteran of the airways, a record breaker in her own right. Her most spectacular feat was in setting the world's altitude record for women, gaining 32,000 feet, promptly fainting, and then regaining consciousness at 27,000 feet. When she came to us...by plane... Elinor had been ordered by her physician to rest for a week. He had told her to stay on the ground and travel at leisure. But she had flown. She was like that. She had her week of vacation and rest, but not all of it on the ground.

CHAPTER 20
MAN FROM LEROY

Roscoe Turner spent most of the night of December 8, 1927, trying to persuade me to fly to Los Angeles with him. Lionel Herrmann, a Wantagh pupil of mine, and I had landed at Turner's field at Richmond, VA, on our way south. We started from Wantagh, L.I. in sub zero weather, landed at Washington in four hours and 50 minutes on December 7, then made Richmond the next day. That night we stayed at Turner's place, where for hours he painted for me a rosy picture of flying in the West. But I was Florida bound and even Roscoe could not change my course.

What that course might have been had I followed this advice I do not know. But there are few laymen today who do not know who Roscoe Turner is....winner of a hundred air races, holder of many records; handsome, dashing, airman, one of the best of all pilots. He was the ideal man for the job he held at Indianapolis as head of one of the largest training schools in the country.

After Herrmann and I left Richmond, we reached Jacksonville by way of Fayetteville, Columbia, and Savannah. At Jacksonville, Dorothy joined me and I spent the rest of the month carrying passengers and teaching there. After Christmas, we moved further south and met Bill Lindley.

It seemed that whenever we met Bill, things happened. This time his idea was to go barnstorming in Cuba. So it happened that by mid-January we were at Key West, trying to muster courage to hop the 90 miles over the dangerous waters between Key West and the Pearl of the Antilles. We had confidence in our Waco Tens' OX5 motors over land, but no idea how they might perform on a 90 mile run across the ocean blue.

We started out just ahead of Ed Musick in Pan American's tri-motored Fokker. Land had just drifted out of sight behind us when the Fokker tore past, making us feel as if we were hanging motionless in mid-air. It was then that I lost confidence not only in myself but in the Waco and the Curtiss motor. Every minute seemed an hour long, packed with the imagination of all sorts of mechanical horrors. I could almost hear the motor developing drum-like knockings, and feel the valve tappets loosen, one by one.

But in reality the trusty OX5 was purring smoothly, and it was only a short time before I sighted land and knew that I had made my first flight across ocean water in a land plane. By then I also knew definitely that I would never become a transatlantic pilot, especially in a land ship. But our Cuban junket was doomed to failure. There were too many obstacles to getting permission to carry passengers on the island. Finally, Freddie Lund, who was flying for a newspaper there, advised us to return to the mainland.

On the return flight, the OX5 made strange noises and my heart thumped madly, but as soon as land came into view, the engine seemed to be running smooth as silk. I returned to Miami and Lindley headed for Daytona Beach, the only place he called home.

Not even her boss believed it when Dorothy became the first airplane saleswoman in the world. By February, 1928, I had tied up my Waco at the old 54th Airport in Miami and was flying Curtiss Seagulls for the Rogers Airline, planes like the one wrecked at Sarasota by the hurricane of 1926.

There's a difference between being at the wheel of a real flying boat and being at the stick of a land plane, especially when all your flying is done over waters like those blue, unfathomable surfaces between Florida and Cuba, Bimini and Nassau. I spent a whole month flying those airlanes again and again in a Seagull with perfect confidence and never a qualm about motor failure or weather. There was always the helpful knowledge that a perfect landing field was under me all the time. Only in crossing the Gulf Stream was there anything to worry about, for that is treacherous for airmen as well as boatmen to navigate, especially when a north wind blows against the flow of the mysterious current.

When I joined his airline as a pilot, Harry Rogers was sales agent for the Fairchild people and was introducing a new type high-wing monoplane powered by one of the famous Wright Whirlwind motors, the kind used in most of the transatlantic flights up to that time. The new Fairchild had places for a pilot and four passengers. It cruised at a speed of about 100 miles an hour.

George Haldeman, more or less fresh from this ocean-spanning attempt with Ruth Elder in the American Girl, delivered Rogers' first Fairchild by making a non-stop flight from Long Island to Jacksonville, where he refueled before coming on to Miami. Rogers decided to display the new ship on Biscayne Boulevard in a vacant store in which he had set up a ticket office to sell flights over the city and take registrations for charter trips in his flying boats. The Fairchild had folding wings and was easy to bring into the building. The plane was set up in the store and Rogers asked Dorothy if she would take charge of the display and sell ride tickets. She said, "Certainly, I'll sell rides, and how about my selling the Fairchild?" Rogers laughed. "O.K., the price is $12,500 and if you sell it, I'll give you five per cent commission." "I might fool you," said Dorothy laughing. "I guess we won't worry about that," he replied. "Just you sell rides and I'll be satisfied." So Dot went to work.

A few nights later, we were both at the ticket office. She was selling ride tickets and explaining the fine points of the Fairchild to strolling transients when I heard a flying boat come in over the bay. This was so unusual at night that I walked the few blocks to the seaplane dock and reached it in time to greet George Rummel and a party from Bimini. It had been such a beautiful moonlit night that they hadn't been able to resist making the flight. They had to pay for it, though, by waiting on the dock until morning, when the Customs Office opened and they could be cleared for re-entrance into the country.

When I returned to Rogers' showroom after meeting the seaplane party, Dorothy greeted me a little breathlessly with a laugh in her voice and said, "I sold the Fairchild!" When she showed me a down payment check for $1,000, signed with an unfamiliar name, I was suspicious immediately, and finally we both agreed the check writer must be a jokester. We showed the check to Rogers the next morning. He laughed at it. But finally I said, "Why don't you and Dorothy see this man at his hotel? He really might be serious about buying the plane."

The check writer was a LeRoy, N.Y. man named Donald Woodward, whose great personal fortune had been derived from gelatin desserts. He was sharing a suite at Miami with Bing Miller and Leonard Heimlich. When Harry and Dot called on him, Rogers got to the point at once and asked Woodward if he really intended to buy the Fairchild or if he had been joking. "Why," said Woodward, indicating Dorothy, "I bought the ship last night, from this young lady. Do you have my check with you?" Rogers handed him the $1,000 check and he tore it up.

By that time Heimlich had gotten into the spirit of the farce and told Rogers and Dorothy that the night before when they had walked into the display room, they had misread the "Flight Tickets" sign for "Fight Tickets." He wanted to know where the fight was and when they could get tickets for it.

Rogers had come to the sad belief that the affair was a joke after all when Woodward sat down at the hotel desk and wrote a check for the full $12,500 purchase price on the Fairchild, handed it to Harry and asked him how soon he could have the plane and where he could get a pilot. The sale was concluded the next day, with news pictures showing Dorothy transferring the papers to Woodward in a deal that made her the first woman airplane salesman in the world.

Woodward wanted me to pilot for him, but I still hankered for my own field and school and told him I would only take the job until he got a regular pilot. Rogers recommended Harry Smith for the job. After a month of flying for Woodward, I was ready to break Smith in with the Fairchild. But here that fate which dogs so many airmen from day to day until it finally pounces on them, stepped in and changed all our lives. Woodward and I were discussing Smith's possibilities and watching him take off a Fairchild equipped with pontoons. He got the ship off the water, turned too quickly with too little speed and crashed.

After Harry Smith's crash, Woodward again insisted that I come on as his full-time pilot. I told him I still had my heart set on operating my own field and flying school, whereupon he brushed aside all my arguments with this: "Come north with me and I'll let you build an airport and have your own school, and what's more, I'll back the whole thing." If someone had told me I had just designed and built the first foolproof airplane in the world, I couldn't have been happier. We closed the deal then and there.

Being a man of action, Woodward wasted no time making his word good. He hired John Pike of Rochester to do the contracting, and put his farm supervisor, Ernest Button, in charge of land clearance. Button advertised for field labor and the dirt began to fly. He felled trees and filled in hollows, leveled, landscaped, scraped and rolled. I drew a design for a hangar on the back of an envelope and Pike's draftsman put it into blueprints. I laid out the runways and for days did nothing but direct a stream of trucks which brought in crushed stone for them from Heimlich's quarry near the village. Meanwhile, Woodward's Fairchild and my Waco, flown north for me, were housed in remodeled barns on the north side of the airport side, pending the construction of the hangar.

I hired Kenneth Hebner as a mechanic to service the planes, and devoted all my time to superintending the construction of the airport, happily bearing in mind that Woodward had said he wanted an airdrome second to none and that no time nor expense need be spared to make it so.

Then Woodward bought a Curtiss Seagull from Harry Rogers and George Rummel delivered it. We built a ramp on Lake Ontario, and then I found myself chief pilot of three planes....Woodward's Fairchild and Seagull and my own old reliable Waco.

Ruth Nichols visited Woodward in July to explain the aviation country club plan to him. She had learned to fly in one of Rogers' flying boats but wanted to know how to pilot a land plane as well. So she learned in my Waco. Ruth, as everyone knows, later became a skilled pilot, one of the best of the women flyers. Her career was temporarily halted by the crash which caused the death of Harry Hublitz, one of the pals of my airmail days, and which brought her such serious injuries that physicians told her she would never fly again. Courageous and full of fight and stamina, Ruth Nichols won out. Later she flew for the Relief Wings and did a great job.

Shortly after Ruth left LeRoy in July, the new airport had advanced enough to be used for flight instruction and passenger hopping. Woodward bought a fleet of planes and we opened for business.

Our busy routine was broken only by a mercy flight, made when Casey Jones sent out a hurry call to all upstate New York pilots to search for Merrill and Romme, believed lost between Buffalo and New York. I had scoured the Lake Country for them for hours when I heard the sad news that they had crashed in the hills just west of Port Jervis.

By that time, our new airport was buzzing like a test field. The Woodward fleet was composed of Fairchilds, Robins, Sterns, Wacos, and the Curtiss Seagull. Not only was there immense satisfaction in being the boss pilot of this shining squadron, but there was much pleasure in seeing the ships, all but the flying boat, housed in a hangar of my own design. Practical experience went into that design, experience which in more than 15 years of flying had taught me where the shop should be, that there should be an overhead rail with cranes to swing the motors from the hangar to the shop. The building had a classroom for the flying school, an office and a pilot's lounge. Everything was pointed toward the opening ceremonies, set for October 12, 13, and 14. Woodward flung himself into preparations for the dedication program with great zeal, put up $5,000 in prizes for air races, planned a series of evening boxing matches, and an elaborate clambake.

By the first of October, the field was done. It had taken shape even better than in our fondest dreams. We knew it was the finest private airport in the world. The townspeople of LeRoy took immediate and consuming pride in it and would even argue with New Yorkers that they had a better field than the metropolis offered.

Weeks before the opening program, Woodward sailed for Europe, taking with him Harry Rogers and his mechanic, Eddie Bowen. In Europe, Woodward purchased the Friendship, the famous tri-motored Fokker which had carried Amelia Earhart, Wilmer Stultz and Lou Gordon across the ocean, thus making Amelia the first woman ever to fly the Atlantic. She in her tri-motor had succeeded where Ruth Elder and George Haldeman in the gallant little American Girl had failed. The Friendship was shipped to New York and overhauled, and on September 29, Otto Enderton and I flew it to LeRoy, where we were greeted by the school band, the town officials and most of the townspeople.

Gordon, Enderton, Holderman, "Friendship" plane
Photograph courtesy of LTC Brian J. Duddy

Even before the airport's opening ceremonies, planes began to come in from all parts of the country to participate, among them Army and Navy planes, speed planes, stunt planes, and long distance planes.

I have had few greater thrills from flying than in driving up to that field on the morning of October 12, seeing glittering planes lined up around it, shining in the sun under a bright blue sky and watching flags of many colors wave in the early morning breeze. I felt that a dream had come true and that many years of working, sweating, and taking chances at last were paying off in satisfaction. For out of the rolling farmlands that before had known only the plow and harrow and had been split by stone and wire fences, had been created a model little airport. I had Woodward, Heimlich, Button, Pike and their men to thank for that.

Our pilot's register that week read like an aviator's "Who's Who." It glittered with famous names and with the names of just plain, good pilots who were contributing as much to aviation as many whose exploits had brought them into the limelight. Among those registered were:

Charles Dallas, Dick Bennett, Vern Roberts, E.W. (Pop) Cleveland, Eric Woods, George Reese, Bill Dunlop, Guy Stratton, Al Heller, Jim Ryan, Pete Brooks, Spencer

Punnett, Robert Moore, Beckwith Havens, Mike Steffer, Vic Evans, Gardner Nagle, Leon Brink, Harry Rogers, Ernie Hannem, Joe Dottawick, Ruth Nichols, Leo Chase, Swanie Taylor, Cy Caldwell, Senator J.G. Webb, W. E. Doherty, D.W. (Tommy) Tomlinson, Jack Little, Lieut. Ford Lauer, Lieut. Charles Overacker, Stanley Olmstead, Lieut. A.J. Isbell, U.S.N. and Lieut. A.L. Stephens.

Woodward wanted everyone from anywhere to come to see his show. He refused to charge admission. He wanted to launch the D.W. Airport in the view of as many people as possible, to build an interest in flying not only for the sake of passenger service, but also for the immense potentialities in student instruction.

Attendance shattered all expectations on the first day. Roads were jam-packed, and the field was encircled by a deep and colorful crowd of spectators. The day's events went off without mishap, and the onlookers stayed until the last ship was safely in. The second day was rainy and the sky was heavily overcast, but the news had gotten around and there was no holding people back. They came in droves. We highlighted that day with an airmail flight from LeRoy to Rochester, where a special sack of souvenir mail was placed on the regular mail plane.

Woodward shot the works that night on a colossal clambake, with all the trimmings....lobster, chicken, corn, everything. All flying guests were given engraved cigarette lighters. Army and Navy pilots were given traveling clocks.

Sunday, the final day, was designated as Army Day in tribute to the U.S. service flyers. The day dawned clear and bright and spectators began flocking in as early as 7 a.m. By 2 o'clock in the afternoon, thousands were still miles away but unable to get nearer because the roads were blocked in every direction by the autos of earlier arrivals. At the height of the program, the crowd was estimated at 40,000. Only one disappointment marred the entire affair. That was the failure of Tommy Tomlinson to appear. He had registered and was expected to land any minute. But there was no word from him. Clarence Young, head of the Aviation Branch of the U.S. Department of Commerce, officially dedicated the field. Charles Miller, Edward Perkins and the flying senator, J. Griswold Webb, made addresses. But no sign of Tommy Tomlinson.

One of the Navy's outstanding pilots, and leader of the famous Sea Hawks, greatest of all formation stunt pilots, Tommy had left the West Coast in his own OX5 Curtiss Jenny on October 10, hoping to reach LeRoy in time for the meet and in time to visit his parents, who lived in nearby Batavia. On the way east, he struck sandstorms and strong headwinds and made several forced landings. He never arrived until the meet had been over for a day. Tired from his arduous trip, he came in late in the afternoon of October 15, and landed in a cloud of dust, amidst a rending of wood and metal.

The fact that he was known to be so skilled a pilot only horrified us more when we saw his Jenny pile up flat on our new airport. We found him standing by, surveying the wreckage with a baleful eye. His jaw was cracked and four teeth were gone, but he managed painfully in true Tomlinson fashion to force out an apology for messing up our nice new airfield. Despite his bodily injuries, I think his pride was the greater suffered. He had been doing low stunting exhibitions for years and had put high-powered pursuit planes through every known kind of maneuver, sane and otherwise, on the West Coast, and yet flying a low-powered Jenny, he had cracked up, right in front of his parents.

He said he had been so tired and weary from his flight east that once he got over the airport and circled, he had strangely run out of both flying knowledge and air speed, and the crackup was the result. One of our best known pilots, Tommy has since done invaluable test work for TWA and is now back in the Navy as a commander. Just as Jimmy Doolittle, he is putting great skill, experience and courage where they will do the most good for the greatest number of the best people.

After our opening meet at LeRoy, Woodward placed an order with Beckwith Havens for delivery of a Loening Air Yacht. He sent me to New York to meet Havens. "Becky" and I took the new ship off the East River and piloted it across upper Manhattan to the Hudson. He was at the controls and I was sitting at his right. We were over Irvington when we first saw smoke shooting out of the motor. The smoke was accompanied by a great jet of oil, which struck Havens in the face and blinded him. He yelled for me to take over. I ducked behind the windshield and cut the motor. Smoke billowed from all sides of the engine, pouring out in a dark, steady, blinding stream as I brought the ship down to water, skimming the housetops of Irvington in order to land as close to shore as possible. We were towed ashore, where we notified Pratt and Whitney to come look at their broken motor. Then we went on by train to Rochester, where we were greeted by newsboys vending papers with these headlines:

"LeRoy flyers crash, D-W aircraft blazes, Dives flaming into Hudson River."

No one was more surprised than we were. Someone had seen the smoking plane diving toward the water over the housetops and had telephoned a description of it to the press. Misguided imagination had done the rest. I still have the newspaper clipping describing the crash that never came and the fire that never was. That smoky landing on the Hudson far from finished the career of the Loening.

We took it to Florida that December, met Woodward there and began a series of flights to Long Boat Key, Bimini, and Nassau. In the next three years, we flew it tens of thousands of miles without a mishap, on long cross-country flights out of LeRoy, many times to the Thousand Islands, where the sight of those indescribable emerald dots of land standing out of the broad, rolling, blue St. Lawrence was always worth the trip. We learned that no one has really seen the true beauty of the islands until he has seen them from the air.

One summer at LeRoy, I took the Loening up with a young unmarried couple 5,000 feet into the clouds and brought them down, man and wife. Bride, groom, minister, best man and bridesmaids were present at the ceremony in the clouds.

The following winter we set a record for the LeRoy-Florida flight by gunning the Loening from LeRoy to Jacksonville in a little over 13 hours flying time. We saw much of Bimini that winter of 1930-1931, living on Woodward's ocean going yacht, Murdona, and using the Loening for quick transportation, flying to Nassau and many of the Florida Keys for fishing.

We started north in March, stopped at Norfolk, Camden, N.J. and Philadelphia, where we landed at Pitcairn Field and bumped into Jim Ray, who demonstrated a new auto gyro for us.

We flew to New York from Philadelphia, landing at North Beach Field, site of what is now the $50,000,000 LaGuardia Airport. I little knew what lesson was ahead of me or on what adventure the Loening was about to embark. Bad weather set in almost immediately, and the Woodwards headed for home on a train, leaving Dorothy, George Cheetham, our co-pilot, and me to bring the Loening on to LeRoy. We waited for 5 days for clear enough weather to take off, finally got up and pointed the Loening's big nose toward LeRoy. We followed the Hudson River north for a while and as we came over the majestic stream cutting its way through what looked like solid blocks of rock, we saw that it was scalloped with white caps, indicating a very strong wind.

Following a procedure we used down South in a strong wind, we descended until we were skimming along only about 10 feet above the water. The wind generally is not so strong at that altitude, and aided by the cushion of air between the plane and the water, it's easy to gain speed that way. Dorothy sat alone in the cabin, strapped in tight because the going was rough and bumpy. Cheetham and I, up front, were having a great time, passing alongside startled boatsmen. The going got rougher as we progressed north on our course, and we both tightened our safety belts another notch and tended more to business.

Just south of West Point, where the rock rises sheer out of the gleaming water like mountainous sentinels, we hit a series of up drafts and down drafts, which beat anything I had ever struck before. I was thankful then for the Loening's great structural strength, because a lighter ship's wings would surely have been ripped off.

By that time neither George nor I was smiling and we had settled down grimly to serious work. The wind was so strong against us that we had trouble matching the pace of the New York Central passenger train, which followed the shore at one side. It was only when I took the ship up to 100 feet for safety's sake and tried to keep it on even air keel that I realized my great mistake. I knew by that time that I never should have brought it into the mountain territory at such a low altitude. By then it was too late to do anything about it, and I knew that if I tried to climb higher than I was, the down drafts would be stronger. I was afraid to try a landing because I feared we would hit too hard and crack up.

There we were, between the wind blown sky and the tumbling waters, three people in a frantically battling machine. Then we hit such a down draft as I never hope to meet again….a clutching, yanking, pulling vacuum that carried us down with sickening swiftness. We all but struck the water, but miraculously missed it and then gained enough altitude to stay level above it, if only for a few moments.

George looked into the cabin and saw Dorothy lying, a motionless heap, in one corner. She was unconscious. George prodded me. I was too busy to look but I guessed what he meant. I headed for the lee of an island and landed with an awful bounce, the impact making such a loud smack I thought surely the bottom had been ripped from under us. Certain that the bottom was shattered, I was afraid to stop for fear that we might sink immediately, so I kept on going, keeping the plane on its hydroplane step. George went back and helped Dorothy to a seat in the cabin. Aside from painful bruises and shock, she seemed otherwise uninjured.

We never did land on the Hudson. I kept taxiing on the step around the island past West Point until we passed the mountains where they pushed highest into the sky. North we went, over the river, unable to gain decent altitude. We flew under Poughkeepsie Bridge, much to the amazement of the riverside citizenry, finally reached fairly flat country and climbed to 4,000 feet, where the air was smoother and the wind stronger, but not so full of pockets and up and down drafts. We arrived in LeRoy after a flight of 4 hours and 15 minutes, a thoroughly chastened pilot, co-pilot and passenger.

Dorothy told us that when we had hit that gigantic down draft that almost wrecked us, her seat had torn from the floor, bounced in the air and struck the ceiling and then tumbled into a corner, with her still in it. Thus I learned my lesson about flying low around mountains in a high wind.

The air yacht bore us safely on countless other flights, and five years after Woodward bought it new, was sold to Charlie Collar in March, 1933. He used it for several years after that at Nassau. By late spring, 1929, we had a fleet of 14 planes at LeRoy, all gotten in readiness for us by Bill Irving and Ken Hebner during the winter months while Otto Enderton ran the airport and school while we were in Florida.

We had four instructors…Otto (later Civil Aeronautics Administration Inspector for Western New York), Tim McKay, Roy Duval and myself. Irving and Hebner handled all the mechanical work, a considerable assignment with 14 ships to keep in flying condition. Frank Koehler ran the office.

Bill Irving has been with me since that spring of 1929. He's like having another arm, or an extra motor, or a sound wing to take the place of one that goes bad in the air. As long as he is my mechanic, I shall never worry about a motor or any other part of a ship. No mechanic can touch him in Western New York and I doubt if there are many in the country who are his peers.

That summer, Otto Enderton and I entered the first of a series of many races for OX5 motors. The first of these was flown at Bradford, PA. Otto and I tossed to see who should enter. I won both the toss and the race, the latter after one of the roughest, bumpiest rides I have ever jounced through.

The D-W Airport's second annual air meet was held on October 11-13, 1929. Large prizes drew flyers from far and near, and the flyers drew spectators from hundreds of miles around. F. Trubee Davison of the United States War Department, then campaigning for a governorship, came up to speak and wrote in the airport's official register: "A big job this airport in a big way."

Lou Gordon and Wilmer Stultz (pilot for Amelia Earhart on her flight across the Atlantic) were there, and the registry bore a new list of names, names of daring airmen, many of whom have passed on, almost all of them in the performance of their flying duties. But the others carry on and they fly the torch high, some in bomber ferrying, others in Civil Air Patrol work, others as instructors of younger men who will soon pilot fighting planes, still others as airline pilots, keeping America's gigantic network of big, swift passenger planes clicking.

Freddie Lund and his wife, Betty, were there. Dick Bennett came, and Eric Wood. Spencer Punnett came for the second year. He is now with the Royal Canadian Air Force, and after two years of flying in Squadron Leader O.H. Madden's ferry squadron, holds a job of importance as an RCAF dispatcher at two Montreal air fields.

The list is long, and now it's full of memories:

L.N. Merrick, Harry Gublitz, Jimmy Taylor, Guy Stratton, Kiddy Barrows, Major M.K. Lee, Bill Dunlop, Peter Brooks, Al Heller, Sonny Harris, Paul Wilson, B. Sergievsky, Fred Taylor, Al Laverty, N.J. Gillis, Emil Burgin, Win Sargent, Betty Hugler, Duke Jernigan, Vic Rickard, N. B. Lenhard, Leo Chase, Lou Gray, Vern Roberts, Asbury Meadows.

I still have that register. It bears the signatures of many flyers who will never write their names in ink or smoke again. It helps a veteran reminisce. Freddie Lund walked away with top honors at our second LeRoy meet. Not only his star performance, but his vivid personality made him the idol of the crowds. Even now when veteran pilots get together, they sometimes talk about the race between Lund and Vern Roberts, which very nearly spelled the end of everything for both.

They flew like men possessed, and rounded the pylon in front of the grandstand at high speed, both planes making the turn at 90 degree banks, the ground wheels of one whizzing ship all but touching the top wing of the other. And they were no more than 50 feet off the ground! Neither would give an inch. Freddie won, and death walked away in disappointment. But it had come close to enlisting two new recruits.

In the same meet, Freddie skeptically surveyed a glider I had flown and promptly informed me I was crazy to take so many chances in it. "You should talk," I told him. I miss Freddie Lund. He was a great guy. He went the pilot's way…killed in an air race much like his race with Roberts at LeRoy, killed when Scotty Burmood's monocoupe got too close and chewed the tail off his ship in a race at Lexington, KY.

Despite the spectacular stunts at the second annual meet, despite Louis Meier's thrilling skywriting exhibition, and Peter Brooks' winning of the cross-country race from New York, which opened the meet, the greatest stir at LeRoy that fall was caused by the arrival of a big monoplane on October 25. It was the Columbia, the big Bellanca that had carried Roger Q. Williams and Lon Yancey all the way from New York to Rome, and previously was flown to Germany by Carl Chamberlin. LeRoy went crazy over that ship when the two famous birdmen brought it down on the D-W field.

Otto Enderton and I won many races that year by the simple expedient of feeding our OX5 Curtiss motor a full meal of speed soup. Wanting a motor that would give us speed and performance we shipped the OX5 to Kirkham, the Curtiss Company's engineering genius, who had designed not only the OX5, but the famous C6 series for the company. If any man knew how to soup up a motor, give it extra ginger, more power and consequently greater speed, he was the man. He tore our engine down, installed new pistons and new rocker arms and reground the camshaft. When it was reassembled, instead of turning up its old time 1,400 RPM's, it turned up an amazing 2,200.

Kirkham, knowing his motor, warned us that it should have a heavier crankshaft to run at such a speed, and told us never to open it up wide except by absolute necessity.

Otto and I piled up many firsts with that engine. I started the string off during the previous winter by winning the OX5 contest at the All-American Races at Miami. Otto won the first event of the summer at LeRoy. Later that fall, I took the ship to Perry, NY for an air show that opened the town's new airport.

Our closest competitor in most of the OX5 races up to that point had been Dick Bennett of Binghamton, whose OX5 motor had been stepped up until it was as fast as ours. But Dick generally developed motor trouble somewhere along the line and up to the time of the Perry race hadn't been able to beat either Otto or me. But we had not opened our motor up full, bearing Kirkham's warning in mind.

Ken Hebner came to me before the Perry race and said, "You've had good luck with that motor all winter and summer, but I think you'd better let me take it down and check it over thoroughly before you race with it again." I told him he was probably right but that I only wanted one more race and then he could do what he wanted about overhauling the thing.

Five ships lined up at the starting line of the Perry race November 9. It was Dick Bennett's last chance of the year to beat our ship and he was out for my hide. He said his motor was running perfectly and that he was sure to win this time. Down went the flag and off we went. At the first pylon, a water tank just west of the town of Perry, I took the lead, and as I turned the second pylon, a chimney on the east side of the village, I saw Bennett right on my tail. I opened up the motor a little and streaked for the home pylon. The race required five laps in all and at the third lap, I felt Bennett gaining perceptibly, so I pushed the motor until it was nearly wide open.

As we rounded the home pylon for the fourth time, Dick and I were almost neck and neck. He lost ground on the first pylon, regained it on the second and as we zipped toward the finish line, three miles distant, we were flying side by side. At almost the same instant, we both nosed down to dive fast for the finish line, and as I did so I opened up full throttle and my souped-up OX5 turned up 2,400 RPM's, 1200 more than it was designed for. I knew it was too much, but I wanted to beat Dick Bennett. We were only about 50 feet off the ground and I began to gain, and nose ahead of him.

Then suddenly I felt as if the whole world had exploded in my face. There had been no warning other than the 2,400 RPM's turned up by my motor. That should have been enough. The whole front of the plane flew in all directions. A wave of oil from the outside and inside, dashing dirt and muck and hot grease, was flung in my face and covered me completely, coating my goggles.

All this happened at 50 feet, at more than 100 miles an hour. I think it was instinct that made me reach for my goggles and rip them off. I was still in the air, skimming a farm at 20 feet. The shattered plane was tail heavy. One side cowling was flat against the flying and landing wires on the left and threatened to put me into a spin. A spin at 20 feet is as surely fatal as being hit by a train. I jiggled the plane and the cowling fell off. I slipped to the left. Straight ahead, almost close enough to touch, was a grove of trees, much too close to miss hitting, I was sure. I booted the rudder first to one side, then to the other with frantic kicks. This gave the plane's tail a wagging motion like a whale's tail in the water. It killed my speed pronto. I pulled the stick back and pancaked to a perfect landing a scant few feet from the trees.

It all happened so quickly....the explosion of the motor, the deluge of oil, the threatened spin, curting the speed and landing suddenly and flat to miss those trees, that I was out of the ship and inspecting the damage, before I realized what perhaps subconsciously thinking of what to do in just such an emergency had pulled me out of it, nothing else. I was standing there when the ambulance and a caravan of cars rushed up from the airport. The crowd and officials had seen my motor explode, had seen the smoking plane disappear behind the trees and then had seen no more. They expected to have to pull my charred body out of the wreckage. As I looked at that ship I knew how right Kirkham and Hebner had been.

The crankshaft had broken just back of the first two cylinders. The front of the motor, the propeller and all the cowling had ripped off. Seven of the eight bolts holding the motor to the plane had broken, leaving one to keep it from falling out. My good fortune had been in not losing all of the motor, for without it, the ship would have been too heavy in the tail to control and would certainly have crashed. One small bolt had saved me from such a fate. They cheered when I reappeared at the airport unscathed. But death had its innings finally that day. It almost got me and almost got Bennett when parts from my ship whizzed past him.

Amos McGuie, the parachutist, went up for an exhibition jump and left the plane with an improperly packed parachute. It failed to open completely and he fell from 1,500 feet to his death. Thus our 1929 season bowed out with a coffin on its back.

CHAPTER 21
MOTORLESS MOMENTS

After 16 years of flying, everything that had a motor in it.....from Fred Shneider's biplane and World War Curtiss Jennies to speedy Wacos and the big, substantial Loening air yacht, I went back to gliding. Don Woodward bought an Alfara glider in September, 1929, and in it I made my first glider flight since long before the World War, this time sitting in a seat and gripping a rudder control and stick, instead of hanging underneath and dangling almost helplessly.

The Alfara was a far, far cry from the Chanute hangtype glider I had flown 17 years before, but it was nothing as smooth as the sailplane we were to know later. On that September day I made four auto-towed flights with considerable more success than Lawrence J. Lesh had in that first air meet at Morris Park in 1908, but like Lesh, I felt as if I were taking off "on nothing in nothing." Gliding is like that, especially to one whose nerves and ears have been conditioned over the years to a motor's roar and high speed.

Each Sunday afternoon thereafter until the time of the D.W. Airport's second annual meet, we staged gliding exhibitions, achieving greater altitudes by lengthening the tow cables and hitching the glider to faster automobiles. One Sunday with a 1,100 foot cable, I reached a 700 foot altitude, towed by a powerful car. I cut loose at that height and turned too sharply, finding to my horror that the aileron and rudder failed to respond. The glider fell into a half spin and half spiral, out of control. The ground grew big below. I pushed the stick forward in desperation. Luckily, I had enough altitude, and gained enough speed to get control just as I was about to hit earth and become a part of it for good and all. From then on, I flew the Alfara glider with caution and respect.

A year later, in October, 1930, we staged New York State's first all glider air meet as our third annual D-W Airport Show. The meet drew 15,000 people the first day and 20,000 the second, demonstrating that we didn't have to have motor racers to attract the crowds. Our show drew some of the best glider pilots in the country and with them Wolf Hirth of Germany, holder of many world's records.

Second Annual

Air Meet

Donald Woodward Airport
Le Roy, New York

FRIDAY
SATURDAY
SUNDAY

OCTOBER 11 to 13

1930

$4500 CASH PRIZES—ALSO CUPS

Races–Stunting–Gliding–Dead Stick Landing. Special Long Distance Race

THIS IS ONE OF THE FINEST PRIVATE AIRPORTS IN THE WORLD
and it's events attract the participation of leading air men

Adding his talents to the program was Wallace Franklin, one of the first pilots to make an airplane tow, and on the second day of the meet, I towed him to 6,500 feet, from which he cut loose and stayed in the air for 45 minutes. His was the outstanding performance of the meet.

Gliding's foremost teacher, Hawley Bowlus, was a participant. He had taught Anne Morrow Lindbergh and many others, among them my own wife, who became a record breaker and holder in her own right. I hadn't realized the great skill of American glider pilots until they all gathered at that meet, among them Gus Holler, Eddie Allen, Jack O'Meara, A.P. (Duke) Artran, E. K. Doe (no relation of John Doe), Warren Eaton of Norwich, Johnny Sanford, and Martin Schempp. Wolf Hirth's entry in the log book said: "A wonderful place and surprising for the size of LeRoy, better than many airports in Europe. I like to land always on such a field."

Duke Artran stayed on a few days after the meet and introduced us to that grand little sailing plane, the Franklin glider. It was a pleasure to fly a glider that made you feel as if you weren't starting out "on nothing," as the Alfara pilots always said of their gliders. The Franklin was built more or less like an airplane, with a strong metal fuselage and real controls. It was constructed sturdily enough for stunting and airplane tow work and after one ride, I wanted one.

On May 10, 1931, a new Franklin came to roost with the Woodard fleet of air birds, and four days later I was granted permission by the Department of Commerce to make an airplane tow.

Piloting a Fleet, Vic Evans, later a captain with American Airlines, took me up 3,000 feet, where I cut loose. It was a wonderful, indescribable feeling, perhaps more startling to one who had flown power planes for years after short and bumpy rides in old fashioned hang-type gliders, than to one who takes up gliding with no other flying background.

Evans was towing me at about 80 miles an hour when I freed the glider. It slowed to a peaceful 30 miles an hour. The loud whistling the wind had made through the glider struts behind the plane dropped to a whisper. I seemed to be hanging motionless in space. No spitting, roaring motor blasted in on my hearing. All was quiet and serene. The sturdy little sailplane was a silent servant, quick to respond to the controls, willing at the slightest touch to dive, turn and climb. I brought it down gradually in graceful circles and flew over the airport in wide arcs, finally getting it down on its single central wheel. It rolled up to the hangar and stopped only when I applied the brake.

We hired Hawley Bowlus as glider instructor and ordered a second Franklin. We got a new tow car and soon Bowlus had more gliding students than he could comfortably handle. Dorothy was one of the first and within a short time she was making auto-tow flights all over the airport. After a single week of instruction, she was granted a gliding license by the Department of Commerce, thus becoming one of the nation's first licensed woman glider pilots. George Cheetham, later chief pilot for Braniff, got his license the same day.

Our Sunday airplane tow shows brought increasingly larger crowds to the airport. One of the first two-glider tows was staged by Hawley Bowlus and me, with Vic Evans piloting the tow plane. When we cut loose, Bowlus and I flew so close together we could carry on a conversation. July was strictly a glider month for us. We made countless flights, in one of which I cut loose at 5,000 feet.

Dorothy, meanwhile, was training to take part in the second National Soaring meet at Elmira, scheduled for August. We both planned to compete, being eager to qualify for our Class C soaring licenses, which were granted only to those who could accomplish soaring flights of 30 minutes or more above the point of takeoff.

Bowlus, Dorothy and I left for Elmira, together. Cheetham, Lee Burling and my brother Wilbur (named after Wilbur Wright), arrived the day after us with the glider packed in a special truck trailer. They were our ground crew, and set up the glider at the foot of South Mountain on the Elmira Airport. Dorothy and Mrs. Ralph Barnaby, whose husband became a navel commander, stole most of the limelight, being the only women entrants in a field of some 60.

Barnaby was a friend from way back….back to the days of my first glider experiences on Staten Island. He, too, had been a member of the old Aero Science Club of New York, along with Cecil Peoli, Percy Pierce and the rest of us.

Soaring conditions did not come up to standard until the second day of our stay and even then they left something to be desired. Bowlus was set against Dorothy's soaring that day. I had the glider towed to the starting point on top of South Mountain. Aided by additional crew members, I was "shock cord" launched, which is like being shot from a hugh slingshot, and found myself soaring along the mountain range with the valley of Elmira about 800 feet below.

My first fear was that I should hit the mountain ridge, but at the east end the air currents gave me a relieving lift and after the turn and the flight west, I soared over the starting point and began to gain altitude. I felt right then and there that I had discovered the finest and most thrilling sport in the world, the cleanest, most refreshing and exhilarating fun I had found in a career in the air.

I soared to my hearts content until Bowlus signaled that I had been in the air more than the required 30 minutes, so I went down, was rewarded with a wifely kiss from a wife eager to be soaring herself. I told her, before she started out, that she had never really known what flying was until she had soared over that Elmira Valley and felt the clean strength of the winds and air currents buoying up the glider without effort, without noise.

Dorothy received detailed instructions from Bowlus before we let her make her first soaring attempt at Elmira, two days after I made my first flight. I was certain she could make the grade, but I knew that the sensation of being shot off the top of South Mountain was so startling that the pitfall lay in not letting surprise get the best of you and make you lose control.

She was propelled into a strong takeoff by the shock cord. The glider zoomed, then flattened out on a level course, and soon she found the updraft and the wind bore her light weight high above the ridge. That eased the tension for us on the ground, and it was with pride and relief that we watched her soar back and forth as calmly and as gracefully as could be. She was signaled after 30 minutes and she brought the glider in perfectly within the white circle drawn on the ground for spot landings. Mrs. Barnaby had made the flight an hour before and thus Dorothy became the third woman to receive a soaring license. The first was Mrs. Charles A. Lindbergh.

Four days after Dorothy qualified, I made a flight of one hour and 35 minutes and two days later I stayed up an hour and 10 minutes. By that time, the newsreels were howling for Dorothy, so she was shot off the hilltop again while cameras clicked away. She stayed in the air for 56 minutes, a record that held for the next two years as the woman's endurance record for soaring.

When we returned to LeRoy after the Elmira soaring meet, Warren Eaton visited us with his glider. Bowlus immediately suggested that we try a three-glider tow. Up we went, with Vic Evans piloting the tow plane, and accomplished what we were pretty certain was the first three-glider tow in V formation ever flown in America.

Somehow newsreel companies and newspaper wire services heard about it and requested a special exhibition for feature story and picture purposes, so we duplicated the stunt a few days later. News articles on it bore the word to Cliff W. Henderson, managing director of the National Air Races at Cleveland, who suggested that we try the same feat at the races in September. It was the first three-glider tow ever performed in public in this country and we did it for seven successive days at the Cleveland meet.

Thus was born, I suppose, the American version of a new gliding technique… the multiple tow for three gliders. It was an experiment born of Hawley Bowlus' expertness as a glider pilot.

George Stead, former Army flyer, was our plane pilot at Cleveland, and he performed his part of the act perfectly. I'm sure we put on a good show. Ralph Kelly wrote of it in the Cleveland Plain Dealer for September 29: "Three small and fragile-looking gliders competed successfully with roaring motor ships for the attention of the crowd at the National Air Races at Cleveland Airport yesterday afternoon when they flew in formation for the first time at a public exhibition in the United States. For ten minutes the three held the attention of the crowd until they moved slowly to a landing in perfect V formation before the grandstand to make room in the sky for stronger and faster ships." We felt triumphant.

Even Bowlus and Eaton, with their vast soaring experience were pleased as punch with the success of the show. Eaton, who had flown with the Lafayette Escadrille in the first World War and later was president of the Soaring Society of America, had established an unofficial World's glider record at Elmira that year by staying in the air for seven hours and 21 minutes and soaring to an altitude of 2,409 feet. He was later killed in a Florida crash, a great loss to aviation, and especially to gliding and soaring. Bowlus was a true veteran, one of the first Americans after Wilbur Wright to stay in the air in a heavier-than-air machine for more than nine and five tenths seconds. As Ralph Kelly pointed out, Bowlus was in the air 15 minutes in our glider stunt.

It was while we were at Cleveland that Bowlus was informed that his sailplane, in which he had broken several gliding records, was to be exhibited by the Smithsonian Institution at Washington, close by Charles A. Lindbergh's Spirit of St. Louis. There was great personal satisfaction for Bowlus in this because as production manager of the Ryan Company factory in St. Louis, he had supervised the building of Lindbergh's ocean-spanning little ship. It was three years after our Cleveland exhibition, at the National Soaring Meet at Elmira, 1934, that we executed a four-glider tow, with Harold Brown of Norwich piloting the tow plane, and Warren Eaton, Jack O'Meara, Dick duPont and myself bringing up the rear in four gliders in formation. To what uses has this technique been put today!

When Germany invaded the lowland countries of Europe, German transport planes towed gliders packed with men 15 or 20 miles behind the fighting lines. The gliders were cut loose, and German soldiers landed behind the Allies. Again in the battle of Crete, Germany demonstrated the state to which she had advanced the glider as a military weapon. At that time, she was towing gliders 50 feet long, with wingspreads of 80 feet. By now, military gliders of even greater size are being perfected, and experts predict that a glider able to carry 50 men or a small tank might soon appear in the fight for world supremacy.

Germany has been towing formations of from three to six gliders across the Mediterranean to supply Axis' North Africa forces with men and material. Fifteen German soldiers, each equipped, and two tons of supplies are flown in each glider at a great saving in fuel and airplanes.

Despite such examples as we set in our three and four glider tows years ago, and despite the great potential national interest created at the soaring meets at Elmira annually, America has been tragically backward in developing the glider as a military instrument. Experts such as Dr. Alexander Klemin, who was consultant for the United States Airmail Service back in our post-war airmail days, have long advocated concentration on the glider's possibilities for silent, economical transportation. The glider has advanced in design and maneuverability almost as rapidly as the airplane.

From the early sailplanes of the great German expert, Otto Lilienthal, and his American counterpart, Octave Chanute, have been developed soaring machines, which seem almost alive in the air, like birds. Up to the present moment, we have fallen far behind some other nations, particularly, the Germans, in soaring and gliding.

After the first World War, with Germany's many aviators grounded, those conquered but ambitious Teutons took up gliding with a will and determination. They studied all its possibilities, developed it from every angle.

While men like Jack O'Meara, Warren Eaton and Ralph Barnaby, who demonstrated that a glider could be launched from an airship by taking one off from the dirigible Los Angeles, kept American gliding from total decadence, Germans such as Wolf Hirth developed new techniques.

Hirth, who participated in our first all-glider meet at LeRoy, demonstrated that a sailplane needed neither hills nor strong winds to stay in the air. It was he who discovered the technique of soaring by thermals, which are wind currents created by the differences in temperature at various altitudes above the earth. By careful study and manipulation of his sailplane, he kept it up until he had soared 465 miles, an almost unbelievable distance, in one flight.

Flights such as Hirth's attracted the attention of such air-minded and power-lustful Germans as Wilhelm Hermann Goring, on whose broad shoulders and fat neck the National Socialist Party had placed the responsibility for developing the most powerful air force the world has ever known.

Through Goring's sponsorship, Germany developed 300,000 qualified glider pilots, had them ready for any kind of action when the Nazis touched off the Second World War in September, 1939.

We are fast catching up on the kind of gliding our enemies have demonstrated for us. American Army officers are now being trained at the Elmira headquarters of the Soaring Society of America, where Lewin Barringer, a great man for the job, is directing the training program. The way was opened to the United States by men such as Barnaby, O'Meara, Eaton, Barringer, and Hawley Bowlus. Whether this nation and its allies can match the Germans in their development of the glider's use in warfare remains to be seen, but no one who has seen how readily Americans take to soaring can doubt for a moment that we are on the road to success.

Nor should the great sporting element in gliding and soaring be forgotten, for in the sport of soaring new techniques may be discovered and developed. Soaring is to power flying what sailing is to speed boating. There is a thrill in all of them, but the exhilaration comes without the motor. Soaring or sailing, you have harnessed nature in its cleanest, strongest form, have made the winds pliable and have bent them to your will, yet still you are completely dependent on them. Like all the other forms of air travel, gliding is being adapted to military use in these times. It is proving its worth as a transportation method. Tow gliding such as we did at LeRoy all that summer is now being done with gliders passengered by troops, to be landed noiselessly and swiftly on foreign fields of battle, behind the lines, behind the enemy, more safely and in greater numbers than by parachute. Out of the war will come a new and stronger interest in gliding. There can be no doubt of that. As a sport, it is inexpensive. As a thrill producer it is unequalled.

I have always been so proud of my wife's prowess as a gliding pilot that I still look back on the summer of 1932 and give myself a mental kick in the pants for what happened. I was getting a Stinson out of the LeRoy hangar for a trip one day when I wheeled it around without noticing what Dorothy was doing, ran over her foot and fractured her instep. That put her on crutches and out of the 1932 National Soaring Meet at Elmira. But her record of 56 minutes of sustained flight stood through the meet and she remained a champion without even competing.

In June of that year, we arranged a special glider tow exhibition at Niagara Falls. George Cheetham towed me from LeRoy to the falls and return. It was a different experience....a cross-country flight by glider. Frank Hawks had demonstrated his skill and the practicality of cross-country glider tows by piloting a towed glider coast-to-coast. At LeRoy, our further experiments with gliders led us to test the Franklin for stunting possibilities in the summer of 1933, and on August 4, I took it up for five consecutive loops. At that time, the holder of the loop record for gliders was Jack O'Meara, whose record of 17 consecutive loops was attained that July over Chicago.

Bent on breaking Jack's record, I notified the National Aeronautical Association that I would try to set a new mark on September 17. While cameras ground and Ralph Bodger of the NAA stood by as official observer, I was towed off at LeRoy that day and cut loose at 6,500 feet. I put the glider into loops immediately, and made 37 in all, landing from 500 feet after the last one. After that, we put from 10 to 20 loops into each Sunday afternoon glider show. These stunts were always crowd pleasers.

Dorothy went to Elmira to defend her laurels in the annual National Soaring Meet in June, 1934. She was determined to enter if only to try to better her own record of 56 minutes in the air, which had stood for two years. She was one of three women contestants. The others were Mrs. Richard duPont and Gretchen Reighard. Although

Mrs. duPont and Dorothy made several flights for the newsreels, it was several days before conditions were judged good enough to try for record soaring flights.

But when she got a crack at it, Dorothy stayed aloft for four hours and 31 minutes. The mark stood throughout the meet. A new record and the longest flight made in a secondary glider during all of the competition. We wrote additional chapters in our personal soaring histories the next year. In June, I signed a contract with the Toronto Flying Club to give glider tow exhibitions and stunts at the sixth Canadian National Air Pageant. George Cheetham flew the tow plane to Toronto with Arthur Bovill, who was signed up for parachute jumping. Dorothy and I took the glider up by auto trailer. The grandstands were full late on the afternoon of June 15 when Cheetham towed me off the ground at the Toronto Flying Club airport and toward the Thorncliffe Race Track, where the air pageant was in progress.

We were at 3,500 feet when we arrived over the crowd, and circled until we attained 6,000 feet, where I cut loose, and with the band playing "The Daring Young Man on the Flying Trapeze," went through 25 loops in time with the oomphing, booming music. The crowd loved it, but no more than I did. Looping a glider to music was something new and different for me, too.

I had been instructed to land on the infield, but in circling low to come in I saw that the track was wide enough, so I set the glider down on the track and rolled to a stop in front of the judges' stand. The crowd rushed for the glider, and ever since that moment I have had untold respect for the Royal Northwest Canadian Mounted Police. Those tall and sturdy boys saved my glider from being demolished by souvenir hunters. Right then and there I knew that Americans had rivals in the frantic search for souvenirs of any special occasion. Their Canadian cousins are just as enthusiastic and just as hard to handle as we are.

Without knowing it, I had accomplished two things that afternoon.....flown the first towed glider in Canada and broken the Canadian glider looping record.

Dorothy entered the sixth annual National Soaring Meet at Elmira anxious and eager to break her own meet record of 4 hours and 31 minutes of sustained flight. Before the meet was well under way, she took off in unfavorable conditions on a flight purely for the benefit of the newsreels. The wind died and she was forced to land in a small field at the base of the ridge. In doing this, the glider knifed through the top of a tree and was badly damaged. Dorothy telephoned me in New York. I told her to have George Cheetham take the glider to LeRoy at once, and I immediately called the airport and instructed the mechanics to be ready to work night and day on it to get it in shape so that Dorothy could use it at Elmira.

Three days after the mishap, the glider was back in Elmira, ready for action. That afternoon I reached Elmira from New York with Len Heimlich. Dorothy had already been in the air for three hours when we got there. The wind was coming strong from the northwest and it was obvious that she was having hard work. As she passed over the swimming pool on Harris Hill, Heimlich and I waved at her. She waved back, and kept at her work. She told us later that she had been about ready to quit then, but seeing us, had regained confidence and kept on fighting the wind.

In the end, the wind won…..by dying down, and she was forced to land, but only after she had soared for five hours and 17 minutes, had blistered her hands and bruised her body. She had a new world's record, but it took her three days to recover from the experience. She had had a tough time. At one point, the glider went into a spin and only by sheer strength had she avoided a crash.

By then I was convinced that the Franklin secondary glider wasn't really a good enough performer to reach a high altitude on a rough day, so I negotiated with Dick duPont to buy the German Gopengen sailplane he had imported to fly in the meet. The Gopengen was the last word in soaring ships. We were thrilled with it. Dorothy handled it so well she became the first woman in the country to be granted a Department of Commerce license to make an airplane tow. The glider was so perfectly balanced and designed that it could roll, loop, and stunt as well as a power plane. By the spring of 1936, I was so busy that we had no time for soaring and was working out of Rochester's Municipal Airport where the traffic was so heavy that no glider could have been flown there safely. Then I had to sell the sailplane. Paul duPont bought it.

Some day I mean to have one again. It was the greatest ship I have ever owned and gave me more fun than any other. When I do take up soaring again, I know I'll have plenty of company. Soaring, despite its rapid development for military use, is still in its infancy, although it is far older than power plane travel. But it has infinite possibilities for sport and for war. I still hope to get my share of its thrills.

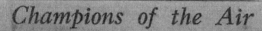

Champions of the Air

The two women who together hold a large share of all the women's flying records of the world greeted each other in The Times-Union editorial offices yesterday. Left is Mrs. Dorothy C. Holderman, wife of Capt. Russell Holderman, manager of D-W Airport; right is Mrs. Amelia Earhart Putnam. Mrs. Holderman set a women's world gliding record in July, 1930, when she kept aloft an unpowered plane for 56 minutes at the national glider meet at Elmira. She is one of three women in America who boast soaring licenses. Mrs. Putnam, of course, is the woman champion of power planes, veteran of two Atlantic flights and holder of speed records.

FLY

Russeell Holderman, Alfara training glider, LeRoy, NY, 1930

CHAPTER 22
SHORT HOPS AND LONG HAULS

From 1929 through 1935, our LeRoy airport prospered, and won itself a good name. Although we caught and pursued the gliding and soaring bug with a will through those years, all was not motorless flight, effortless and quiet. Operating an airport brings many a drudgery, many a thrill, many a surprise.

In the winter of 1929-1930, we were so busy with ground school work we couldn't go to Florida. Our school had won government approval, one of the first five U.S. approved schools and the only one east of the Mississippi.

Students came from all over the country to study flying rudiments there and in the summer we sent many a promising lad away with his certificate. These flaming war years have brought us satisfaction in knowing that many of our students were well prepared for what would be their roles in a war in which aviation plays so vital a part. Many of them are now flying for the U.S. Army and Navy. Some are instructing young, new pilots; others are ferrying bombers to England, Africa and elsewhere, and others are flying the airlines.

In the spring of 1930, after more than 16 years of flying I took delivery of a new plane for the first time at the place of its birth. There are few greater thrills in flying than in bringing a new plane home from the factory. You feel smugness in watching a new and shining ship on the factory floor, standing sleek and ready while mechanics put on its finishing touches. Then they wheel it out, warm up the motor, and there you are, flying something that has never been flown before. It's like taking a hop on the back of a powerful young fledgling eagle. The Stinson I brought home from the company's Wayne, Michigan factory was one of the first of that firm's ships powered with a Lycoming motor.

Flying a new ship like that is one of the few thrills a veteran can enjoy alone. Novice flyers seem to take for granted that each new ship is little different than the last. But a man who once flew Curtiss pusher planes knows better. Each improvement in design, each advancement in motor construction to him means a new and shining chapter in the story he has helped to write through the years....the unended story of aviation.

I had another such thrill at Cortland, N.Y. that same summer of 1930, after I had won several firsts in races at the opening of Cortland's new airport. This was in a new low wing Buhel 300 horsepower monoplane, fresh from the factory, and at the stick of that ship I flew more than 200 miles an hour for the first time in my life.

That July, I joined almost every pilot of my acquaintance in Central and Western New York in the New York State Air Tour, in which we took off from Buffalo for Niagara Falls, Hammondsport, Hornell, Binghamton, Norwich, Syracuse, Cortland, LeRoy, and then back to Buffalo. The tour was a great success, particularly because I met E.S. Rhodes again. Meeting Rhodes always has given me a lift, because Smoky Rhodes was actually the first man to pilot a plane across the Atlantic Ocean. He was the forerunner of all the others, all the Lindberghs, the Chamberlins, the Earharts, and the Williams and Yanceys. For he was the co-pilot of the Navy's NC4 when it became the first airplane in history to achieve the mighty feat of spanning the ocean in a single flight. He was awarded the Congressional Medal of Honor for his feat.

I seemed to learn more in that summer of 1930 than I had in many years. That August Lowell Bayles came to LeRoy. Bayles achieved fame by winning the Bendix Air Race and breaking the measured mile speed record. He was later killed trying to beat his own speed mark. This day he had one of his special Gee Bee planes, and I'll never forget that ship.

Lowell sent me up in it with the challenge that I couldn't make it do a snap roll once and then keep it from doing several more in rapid succession. It was a challenge any pilot would accept. But I found the controls so sensitive that the least bit of movement on the stick and rudder sent the ship into three rolls faster than I could say "Bendix." It took me a long time to get the knack, but finally I achieved a lone roll without being knocked dizzy by a succession of them. All the while, Bayles stood on the ground, laughing at my plight.

RUSS – 'GEE BEE'
RACER

Flying with famous, skillful flyers is like playing golf with professionals. You get a big kick out of it and you learn something.

When participants in the National Air Tour for the Ford Trophy landed at Le-Roy, Woodward staged a clambake in the woods back of Heimlich's quarry for them. What a galaxy of flying names, what a squadron of star pilots that was, and how many hundreds of clams they put away. It was a great bunch, and we will never be together again, headlined by such standouts as George W. Haldeman and Jimmy

Doolittle, Eddie Stinson, Boyles, Bill Gould, Tom Colly, Walter Lees, J.H. Smart, Pop Cleveland, Jack Story, Harry Russell, Captain R.E. Lake, Harvey Mummerl, Captain W. Lancaster, Leo Gehfback, Joe Meehan, Cliff Henderson, Vic Nelson, Senator Webb, W.B. Linkhard, Lon Yancey, Al Heller, Leo Chase, Eddie Schneider, Asbury Meadows, and J.E. Sommers. Stuffed with every item on the menu of Woodward's clambake, until they bulged, they went on to Binghamton the next day, then to Bradford, PA, where I caught up with them.

* * *

Flying up north is no bargain in the winter, and the winter of 1932 was by no way an exception. It was a bitter stretch of gray, snowbound months, and the greatest of these was March, which blustered, snapped and growled with almost unparalleled ferocity.

It was on the morning of March 8 that I got word at LeRoy that two busloads of people were marooned in 10 below zero weather in gigantic snowdrifts on the Rochester-Batavia highway. They had no heat and no food. The larder of the nearest farmhouse could not provide for them all. Snow kept coming down and there was no hint of a temperature rise. The storm had taken two lives in a day and a half. The only way to get food to the marooned bus passengers was by airplane. We collected a large supply of ham and canned soup, thermoses of coffee and bundles of sandwiches and packed them in a big canvas bag. Then we wheeled out a Stinson cabin plane.

As we brought the ship into the teeth of a howling wind, volunteers had to be called to hold it down. Then we pointed it down a gale-swept lane shoveled out of the drifts on the runway. Ken Hebner, Tommy McDermott and Stanley Knight climbed in with me and we reared down the lane of snow and into the full force of the wind, got off the ground and headed bumpily for Batavia. By the time we were in the air, the roads below had drifted so badly it was almost impossible to make them out. Only by following lines of telephone poles were we able to make out which was road and which was snow-piled field and meadow. By the time we picked out the two marooned busses, they were all but invisible under giant drifts.

We circled the nearest farmhouse until its occupants tumbled out into the drifted barnyard, gesticulating wildly. Then we dropped the food, waited to watch them pick it up, and somehow got back to LeRoy. I would almost have rather been one of the bus passengers.

* * *

One of those tall, dark men you read about in mysteries swung up the snow-swept path to my office one day in January, 1933. His appearance at my door was like something out of Poe. Said he, in a voice of thunder, "I am Mardoni, the Magician." I might have guessed as much, for I had read that he was staging his magical show at the local high school that night. He draped his long frame on an office chair and told me that he was interested in flying and already had some hours to his credit. He wanted more time in the air, and asked me to take him up for more instructions as soon as the snow stopped falling.

While we waited for the storm to blow over, he went through a little routine of pocket tricks for the instructors and hangar crewmen. His cleverness fascinated me so much that I offered to exchange flying lessons for lessons in magic. I paid him three hours of flying instruction for one trick alone....Houdini's famous bird cage trick.

Mardoni stayed several days and before he left had made me a more or less awkward but passable magician. I put so much time on the hobby that I finally joined the International Brotherhood of Magicians. Practicing feats of magic, even the more simple routines are great for the nerves, a great steadying and relaxing influence.

No one who flies for a living should be without some pastime he can turn to when he's not in the air. He needs that mental salve, the balm that comes from trying something totally different from flying. I had found it in both magic and music. Years ago when my parents insisted that I learn to play the violin, I balked, but without success. I learned to play the violin, not well, but well enough not to be particularly annoying when I take it out and play along with the radio or phonograph; it eases frayed nerves and calms down a work-weary disposition.

Some airmen play piano. Others have been known to tear terrible tunes from battered harmonicas and banjos. They do this with a zeal and zest given to few other musical hobbyists. Some play as they fly, with reckless abandon. The more careful the flyer, the more precise a hobbyist you will find he is. Up to the time of the present war, when necessity placed restrictions on flying, my magician Mardoni and his wife were still meeting most of their stage engagements in an airplane.

* * *

It was only a few months after Mardoni made his mysterious appearance on our rural LeRoy scene that another magician appeared out of the blue. This time it was Tommy Tomlinson at the stick of a U.S. Navy Hell Diver, the trickiest, fastest thing I had ever flown. When Tommy came to visit us, I had just completed 5,000 hours in the air and was interested in the U.S. Naval Reserve. Tommy left me some application blanks. That August, Earl Carroll, whom I had not seen since our Liberty Loan flight from Hazelhurst Field during the First World War, dropped in at Leroy for a visit, practically unchanged and still on the high road for beauty. Three months later, I was commissioned a Lieutenant Commander in the U.S. Naval Reserve (A.V.T.)

* * *

I got into the newspaper game by landing a glider on a pie plate. It was one Sunday in April, 1934, that Frank Gannett, the Rochester publisher, phoned me to say he wanted a demonstration in an airplane. Six months before I had made what I feared was a futile attempt to sell him a plane. As luck would have it, when he called me that Sunday afternoon, Bill Mara, Stinson's traveling representative, was in town on a weekend call, and he and I gave Gannett a demonstration in Stinson's latest model.

Then I went to LeRoy to fly in a glider exhibition, and Gannett was flown over by Mara to watch the show. I put on my routine stunts and maneuvers and then Tommy McDermott announced over the public address system that I would bring the Franklin glider in and land it within three feet of a pie plate he placed on the apron about 50 feet away from the spectator's stand. I brought the glider in slowly and put it down with its single landing wheel pointed toward the crowd and with its nose on the pie plate. When it was over, Gannett told me that I was the man he wanted for a pilot.

First Gannett Plane

t.-Com. Russell Holderman, ace pilot and
iger of D-W Airport, Le Roy, N. Y., flew
ew Stinson four-passenger monoplane to
hester from the Detroit factory this morn-
At Rochester Airport to accept delivery
Gannett Newspapers were Frank E. Gannett,
sher of Gannett Newspapers and other Gannett executives. Almost immediately Mr.
nett and John J. Connors, advertising direc
Albany Evening News and the Knickerl
Press, took off on the first flight to A
Left to right. Mr. Connors, Mr. Gannet
Pilot Holderman. The plane will be us
facilitate news coverage of Gannett Newsp

Late that week, he bought a new Stinson, with the proviso that I fly it for him. I agreed, but told him it would have to be a part time job because the air school at Le-Roy was doing well, and I had no desire to leave it.

I took delivery of the Gannett Newspaper's new cream-colored Stinson at the factory late that month. It was the first of a series of planes the news chain was to buy to use exclusively for quick coverage of news from the air, in several spectacular promotional stunts and in more than one instance in swift errands of mercy, rushing blood donors to stricken men and women who needed special transfusions in order to live.

Within a few days after I delivered the newspaper Stinson, I flew the far-traveling publisher to Albany, Elmira, Detroit and Chicago. From then on, despite the experience of the years, I knew I was in for enough flying to satisfy even my desires. Late that summer, when I took over ownership of the D-W Flying Service from Woodward, I found myself busier than a P-40 Pursuit pilot in the midst of a squadron of Japanese Zero fighters.

* * *

The International Brotherhood of Magicians came down from Batavia during its annual convention in 1934 to see a special air show at LeRoy. It was during the convention that we first saw the automobile blindfold drive. It was only natural that as a pilot and magician, I should try even a better trick.

On Sunday, September 30, a committee of six solemn judges blindfolded me with a special blindfold, sealed it, and told me to go ahead and fly. I took off, circled the airport several times in my Stinson, landed, stopped and was led to the committee, which examined my blindfold to see if it had moved during the flight. The judges were willing to admit that the first airplane blindfold test had been accomplished.

I did my first slow rolls in a Stinson cabin plane that Armistice Day. The ship had been brought in to LeRoy by Jack Kelly, one of Stinson's test pilots. After that, we added slow rolling in the Stinson to our Sunday afternoon shows.

After Christmas, we spent a day or two in Miami and were back in LeRoy before New Year's Day, landing on December 28th. Three days later, I was bound for one of the most thrilling flights I have ever had. It was dead winter all over the north country, and only those who have lived in upstate New York know what real, raw winter can be like, not Canadian or Arctic, but solid New York State winter, with bitter cold winds and snowdrifts, hip deep, fence deep, sometimes house deep.

On the day we landed on our return from the South, an American Airlines Curtiss Condor carrying four men disappeared northeast of Utica. That meant Adirondack country, no bargain for crashing airplanes, especially in the winter. The hue and cry immediately went up and it was to trappers and flyers that appeals were sent for aid, aid in sighting the ship, aid in helping the survivors of the crash, if any, for it was a certainty that the big airliner was down somewhere.

Ernie Dryer was pilot of the airliner. His brother Dale was co-pilot. With them when the ship dropped out of sight and failed to make its scheduled landing were J.H. Brown and R.W. Hambrook. Dick Hemenway of the Rochester Times-Union's city staff, Joseph J. Durnherr, veteran Rochester news cameraman, and I were dispatched almost immediately, not only to sight the plane for news coverage if possible, but to find it perhaps before anyone else.

Gannett Plane Takes Part in Search

We flew from Rochester to Utica, landed at Utica Airport, and then took off, taking a northeastern course into the foothills of the mountains. We were flying low, almost touching the tops of tall, wind and snow-beaten pines, when we sighted the wreck, half an hour after we had left Utica. The airliner was down in a grove on a steep slope. Across the path it had hewn through the trees was a straight long tree, shattered at the base. The plane's wings were off and its nose was buried in the snow. There were signs of scattered wreckage, but best of all, there were two men standing in the snow back of the tail.

By that time, we had also sighted a rescue party, trudging through drifts about three-quarters of a mile from the wreck. We circled the rescue party and pointed the way toward the marooned flyers and their smashed plane. Durnherr's news pictures from the air and Hemenway's story were national scoops that day.

The Dryer Brothers and their passengers fared far better than the victims of most airline crashes. All suffered from exposure. Ernie Dryer had fractured ribs and a hip injury, congested lungs and frozen feet. Dale had frozen feet and a fractured jaw. Their passengers suffered from exposure and shock. But all were brought out fairly whole, and alive. After that flight across the Adirondacks to sight the crashed American Airlines Curtiss Condor, I was glad to fly south.

I made six round trips in all to Miami that winter and early spring in the Gannett ship. I was beginning to know the route by heart. I almost, but not quite, felt as if I could fly the route by the seat of my pants, as we flew some of the airmail in the old days. We weren't exactly ruralized in LeRoy in all those years, but sometimes I wondered what my veteran pilot colleagues were doing. As Cy Caldwell wrote: "LeRoy is a homelike little town of 5,000 souls, all of whom are sound asleep by 9 p.m. Russ himself sometimes sits up until 10 on a Saturday night, waiting for the bath water to get hot. But outside of that, he leads a quiet life."

It was hardly that serene, but in the spring of 1935 I learned I had been missing something in the way of speed. I reached this conclusion when I went to Newark to get Jimmy Doolittle's latest speed plane. It was like a flying bullet. A ten passenger cabin job, it had borne Jimmy on spectacular long distance hops with great speed. He took it from Los Angeles to Washington, D.C. non-stop, in 10 hours and 22 minutes on February 21, 1935, and March 6, flew it from Los Angeles to Mexico City in 13 hours and 6 minutes.

These records were printed neatly on the fuselage, and I took full note of them when I stepped into the cabin to take the controls at Newark Airport. Walter Bass and

Lee Smith, technicians for the Airplane Development Corporation, Glendale, makers of the plane, were with me.

When we took off and got up before I knew it, I realized how, with skill and daring, Jimmy had been able to fly the ship non-stop from Los Angeles to New York the previous January in 11 hours and 59 minutes. We made Rochester that day in exactly 90 minutes, including a stop in Syracuse. I took Gannett, Raymond N. Ball of the Lincoln-Alliance Bank & Trust Company, Rochester, and Herbert W. Cruickshank, Treasurer of the Gannett Company, back to Newark on the return flight.

What a ship! But what a flyer was Doolittle, anyway! And still is. Tokyo will confirm this. As this is written, the second World War is far from being over, but if any men can win it for the United Nations, men like Doolittle can. His American friends in the flying game, and they are legend, know his true worth. They know what chances he took in 1930 when he won the Harmon Trophy by flying from New York to San Francisco completely blind and bringing his plane in without a bump, and in 1931 when he won the Bendix Trophy Race from Burbank to Cleveland, and in 1932 when he set a new speed record for land planes in copping first in the Thompson Trophy Race.

Learn
FLYING D.W. SERVICE INC
AVIATION
GOVERNMENT APPROVED
GROUND AND FLYING SCHOOL
D.W. LE ROY
D.W. FLYING SERVICE INC.
LE ROY NEW YORK

FIRST GOVERNMENT APPROVED FLYING SCHOOL IN THE EAST
LOCATED AT THE FINEST PRIVATE AIRPORT IN AMERICA

Direct Communication At All Times During Flight

Special Course in Gliding

Aeronautic Explanation

THE D. W. Flying Service, Inc., because of the interest and foresight of Mr. Donald Woodward in building and equipping the Donald Woodward Airport in Le Roy, in 1928, with everything the best that money could buy, is enabled to operate an aviation school under conditions, and with advantages, that are outstanding in many ways. Any young man looking to aviation as his future can find no better place to gain his fundamental training than at this school.

THE AIRPORT occupies about 150 acres of land, open on all sides. The field is T shaped, 3,900 feet long on the stem and 2,600 feet in width across the top. Seven miles of tile were laid to drain the field, and 30,000 tons of crushed stone were used in building the macadam runways, four in number. The runways are from 100 to 225 feet in width. In addition to the runways, and paralleling them, are landing strips of grass turf, free from stones, ditches, or any dangerous obstruction.

Equipment

CONSIDER this plane equipment when you are selecting your aviation school. It is outstanding in the number and the different types.

8 Wacos
3 Birds
3 Challengers
1 24 Curtis Robin, monoplane
1 Stinson, Wyoming motor
1 Eaglerock, cabin monoplane
1 Fairchild, cabin monoplane
1 Loening, amphibian
1 Gliders

Instructors

All flying instruction is under the personal supervision of Mr. Holderman, who began flying in 1913 in gliders and the old type "pusher" biplanes. He served during the World War as flight instructor and after the armistice was one of the early pioneers in the air mail service. Later he organized his private school and taught many of the well known flyers of today. He has had over 5,000 hours in the air and has

HERBERT HOLDERMAN

built up a reputation as operator of one of the finest schools in the country.

HAROLD A. McKAY—All ground school instruction is under the personal supervision of Mr. McKay, graduate of Princeton University Army School, 1917. Commissioned Lieutenant and served in Army Air Service until conclusion of War. He at present holds a transport pilot's license, and is licensed by the U. S. Department of Commerce as approved school ground instructor on all subjects.

THE HANGAR, including the school quarters, is located on a slight eminence. The main building, 100 feet wide by 140 feet long, is of fire-proof construction. The school rooms are located along the west side of the building, and include class rooms and complete machine shop. Ladies' club room and men's club room is located on second floor and club room on top floor of the three-story tower. The building is steam-heated throughout and has every modern convenience, including locker room and showers.

The Spirit of the School

IT is neither our aim or ambition to operate the largest aviation school in the country, but rather to give the very best instruction to a limited number of students. At no time is our class allowed to exceed thirty in number. This enables us to give very close personal attention to each student, to the end that when he gains his diploma he is not only a credit to us, but to aviation.

Our record for students passing the Department of Commerce license tests for 1929 and 1930 was 99%. We do not consider aviation as a thrill or a fad, but as the coming industry of the nation, and this is the background of every day in our school. We invite inspection of the school. All communications from those interested answered at once.

Airplane Assembly and Rigging

Engine Overhaul and Shop Practice

Complete Ground School

Ideal Location

The location of the school is ideal in its surroundings and environment. Le Roy is a village of 5,000 population, healthy, clean, and free from the diversions that are apt to distract the attention of students in city-located schools. We aim to give our very best in instruction and attention to students, and the school does not invite the attendance of young men who are not seriously bent on learning aviation and making it their life's work. The school is located five minutes' drive from the village, and transportation is furnished to and from the airport. Room and board can be had for about $9.00 per week.

M ANY of the most noted pilots and leaders in Aviation have visited the airport and school, including Amelia Earhart, F. Trubee Davison and Army and Navy fliers. Following are a few expressions that have come to us:

"They tell me I have landed on more airports than any other existing pilot. If that be so, I am happy to say that this is without doubt not alone the finest private airport in America, but in the world."
—Lady Mary Heath, Noted English Aviatrix.

"I feel that a young man wishing to learn to fly can place himself in no better hands, no cleaner healthier environment than with the D. W. Flying Service, Inc."—D. W. Tomlinson, Former Lieutenant U. S. N. and one of Famous Sea Hawks.

"Seldom does one man do so much for aviation as has been done here. The Donald Woodward Airport is the envy, and will be the envy for some time to come, of many cities and communities. Mr. Woodward is to be commended, not only for what he has done for Le Roy and this territory, but for what he has done to promote aviation."—Clarence M. Young, Director of Aviation, U. S. Dept. of Commerce.

"A big job, this Airport, in a big way."—F. Trubee Davison, Asst. Sec. of War in charge of Aeronautics.

D. W. FLYING SERVICE, Inc.
Le Roy, New York

Russell Holderman, President   H. Kirk Tennent, Secretary
J. Leonard Heimlich, Treasurer

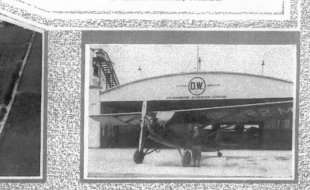

CHAPTER 23
THREE MOTORS

The Gannett Newspapers went airplane shopping in 1935 and came up with a tri-motored Stinson monoplane. It was battleship gray, with burnt red motor cowlings. The finest ship I had ever flown, it had everything….power, speed, comfort, even a couch. It was equipped with blind flying instruments, and after I got my instrument rating, I took it through some thick and soupy weather. It boomed along at a comfortable 165 miles an hour. The first time I took it through rain and fog, the tremendous contrast between that 800 horsepower, streamlined, airtight greyhound and Fred Shneider's old 1913, pusher biplane came home to me forcibly.

In 1913, my only instrument had been a 12-inch piece of string. In the Stinson, a score of precise, unfailing instrument dials gleamed from the dashboard, constant reminders that the plane and everything in it were at the mercy of needles and indicators, electrical circuits, fine little springs and countless other unerring gadgets.

On a flight to Miami in the tri-motor that November, we cut the Loening's LeRoy–Miami time by five hours, making the trip to Miami in eight hours and 30 minutes. In all, we made five round trips to Miami before spring came again, and late in the spring the newspapers sold the small Stinson and added a new gull-wing Stinson to their news covering facilities.

Then I became a full time newspaper pilot, signing up to fly exclusively for the Gannett chain. I regretted having to give up the air school and field at LeRoy, especially when we were having such good luck with young flying students, teaching them the fundamentals of flying by giving them gliding instruction first, then with that sound foundation, going into power plane work.

But the newspaper proposition was too good to turn down, and covering the news from the air with photographers and reporters was one of the great experiences flying had shown me. It was a good feeling to become a regular part of a newspaper organization and still do the work I liked best. I kept my Stinson agency after I signed with the newspapers. On October 19, 1935, we staged a farewell air meet at LeRoy.

The wind was strong and raw and the air was icy, but the show drew a crowd, for the proceeds were to go to Rochester's orphan children at Christmas. Ray Moulton, Jack Jenkins, Otto Enderton, Ralph (Pete) Barton, Guy Stratton and Ray Hylan did the stunting. We went through every trick the wind would allow, and I think the orphan kids got a nice Christmas out of it.

Then with both regret and finality, I turned over the managership of the finest private airport in the world to George E. Meglemre, and closed a chapter in my life. Since then, the D-W Airport has had its ups and downs, but right now it is being used in the best possible way... as a government sanctioned training school for prospective Army, Navy and Marine air corps flyers. It's a beehive of activity, all for the good cause of making America supreme in the air.

$$* * *$$

I've marked the date February 20, 1937, on my calendar with a red circle and have hung a wreath around it. I was flying the Stinson Reliant, the tri-motor under going repairs at the moment, and was coming in for a landing, with every reason to believe I was set to bring all three points down smoothly.

Just as the wheels touched, out of the corner of my eye, I saw our left landing wheel roll gaily ahead of us. Instantly I dropped the left aileron. This raised the left wing and kept us rolling on the right wheel for about 200 feet. Then we lost speed and the left wing settled. The broken left landing gear dug in and the plane stopped as suddenly as if it had struck a brick wall, nosed over briefly, then settled back on its tail wheel.

Holderman's only crackup brought this result. The Gannett Newspaper's Stinson Reliant cracked its left landing-gear strut upon touching down. Holderman taxied the plane on its right wheel for some distance as it lost speed, then tilted forward onto its nose, bending the propeller

I was unhurt, and the sole casualty was Gannett, who without his safety belt fastened, was thrown against the front of the cabin and cut his head. We might not have done such a messy job of stopping if when I had seen the wheel I had also seen that it had taken part of the landing gear with it when it came off. Inspection revealed that the strut had been cracked for some time and that each successive landing has opened the breach a little wider until finally there was nothing to hold it.

Even little things like a cracked strut can spoil a safety record. That one spoiled mine…..8,500 hours in the air without a single crackup. I'm still mad at that strut, 4,500 hours later. But it wasn't long after that mishap that news came to us from Florida that made my crackup with the Stinson seen trivial by comparison. I lost a true friend and commercial aviation lost a great pilot when Bill Lindley, after a stay in Bimini, took off his pontooned ship for Palm Beach unaware that a leak had developed in the pontoons and they were full of water. He landed at Palm Beach, the "foot"-heavy ship dived under, and Bill was killed.

* * *

Many times the tri-motored Stinson bore us safely and swiftly south, through and over storms. It was big and powerful enough to climb over most storms, and its two-way radio and blind flying instruments made bad weather comparatively harmless. The radio beam had been introduced by then and simplified the task of staying on course under any and all conditions.

Gannett Newspaper's tri-motored Stinson

In six months in the late winter and spring of 1936, I spent 450 hours in the air, most of them in the tri-motor, covering the great southern New York State flood, train wrecks, fires, and various other spot news assignments which kept us in the air most of the time. For short hops we were using a new Stinson Reliant. The 1936 model was turned over to the Hartford (Conn.) Times for news coverage use.

Gannett Newspaper's second tri-motored Stinson

We were some hours out of Rochester on our way south one day in 1937 when a twin-motored Lockheed passed us like a rocket and disappeared from view. Later, in Miami, I learned from Eddie Nehemeyer, Powell Crosley's pilot, that Crosley's Lockheed 12 was for sale. Gannett sold the tri-motor and bought it. I went to Cincinnati to take over the Lockheed from Eddie, with whom I had flown as far back as 1927. Eddie went with me on a couple of landing practice flights, and then turned the ship over to me to take back to Rochester.

Two Wasp motors, most reliable engines of their day, and still going strong, pulled the gleaming silver plane up 1,500 feet a minute. I leveled off at 7,000 feet and gunned for home at better than 200 miles an hour, happy as a kid with a new electric train. There were regrets in turning over the tri-motored Stinson to a new owner. It had been a wonderful trip.

On one of the last trips from Miami, where we had housed it at the No. 1 hangar at Miami Municipal Airport, I flew it to Rochester with George Cheetham as co-pilot, and Rochester's chief of police, Henry T. Copenhagen, and Clem R. Franklin, general auditor of the Gannett Newspapers, as passengers. A day after we arrived home, fire destroyed the No. 1 hangar at Miami and the 14 planes in it, causing some $700,000 damage.

I patted the tri-motor almost affectionately when I got the news, but with many other pilots sadly learned the full details of the destruction. Gone up in flames were M.L. Bendum's $120,000 Lockheed Electra, in which Jimmy Mattern conducted his Arctic search for lost Russian flyers; Gar Wood's $65,000 Graumann amphibian, and Major Alexander P. de Seversky's $250,000 experimental ship, in which he had set several speed records.

When we sold the tri-motor, I had flown it more than 130,000 miles. It is now in Alaska, doing transport duty for Pan American Airways, and pulling its weight, I'll bet my bottom dollar.

But how that new Lockheed could go! It was much like the model that Howard Hughes flew around the world in 3 days, 19 hours and 8 minutes.

On its first Rochester-Miami trip it got us there in six hours and 40 minutes, a speed executed with such solid comfort that when we landed, both Gannett and I wore broad smiles of satisfaction.

Our trips to New York, about 250 air miles from Rochester, averaged an hour and 15 minutes. One day, with a strong tail wind, I made the distance in two minutes over an hour. I never got the chance to try to make it in an hour, but the temptation was always there, and the quick and powerful Wasp motors were always ready and willing to be given the gun. On one flight to Spokane, where Gannett had a speaking engagement, we did 2,020 miles in 11 hours and 40 minutes, with head winds giving us a battle most of the way.

When Douglas (Wrong Way) Corrigan came back to America and to the most enthusiastic receptions since Lindbergh's, in August, 1937, I flew to Albany to meet him on August 16 and to escort him from Albany to Utica, Syracuse and Rochester, where hundreds of thousands wanted to greet him. We spent the evening of August 16 together, talking mostly about Corrigan's future, He was having a grand time, lionized by larger crowds than he had ever dreamed existed, enjoying himself thoroughly, liking the receptions, liking the confetti, liking the glamour of being a public hero.

But if his heart was in the clouds in his miraculous flying crate, his feet were on the ground. Out of all the glitter and the glamour of his reception across the nation, he was thinking seriously of his future. He told me frankly that what he really wanted was a job that would give him a chance to fly and at the same time an opportunity to tinker with airplanes.

Corrigan was a great kid with a reckless, adventurous spirit and his feat of flying to Ireland in a rickety plane seemed all the more remarkable to those of us who had flown the same kind of ship long years before. Leading the wayward hero across upstate New York was a pleasure. Utica went mad over him; Syracuse yelled itself hoarse, and Rochester broke down and filled its streets with shouting and confetti.

Forty days after we watched Corrigan's little plane disappear in the west out of Rochester, we were winging east, bound for New England, where the September 27 hurricane had struck with unparalleled force and taken its terrific toll of life and property. It was a newspaper assignment in the strictest sense of the word.....getting out the news despite all obstacles. Hank Wetherell, pilot of the The Hartford Times' Stinson, was doing a yeoman's job of flying out newspapers across the Connecticut River. The bridge was out at Hartford and Wetherell and the plane were the sole means of delivering a large part of the out-of-city circulation. Hank was doing fine, but he needed help in the great emergency of the moment. Thus the Rochester plane turned serial carrier boy and never missed a delivery.

That November, the Lockheed rang up three of its fastest flights to Miami, and a month later, I got the race tingles again.

CHAPTER 24
THIRTY-SIX SECONDS

I told the boss I thought the newspaper Lockheed might have a chance in the New York-Miami air race, which was to feature All-American Air Races in January 1938. The race was open to ships of all classes which had "X," or experimental, licenses.

We got a nod from the boss on entering the Lockheed. Bill Irving installed extra gasoline tanks so we would have enough fuel for a non-stop flight. Then we painted "Visit Rochester, The Convention City" on her sides. We streamlined the ship even further by removing some of the radio antenna. Then, with Dick Richards as co-pilot, Cheetham since having joined Braniff Airlines, we took off from Rochester Municipal Airport on January 6, landed in New York and went through the usual press photography rigmarole.

On the following afternoon, we made a two-hour test flight to determine speed and the rate of gasoline consumption at high speeds, and later we met the other contestants, along with newspaperman, in the office of Ken Bahr, manager of Floyd Bennett Airport, the starting point of the race. New York newsmen told a Miami press agent that they were holding flash stories pending the arrival of women entrants in the race. But none came.

At the last moment, Jacqueline Cochran was unable to participate as she had planned, so she sent her special Beechcraft along anyway, with Max Constant to pilot it.

Dorothy had come down with us to watch the takeoff. Someone suggested she act as my co-pilot, to give the race a properly feminine angle. This was ruled out immediately, because she had no pilot's license. But when it was suggested that she go along as a "stowaway," the newsmen chorused, "A swell idea!" and their eyes brightened.

Dorothy received this suggestion coolly. It took high-pressure salesmanship by several of New York's fastest talking news hawks to convince her that the idea had any kind of merit. In the end, she gave in. To lend credulity to the stowaway story, she posed for farewell pictures, kissing me goodbye while cameras flashed. She insisted that the only reason she was going through with the stunt was that she actually wanted to ride along with us, but she said that if the finish were close she would blame herself. I told her a close finish was next to impossible because Max Constant in Jacqueline's

Beechcraft was a good pilot in undoubtedly the fastest ship and we should count our-selves lucky even to place second.

On the morning of the race, we got our weather reports. The prospect was for clear weather all the way, with variable light winds to spice things up a bit. We were a strange and eager set of pilots, anxious to start the fun along the 1,175-mile race course.

Besides Max Constant in the Beechcraft and us in the Lockheed, the starters in-cluded Frank (Sonny Harris), Dorothy's brother, piloting a Northrup Delta with a 700 horsepower Wright Cyclone motor. With him was Jack Loesing. Other starters includ-ed Arthur C. Bussey of Potstown, PA, at the controls of a Beechcraft with two Pratt & Whitney engines; George Pomeroy, who figured his Beechcraft would probably beat us in the long stretch with his two motors matching ours; Wallis Bird of Oyster Bay, also with a Beechcraft powered by a 450 horse power Wasp plant; and Lewis Brewer of Brooklyn, whose Beechcraft also had a Wasp engine.

Sonny Harris' wife and three children were there at the takeoff, pretty much de-cided that they wanted "daddy to come in first and Uncle Russ second." That would have been all right with me. It didn't quite work out that way. Ken Bahr and Grover Whalen, as president of the New York World's Fair, which was offering a special trophy to the winner, were starters.

Constant drew first place starting time, and after pictures were flashed, Whalen and Bahr dropped the checkered starting flags and off Max went, Miami bound for Bernarr MacFadden's trophy and $2,000 first place money, as well as the World's Fair Trophy. We followed Constant's Beechcraft three minutes later, properly failing to no-tice that Dorothy opened our door and slid in stealthily just as we were about to roll down the runaway on the takeoff. Neither Bahr nor Whalen saw her, and to all intents and purposes, neither Richards nor I discovered she was in the after part of the Lock-heed until we were well on the way.

The stowaway gag was truly a hoax and there is no reason now to cancel what happened. Nevertheless, Dorothy's fears about the race were confirmed. It was a long haul, and a fast one, and of course we sighted none of our fellow contestants. All we could do was give the Lockheed her head and trust to luck she would outrun the pack. As soon as we were well away from New York, we set the ship on a compass course and held it there.

We had plenty of weight. The only seat in the cabin was occupied by our "stow-away." The rest of the space was crowded with gasoline tanks, one large one and a dozen five gallon containers. We averaged 210 miles an hour when we winged over Norfolk, VA. The day before, I had wired Civil Aeronautics Authority radio stations along the race route, asking them to be ready to supply us with wind information when we queried them during the race. They complied splendidly and we had up-to-the-minute wind velocity readings all the way.

The cities, towns, and villages of the southern coastline slipped by under us as the Lockheed chewed up the miles toward the finish line. We left the coastline just west of Cape Fear and I checked drift and variation with familiar landmarks. As soon as we were out of sight of land, I set a compass course again. We crossed the east leg of the Charleston radio range about 40 miles east of the coast and our estimated time checked exactly with the actual time consumed thus far in the run. By then I knew things were running as smoothly as possible.

Almost before we knew it, we were only 80 miles off Savannah, and shortly afterward we whizzed across the eastern leg of the Jacksonville radio range, all according to plan. We were at 7,000 feet then and when Jacksonville reported the most favorable winds were at 3,000 feet, we knifed down through the clouds at better than 230 miles an hour until we leveled off at 3,000 feet and streaked for Florida. There was always the possibility that we had drifted more than we calculated, and missing an entire state the size of Florida wasn't an impossibility. So we changed our course five degrees to the west to be sure to have the Florida coastline under us.

There was still no sign or word of our competitors when the familiar landmark of Stuart, FL, shot by under us. We were over Palm Beach when I called the CAA radio at Miami and gave our position, estimating the time of our arrival at the finish line at 3:05 p.m. A few minutes later, I heard the Miami operator repeating Max Constant's estimated finish time, 3:00 p.m., right on the nose. I also heard him say that Max was having gas line trouble in the Cochran Beechcraft.

First news of any of our fellow racers, that was surprising information for us, because we had left New York only three minutes after Max and figured he would have landed long before us because of this ships' greater speed. As soon as we heard his estimated arrival time, I opened the Lockheed almost as wide as it would go, which was plenty fast. We had been running at three-quarter throttle all the way and never once had we given the ship its full head.

We almost left a groove in the sky as we streaked across the state, saw Miami suddenly come into sight below. Then the airport appeared and we crossed the finish line in a terrific dive, the air speed indicator showing 250 miles an hour. The big ship took the dive like a bullet-nosed racer, roared across the line and then zoomed up to wait for clearance to land.

Grover Whelan drops the starting flag as the Gannett Newspaper's Lockheed 12 gets underway from Floyd Bennett Field en route to Miami on January 7, 1939, with Holderman as pilot, Dick Richards as co-pilot, and Dorothy Holderman as "stowaway." Holderman lost the race by 36 seconds to Max Constant in Jacqueline Cochran's plane.

When we landed, Bernarr MacFadden, Miami city officials and race officials rushed up to greet us. Cameras clicked and newsreel men angled for shots. We were congratulated as the winners. It was a great feeling, but I had been in too many races in the old days, and knew too much about the vagaries of fate ever to trust in first hand announcements. I was all for waiting for the official announcement.

This came several hours later and revealed Max Constant as the winner over us by a mere 36 seconds! But stowaway and all, we had won second prize money along with the Maynard Page Trophy. Max took $2,000, the LaGuardia World's Fair Trophy, the MacFadden Trophy and most of the honor and glory.

We were well pleased with the Lockheed's performance nevertheless. In approximately 1,200 miles of flying, she had done the stretch in five hours and 44 minutes, sensational time for a big news hawk.

Constant told me that with his single motored plane he had followed the coastline, a smart procedure with one motor, and consequently he had covered more distance than we had. That was why, even with his faster ship, he was able to beat us in by only 36 seconds.

Dorothy's immediate share in the publicity was not favorable, for the newspapers declared we had lost the race because of her 118 pounds of added weight as "stowaway." This was untrue. What lost us the race was our failure to open the Lockheed wide earlier than we did. But what angered Dorothy was that her stowing away had been a press idea and the fact that the newspapers mistakenly blamed her for our losing the victory seemed decidedly unfair and unsportsmanlike.

Two days later, when the tumult and the shouting had died, we hopped non-stop from Miami to Rochester, nearly 1,300 miles, in under six hours. Some weeks after that, Ken Bahr wrote me to say that he and Grover Whalen had decided that 36 seconds, the margin by which Constant had beaten us, was as good as a tie as far as they were concerned. A few days later, in formal ceremonies and with all his charm and formality, Whalen presented me with a World's Fair Trophy exactly like Max's. That first New York-Miami race by no means ended the Lockheed's racing career.

For speed and dependability, it was like something out of a book. From the first of June until the end of January, 1939, I flew it almost every day. It averaged 200 miles an hour without a skip, without a slip, without once failing to respond to the slightest touch on the controls. Truly, in that streaking transport ship, the days of Curtiss pusher planes seemed a century away, part of another era instead of the beginning of the present one.

But if the Lockheed's great speed provided a tremendous contrast with that of the century's earlier ships, even greater was its ability to fly in almost any kind of weather in comparison with the feeble attempts most of us used to make in our Jennies and DeHavilands through fog and snow in the days of Heller Field and the early airmail.

Jack Jenkins and I, with Frank Tripp, general manager of the Gannett Company, as passenger, brought it from Chicago to New York in three hours and 25 minutes, in a flight which was mostly made at 11,000 feet, through and over snow storms. We had snow all the way and flew blind on instruments safely and without fear.

The entry blanks for the All-American Races came in again in December, 1939. I showed them to the boss. All he said was, "Better luck this time, Russ." This time the rules for the New York-Miami dash were different. There were to be no "X" licensed planes participating. Entrants had to agree to a visual check over Jacksonville, FL, that is, flying in low enough to get a signal from the ground and to be recognized. This was insisted upon because officials considered it was dangerous to fly over water, especially in some of the smaller, faster and trickier ships. Our course the year before, done in the big-winged Lockheed, had proved that it was the faster route, if not the safest.

We were to be allowed no extra gasoline tanks, but neither could we remove any seats from the cabin. Each ship was required to have an NC Commercial license and to be checked by a CAA inspector before starting. We knew that with no extra gasoline aboard we would have to land at Jacksonville for fuel.

Lieut. Jack Scherer was my co-pilot, and the takeoff was made from Roosevelt Field, site of my first solo flight in Fred Shneider's biplane in 1913. We were the only entrants to start from Roosevelt Field. Permission had been granted to the racers to start from any point more than 1,000 miles from Miami. Several of them started from points in the Midwest to take advantage of prevailing tail winds.

I consulted with Pratt & Whitney engineers before the race to get their opinion on opening up the Lockheed's two Wasps to get the best possible speed on the dash down. They told me I could do it without endangering the motors, so all the way down I gave the ship more power than I had the year before.

The field was fast, and the Lockheed needed practically everything we could give it. We made fast time from Roosevelt Field to Jacksonville, where we lost 13 minutes in refueling, pulling out just as Arlene Davis landed in her Spartan. We crossed the finish line at Miami five hours and 35 minutes after leaving New York, and our average speed was 218 miles an hour. But we were still playing second fiddle to victory.

Walter Beech, head of the Beechcraft Company, and his pilot zoomed in non-stop from St. Louis, averaging 234 miles an hour and easily winning first place. This was an amazingly fast speed for a commercial Beechcraft, and aside from the surprise I felt in learning they had made the trip without stopping to refuel, I thought nothing more about it.

But the next day, I walked past Beech's ship and by coincidence looked inside. I saw two large oil drums with temporary copper gasoline lines running uninsulated all over the place. The ship's rudder bore only its plain NC license. A CAA inspector agreed with me that the ship had no business having a C (Commercial) license with all that extra equipment inside. Urged by other pilots, I filed a protest with the Contest Committee along with a $100 protest check, required in all protests and forfeited if the protest is not allowed.

But as it turned out, Beech was technically qualified to race the ship as I had found it. It had been licensed by a St. Louis inspector who passed it as an NC ship despite the fact that it had extra, uninspected gasoline tanks. So my protest was disallowed, much to the embarrassment of the Contest Committee. But my check was not accepted.

The chairman said, "Here's what I think of all this!" and tore up the check. But revenge can be sweet, if patience holds out.

Three Beechcraft were entered that afternoon in the Curtiss Trophy race, a 25 mile contest, five times around a five mile course. One of the Beechcraft was Wasp powered and figured to be fast enough to win, hands down. I told Jack Scherer, "Let's go in. I'm sure the boss wouldn't mind, and, boy, would I like to beat those Beechcraft!" So we entered.

There remained the not inconsiderable problem of breaking the news to my wife. This was a little difficult, for I had spent years telling her how dangerous pylon racing was, and I had to undo all my sermonizing to convince her that everything would be all right.

I had begun to feel as if I were going into a motorcycle race again after 25 years. A pre-race tingle was dancing up and down my spine. I was as jumpy as a schoolboy sprinter. Whether Dorothy saw all these signs and portents, and sympathized with them, I do not know, but she reluctantly gave in and promised not to worry.

Still, I knew we had entered against our better judgment. I told Scherer, "Jack, I haven't flown a race like this in a long time and I don't know how the Lockheed will handle on the turns. If you'd rather not come along, it will be all right with me. I can handle her alone." There was no shaking Scherer. "Where you go, I go, mister," he said. "Let's get going."

There was only one way to find out how the Lockheed handled on sharp turns, so Jack and I took it up and headed for the Everglades, 10 miles out of Miami. Away out in that dense and swampy wilderness we found a lone, tall pine tree. For half an hour we did nothing but make turns around that tree. We were surprised and delighted to find that the big, eight place ship handled like a whippet around the bends. I began to feel better about the race. But Dorothy didn't.

We were lining up and she was in the grandstand, misty-eyed and nervous. Behind her sat Johnny Livingston, a longtime friend of mine and a famous racing pilot. Not knowing Dorothy was my wife, he said to his companions in a voice like Stentor's, "Be sure to watch this race, because Holderman's a very conservative pilot. He hasn't raced in a long time, and that big Lockheed will be tough to handle on a five mile course with four pylons." Dot was almost frantic.

The Lockheed, three Beechcraft and a Spartan line up for a "race horse" start. The flag went down and we all gunned our motors. The Lockheed took the scattering pylon last, pulling much greater weight than any of the others. The Spartan immediately zipped up to a high altitude. We stayed low, and at the second pylon passed the first of the three streaking Beechcraft. We gained the lead on the second lap. I throttled the motor to hold the pace, staying below the pylons to be sure not to foul them, with the result that we were flying close to the ground and making 90-degree banks around the turns.

By that time, the grandstand crowd was on its feet. Spectators told us later that the Lockheed was a beautiful and thrilling sight, streaking like hell bent for leather, almost skimming the trees, big, fast as lightning, the mechanical personification of power. Somehow, the Beechcraft got out in front. I knew then we needed a sweet burst of speed if we were to win in the stretch.

Jack and I gritted our teeth. The thrill was coming back. I opened the throttle wide and the motors roared in response. Pulling us in a silver streak over the stretch, the two Wasps made the sweetest sound in the world, the sound of motorized power, of thousands of explosions timed to the tenth of a second, each adding its full quota of strength and speed to the overall task. At the start of the fifth lap, we lapped the three Beechcraft.

At the beginning of the race, Jack had clutched five pennies in his hand, and each time we rounded the home pylon, he threw one out. Now he had but one, and then the home pylon loomed up ahead and we flashed by, a winner. I gave the Lockheed the up signal and she climbed like a comet. Never have I flown a ship that climbed so fast. We disappeared into the 1,500-foot overcast in a matter of seconds. Then we landed. I was wet with sweat. I had shed weight. But I was happy. Dorothy was overjoyed, but I promised her I would never do it again. We took home $2,500 in prize money, along with the big Curtiss Trophy.

CHAPTER 25
TWO-MOTORED CAMPAIGN

The memory of the 1940 Presidential campaign is etched in my mind in terms of tremendous distances. When he entered the race for the Republican Presidential nomination, Frank Gannett mapped out for himself the most extensive and exhaustive campaign of any of the candidates. One of the most important aspects of his plan was that he should conduct a whirlwind speaking tour the length and breadth of the land.

Thus the Lockheed 12 became a campaigner, for so numerous and far-flung were the boss's engagements that only by air could he fill them all, and by air he did. Gannett's campaign manager, Nelson Sparks, mapped all the arrangements weeks in advance, the time and place of each meeting, each speech, and each rally. Our schedule was so exact that we had to organize the flight like an airline to meet crowds on the dot, to make airports on schedule, to take off on time in order to fill the next engagement without a hitch.

The Lockheed covered great distances without batting a wing, Albany to Reno. To San Francisco, Tulsa, St, Louis, and Little Rock; to Portland, ME and Seattle, WA. To Richmond, Charleston, Jacksonville and Miami. To Fargo, Superior and St. Paul. To Milwaukee and Minneapolis, Oklahoma City and Phoenix. To Tucson and Los Angeles. To Palm Springs and San Diego, Washington, Memphis and Dallas. To El Paso and Boston and Bangor, ME. To Denver and Omaha.

We started out on January 12, 1940. Jack Scherer carried so many maps he looked like a paper hangar. We had regional and sectional airways maps of the whole United States. We had charts, books, and pamphlets. In the next five months we were to crisscross the United States in a swift series of flights to every corner of the land.

The first few days are a fair sample of what followed. We took off from Rochester, landed in Akron in one hour and 20 minutes, made St Louis three hours and 10 minutes later in time for the first speech, headed for Cheyenne the next day, followed that with a flight to Spokane, stopping at Billings, MT for gasoline on the way. The Spokane rally was an evening affair. We were handed a gloomy weather report the next day. Fog had set in and we were told it would probably last for three days, that being the beastly nature of Spokane fogs.

The next day upheld the weatherman's prediction. By that time the fog was so thick even the "seagulls were walking home." The third day was still foggy, but somehow we had to get to Seattle. Late that afternoon, the fog lifted to about 200 feet and we learned it was clear weather further west, so we took off on instruments and came out into the clear at Ephrata, 100 miles from Spokane. We landed at Ephrata and took off the next day for Seattle, but had to climb to 10,000 feet to clear the mountains. Our weather information told us it was raining in Seattle, where the ceiling was a scant 1,500 feet.

We arrived over the city's range station at 8,000 feet, got permission to come in on instruments on the beam. We broke out into the rain and after some trouble finding the field, finally set the Lockheed down on solid but slippery earth and climbed out.

The first person to greet us was George Haldeman, who was testing new Stratoliners for Boeing and the Civil Aeronautics Authority at the Seattle airport. I said to him, "This is lousy weather you have here, son." "Hell," he replied, "this is the best day we've had in a month."

Shortly after 2:30 p.m. that day we were headed for San Francisco. As the sun went down behind the Golden Gate we came in sight of the city, landing after dark. Two days later we hopped to Reno for a night meeting, then to Salt Lake City, across great mountains and green valleys, rivers and canyons that seem to split the earth in two.

We hit Minneapolis after that, then Chicago, and then Rochester, and that ended the first leg of the campaign. But it was only the first of many.

There were weeks and weeks of flying ahead, each with a score of dates to be met…on time. We made so many flights and stopped in so many scattered cities that I think I met almost everyone I had ever known in the flying game. I celebrated February 26, my birthday, by flying from Little Rock to Tulsa in an hour and a half. At Tulsa, Gannett visited the beautiful memorial to his longtime friend Will Rogers, killed in an Alaskan air crash with Wiley Post, whom I had known well in the old days.

When we landed at Dallas on February 28, one of the first people I saw was Asbury Meadows, a pal of long past flying days who was Department of Commerce inspector when the LeRoy Airport was first opened. That same day we ran into George Cheetham, our former co-pilot, who was now a co-pilot with Braniff Airlines.

I had never comprehended the vastness of Texas until we took three hours and five minutes to fly from Dallas to El Paso. The crew went sight seeing that night in Mexico.

The perfection of the weather up to the point we reached Phoenix amazed us. When we took off for Palm Springs on March 1, visibility was still exceptionally fine. One incident is enough to prove this. We were about 25 minutes out of Phoenix, well on our way to Palm Springs, when I saw ahead what looked like a small group of cumulus clouds. Soon I discovered that it was a snow-capped mountain top; I asked Scherer how far away he thought it was. "About 25 miles," he said. I said it seemed nearer to fifty miles. We were doing 200 miles an hour, so we glanced at our watches to time the distance it took us to reach the mountain. It took us an hour and 10 minutes to reach it, and when we got there, we discovered we were over Palm Springs. That's what is called exceptional visibility.

Even for one who has watched the panoramas of the whole vast continental United States unfold for him one by one in a thousand flights in more than 25 years, coming upon Palm Springs from the air is an unforgettable experience. It is a truly gorgeous sight, a marvelous work of matchless architecture, landscaped with grandeur and sweep, colored as no artist could or would even dare to color it.

Palm Springs lived up to its reputation. The sun was hot on the sandy airport as we brought the sizzling Lockheed in, an hour and 35 minutes out of Phoenix. We were whisked to a cool luncheon table close by a blue and inviting swimming pool. Out for an after-lunch stroll through the hotel garden, I met Arlene Davis, a grand sport and fine pilot. I hadn't seen her since she had flown in the last Miami race against me. It was tough, pulling out of Palm Springs. Some day I mean to go back when no exacting calls, when no presidential race is on.

We took off from the sandy field and climbed to 11,000 feet to cross the rugged mountain ridge behind the city, and within 35 minutes, the California coast of the broad Pacific was in sight and shortly afterward we taxied in on Lindbergh Field, San Diego. We pulled out for Burbank the next day and that afternoon I took the plane to the Lockheed factory and left it in the hands of plant mechanics, with instructions to give it a thorough going over. The job had to be done in three days and fully a score of men went to work on the ship.

While this was going on, Los Angeles was ours. Through the efforts of Edward P. Curtis, of Rochester, a World War flyer with six German planes to his credit, and at this writing a Major in the United States Army Air Force, we were given a true Hollywood welcome. Curtis was Eastman Kodak Company's Hollywood division sales manager. Through him Paramount took us under its wing, trotted out many a star for us, brought us face to face with Bing Crosby, the horse and croon man; Gloria Jean, the little singer, and a small individual of infinite charm called Baby Sandy.

We left Hollywood's glitter behind on the morning of March 6, getting a slightly late start because of last minute adjustments on the ship. I was sure we could make Topeka by nightfall. There was no rally there, but Gannett was expected by Alfred M. Landon. We hit Albuquerque, N.M. after 3 hours and 45 minutes, took on gasoline, and headed for Oklahoma City in clear weather. It occurred to me at that point that we had struck nothing but perfect weather since leaving Birmingham, AL many days before.

As we passed over the emergency landing field at Tucumcari, the weather was so good that I took off my ear phones and enjoyed sailing along merrily as I pleased with apparently nothing but calm and bright weather ahead for us to use. Without warning, we ran into low overcast. I hastily replaced the earphones and decided to fly contact, under the overcast. But with the phones off I had missed the hourly weather reports out of Amarillo, TX. I hurriedly called the station there and asked for a report. The operator startled me with the information that the Amarillo airport was closed because the ceiling was only 300 feet, that the overcast was "very bad." He advised us to return to Tucumcari at once. I didn't argue.

By that time the snow was coming down fast. I reversed our course. We soon ran out of the snow and set down at the emergency field, a most blessed, but bumpy piece of terrain, but as welcome as an oasis in the desert. The operator at the emergency port said he had been trying to call me ever since we had passed over but had had no luck because in my blissful ignorance of what unexpected things southwestern weather can do, I had been flying without the earphones.

It was cold at Tucumcari, and after we tied the ship down, we huddled around the fire in the office, waiting for a cab. We had to make St. Louis for a meeting the next night, and took off early in the morning, heading for the Missouri metropolis at 6:30 a.m., with the first stop Oklahoma City.

Oklahoma City was still 100 miles away when I noticed we were using an excessive amount of gasoline. It soon became evident we hadn't enough to make the city. While Scherer took over the controls, I studied the maps, looking for an airport. The only one I could find on the maps was at Chickasaw. The airport list showed it to be a small field with day service only. But it was our only hope, so we changed our course to find it, southwest of Oklahoma City. When we got over Chickasaw and looked for the airport, it wasn't there. The gasoline dial registered a hair above the empty mark, an indication that there was no more than 10 gallons left in the tanks. Still we could find no Chickasaw airport. We circled the town several times and then picked out the best-looking piece of pastureland we could find on the outskirts.

Down we went and came to a stop on the field, which we soon discovered had actually been an airport at one time. The hangar was being converted into a farm shed. Our tanks were bone dry. Inspections showed a broken gas line was responsible for the unexpected fuel famine. We soon fixed the line, but the next problem was to get gasoline. We had to be content with enough automobile gasoline to take us to Oklahoma City. The Lockheed drank it up thirstily, and we took off from Chickasaw's ex-airport pasture and hastily winged for Oklahoma City, landing in plenty of time.

A few days later, with a single stop at Charleston, we flew from Miami to New York in six hours and 20 minutes, rested for a day and then started the New England tour. By that time I was beginning to know my native land like the back of my hand. Famous rivers of song, poem and story….cities, villages and towns, mountains, battle-fields, highways, turnpikes, forests passed under us in a never-ending but always thrilling kaleidoscopic scene. We had been in the air so long I half forgot what living on earth was like.

One day we were in Boston and it seemed only a few hours later that we were circling Pike's Peak and its mining towns, then pointing for Lincoln, NE. We were back in Rochester on April 6, and five days later, after Bill Irving had checked and serviced the motors, we went to Miami, stopping on the way at Washington and Jacksonville. But we were back in Rochester on April 19, on the 20th were in Charleston, next in Washington, next in New York. Local flights around New York were followed by another return to Rochester. By that time they were practically keeping the coffee pot on the stove for Jack Scherer and me at the airport restaurant.

April 29 saw us off again. There were more long stretches, more landings and meeting people unexpectedly. We saw Roscoe Turner at Indianapolis, had only time for a brief chat before we took off for Topeka. We were in the air eight hours and 20 minutes that day.

Next day I saw Tommy Tomlinson, fit as ever, in Kansas City. I sprained an ankle several days afterward trying to take pictures from the top of a pile of tables at a church supper. It gave me the flying miseries for the next few days, being distinctly unpleasant when we hit small fields and I had to apply the brakes.

We started another long leg from Rochester on May 12, hitting Memphis and Fort Worth in a single day, meeting Cheetham again at Fort Worth. By that time he was a Braniff captain.

We landed in San Antonio, Eddie Stinson's hometown, on May 14, hit Houston the next noon and Atlanta that night. By that time, the staunch Lockheed had me a little worried. I was relieved that the Atlanta meeting was to be the last leg of that leg of the campaign flight, because on our last takeoff from Rochester, Bill Irving had told me the engines should have been overhauled 100 flying hours before. We left Atlanta for Rochester and took the route around the mountains instead of the shorter, direct cross-country route over the ranges. Flying over mountains with unsure motors is a risky business.

The right hand motor set up a terrific fuss and vibration 40 miles west of Spartanburg. We knew something had let go. I cut the switch, made a 180-degree turn and headed for Spartanburg Airport on one motor, which tugged us in safely. The failing motor had broken an exhaust valve, which had wandered and dropped into the cylinder, smashing the piston and breaking the cylinder head. A fine mess.

Pratt & Whitney airmailed parts special delivery from Long Island; a mechanic flew out from Norfolk to service the plane, and three days later, we were in Rochester. We were off again late in May. At Moline, IL, on that leg I met Vern Roberts who with Freddie Lund, had staged that most spectacular of all our races at LeRoy. Roberts was managing the Moline Airport.

We were in Rochester again on June 12 when Gannett asked me if Jacksonville, IL had an airport. There was none on the map and none was registered in the book of airports. He telephoned the chairman of the committee planning his reception there and was told that a field and hangar actually were in operation at Jacksonville.

A heavy rain had fallen by the time we were over the so-called airport. The field looked postage stamp size and its hangar was apparently only large enough to house a light Cub trainer. As I circled the little dot of land, my better judgment told me not to try a landing. But a large welcoming crowd was on hand, so we decided to go down, come what may. I thanked my lucky stars that day for all the training of the past that had taught me how to bring a ship in on a dime, all the hours with the Lockheed that had taught me how to bring it in as short as if it were a Stinson Reliant. A cross wind was blowing and the field was a one-way, narrow affair, only 1,200 feet long from wires at one end to a line of trees at the other.

But, down I went. I put the flaps down and dragged the plane in over the wires with very little speed, settling it so quickly that it struck hard because it was moving so slowly. I stood on the brakes. They set. The plane skidded in mud for several hundred feet and then stopped less than 200 feet short of the trees at the far end of the field.

I told the boss then and there that I was going to take off "light" from that field and that he and the rest of the party had better motor to the next man-sized airport, 25 miles away. He laughed, "OK, anything you say is all right with me after that landing." We were back home again the next day.

By June 15, we were in Philadelphia, scene of the Republican convention, and on the 16th we went to Atlantic City, where Gannett delivered the last address of his campaign. We flew back to Philadelphia that night. It was unbelievably calm, and flying was almost automatic. It was hard to believe that five months of campaigning from city to city and town to town, border to border and ocean to ocean were completed.

Scherer, the Lockheed and I had taken Gannett more than 55,000 miles on an exhaustive journey which was pioneering of its kind, the first presidential nomination campaign ever conducted exclusively by air, and certainly the most vast schedule ever undertaken by any candidate in such a comparatively short time.

But our flying task was far from over when the conventions opened. Each night, weather permitting, Jack and I flew news pictures of the convention to Rochester, took on a load of newspapers, and had them in Philadelphia ready for distribution even before the Philadelphia dailies were on the street. But finally the hurly burly was done, and we all returned home.

Irving and I took the Lockheed to New York for a major overhauling, and Dorothy and I went on to the National Soaring Meet at Elmira, then to Lake George for a rest. For the first time since 1912, I really felt that I had had enough of flying for a while. But 10 days later, Scherer came in with the newspaper Stinson and we went to New York to see how repairs were coming on the Lockheed. The sight of her and I had the urge again. On July 27 we brought her home to Rochester and shortly afterward Gannett and I took off for Elmwood, Indiana, to be on hand when Wendell Willkie got his home town welcome.

Fourth Lockheed 12, 1939

Frank Gannett and Russell Holderman

APPENDIX A
SCHEDULE OF THE 1940 CAMPAIGN FLIGHTS

JANUARY		Time	Mileage
14	Rochester – Jacksonville	4:50	810
14	Jacksonville – Miami	1:55	340
22	Miami –Jacksonville	1:55	340
22	Jacksonville – Charleston, SC	1:20	250
22	Charleston – Raleigh, NC	1:20	260
23	Raleigh – Rochester	3:20	670
23	Rochester – Akron, OH	1:20	250
23	Akron – St. Louis	3:10	600
24	St. Louis – Cheyenne	4:35	900
24	Cheyenne – Billings, MT	2:05	400
24	Billings – Spokane	2:25	480
24	Spokane – Ephrata	0:40	120
25	Ephrata – Seattle	1:35	300
26	Seattle – San Francisco	4:10	800
27	San Francisco – Reno	1:10	300
27	Reno – Salt Lake City	2:15	450
28	Salt Lake City – Cheyenne	2:00	450
28	Cheyenne – Cedar Rapids	3:40	715
28	Cedar Rapids – Minneapolis	1:25	275
29	Minneapolis – Chicago	1:45	340
29	Chicago – Rochester	3:00	530
30	Rochester – Elmira	:30	90
30	Elmira – Jacksonville	4:45	860
30	Jacksonville – St. Petersburg	1:10	200
30	St. Petersburg – Miami	1:05	200

FEBRUARY			
1	Miami – Orlando	1:05	200
1	Orlando – Raleigh	2:55	600
1	Raleigh – New York City	2:25	530
4	New York City – Elmira	1:10	200
4	Elmira – Rochester	0:35	90

7	Rochester – Cleveland	1:30	250
7	Cleveland – Rochester	1:20	250
9	Rochester – New York City	1:10	265
11	New York City – Rochester	1:55	265
15	Rochester – Washington, D.C.	1:20	300
16	Washington, D.C. – Jacksonville	3:20	720
16	Jacksonville – Miami	2:10	400
23	Miami – St. Petersburg	1:05	200
24	St. Petersburg – Atlanta	2:40	430
25	Atlanta – Birmingham	0:50	140
25	Birmingham - Little Rock	1:55	330
26	Little Rock – Tulsa	1:30	290
27	Tulsa – Claremore & return	0:20	60
28	Tulsa – Dallas	1:15	235
28	Dallas – El Paso	3:05	570
29	El Paso – Tucson	1:45	280

MARCH

1	Tucson – Phoenix	0:45	120
2	Phoenix – Palm Springs	1:35	265
2	Palm Springs – San Diego	0:35	90
3	San Diego – Burbank	0:45	125
6	Burbank – Albuquerque	3:35	650
6	Albuquerque – Tucumcari	1:55	280
7	Tucumcari – Chickasaw	1:55	330
7	Chickasaw – Oklahoma City	0:10	30
7	Oklahoma City – Little Rock	1:35	280
8	Little Rock – St. Louis	1:55	390
8	St. Louis – Memphis	1:15	260
8	Memphis – Tuscaloosa	0:55	200
8	Tuscaloosa – Miami	3:25	750
10	Miami – Charleston	2:50	510
10	Charleston – New York City	3:30	670
12	New York City – Boston	1:15	210
13	Boston – Bangor	1:15	220
13	Bangor – Portland	1:00	200
13	Portland – New York City	1:30	300
15	New York City – Rochester	1:45	265
17	Rochester – New York City	1:15	265

18	New York City – Hartford	0:35	100
19	Hartford – New York City	0:30	100
21	New York City – Rochester	1:25	265
22	Rochester – Akron	1:35	250
22	Akron – Milwaukee	2:20	410
22	Milwaukee – St. Paul	1:50	310
25	St. Paul – Superior	0:45	140
26	Superior – Fargo	1:15	230
26	Fargo – Jamestown & return	1:05	200
27	Fargo – Minneapolis	1:20	225
27	Minneapolis – Milwaukee	1:40	310
29	Milwaukee – Chicago	0:35	90
30	Chicago – Milwaukee	0:40	90
31	Milwaukee – Chicago	0:30	90

APRIL

1	Chicago – Omaha	2:15	430
2	Omaha – Colorado Springs	3:00	520
4	Colorado Springs – Denver	0:40	120
5	Denver – Lincoln	2:20	450
6	Lincoln – Cleveland	4:05	780
6	Cleveland – Rochester	1:15	250
7	Rochester – Washington, D.C.	1:25	300
8	Washington, D.C. – Jacksonville	3:20	670
8	Jacksonville – Miami	1:40	380
9	Miami – Charleston	3:15	530
9	Charleston – Washington, D.C.	2:40	470
9	Washington, D.C. – New York City	1:40	230
10	New York City – Rochester	1:30	265
11	Rochester – Washington, D.C.	1:35	300
11	Washington, D.C. – Raleigh	1:10	235
11	Raleigh – Philadelphia	2:10	410
12	Philadelphia – Rochester	1:30	265
26	Rochester – New York City	1:15	265
27	New York City – Rochester	1:25	265
29	Rochester – Camden	1:15	260
29	Camden – New York City	0:30	100
29	New York City – Camden	0:35	100
29	Camden – New York City	0:30	100

30	New York City – Hartford	0:35	100
30	Hartford – New York City	0:30	100
30	New York City - Hartford	0:30	100

MAY

1	Hartford – Rochester	1:30	280
1	Rochester – Cleveland	1:30	260
1	Cleveland – Indianapolis	1:55	480
1	Indianapolis – Topeka	3:25	600
3	Topeka – Sioux Falls	1:30	325
4	Sioux Falls – Wan Soto	0:45	160
6	Wan Soto – Des Moines	1:00	200
7	Des Moines – Cleveland	3:05	620
7	Cleveland – Rochester	1:15	250
8	Rochester – Providence	1:40	340
9	Providence – New York City	1:00	180
9	New York City – Binghamton	1:00	180
10	Binghamton – Utica	0:30	80
10	Utica – Rochester	0:45	130
11	Rochester – Albany, Saratoga & return	2:20	440
12	Rochester – Memphis	4:50	900
12	Memphis – Fort Worth	2:35	465
14	Fort Worth – San Antonio	1:30	265
15	San Antonio – Houston	1:10	220
16	Houston – Atlanta	3:30	720
16	Atlanta – Spartanburg	1:10	210
19	Spartanburg – Rochester	3:20	650
20	Rochester – Louisville	3:35	550
22	Louisville – Akron	1:40	300
22	Akron – New York City	2:30	430
23	New York City – Washington, D.C.	1:10	215
23	Washington, D.C. – Rochester	1:50	330
25	Rochester – Moline	4:00	800
25	Moline – Cheyenne	4:05	800
28	Cheyenne – North Platte	1:05	220
29	North Platte – Moline	2:50	540
29	Moline – Rochester	4:10	720

JUNE

2	Rochester – Indianapolis	2:45	520
2	Indianapolis – Kansas City	2:35	465
4	Kansas City – St. Louis	1:20	240
4	St Louis – Cleveland	2:00	500
4	Cleveland – Rochester	1:20	250
7	Rochester – Burlington	1:25	250

CHAPTER 26
LANDING

They have come and gone swiftly… those three years since that 55,000 mile campaign flight. For these are the war years, and events move at airplane speed, partly because the airplane has become such a swift and terrible instrument.

Into the maelstrom of war the Lockheed 12 went first. It was like a veteran going into the service. It carried us on a score of southern flights, victoriously through air races, safely and swiftly through the 1940 political campaign. In its place we acquired a new Lockheed 12, with de-icers, 125-watt radio transmitter and Sperry automatic pilot and direction finder. It had so many instruments that I began to feel I wasn't needed as a pilot after all.

Then we lost Jack Scherer to the Royal Canadian Air Force. This was because a technicality kept him out of the U.S. Army Air Force. This, despite his background as a Lieutenant in the New York National Guard's Aero Squadron and his experience with multi-motored ships.

One of the crying needs of the RCAF was for instructors who could teach recruits how to pilot bombers. There were plenty of single-motor experts, but men who knew how to pilot multi-motored ships and could teach others what they knew were worth their weight in gold.

Jack Scherer was one of these. Almost immediately, he was made a flight officer, and was flying a Lockheed Electra. He wrote, "I certainly feel at home in this ship. It's like old times."

When a Hollywood motion picture company started out to tell the stirring story of the Royal Canadian Air Force in it's film called "Captains of the Clouds," it was necessary to find a suitable double for the picture's star, James Cagney. Scherer was selected for the role. He did all the flying that Cagney was supposed to be doing in the picture.

In May 1942, Jack Scherer got what he had tried to get two years before….a commission in the U.S. Army Air Corps. Technicalities of the red tape kind that had kept him out before were then waived. Scherer's experience in this country and with the RCAF made him an invaluable addition to the service. He is now overseas.

We took Gene Beattie on as co-pilot after Scherer left us. We got untold pleasure from the new Lockheed, flying it through ice and storms, listening to the de-icers cracking the ice as fast as it formed on the wings, hearing the pleasant "chunk" made by pieces of ice flung off the propellers by the ice slingers. We would set the automatic pilot, adjust the Sperry direction finder and sit back watching the clouds. This was the kind of flying about which I had hoped and dreamed for, for many years, ever since I had soloed in Fred Shneider's biplane. No greater contrast could I imagine than that between the 60 mile an hour Shneider ship with its single 35 horse power motor and its 12 inch string "instrument," and the 900 horse power streamlined marvel that now carried us safely at more than 200 miles an hour, flying blind but flying true, with radio keeping us in constant contact with the ground.

I thought often of all those who had gone before....Bill Piceller, John B. Moisant, Lieutenant Selfridge, Walter Brookins, Max Miller and not the least of all, Bill Lindley.... all the galaxy of brave and curious flying men who paid with their lives to fly ships that were only steps in the development of ships as we know them today. They knew the flaws in their ships. They saw them and did what they could to eliminate them. The result has been that men have built planes truer, faster, better in all ways.

Flying that Lockheed made me want to be able to fly until I am too old to dodder to a hangar. It gave me consuming ambition to be the oldest pilot in the country in which I was once the youngest. Flying blind and safely over Bellefonte, PA, one time "graveyard of lost pilots," where I lost many a friend in the early airmail days, made me shudder to think of the lives lost and the careers blighted all because man up to that point, had developed nothing that would take his airplane safely through fog and mist, storm and overcast.

We lost the second Lockheed in August, 1941, in the best of all causes. Frank Gannett volunteered its services to the United States War Department, and my pride and joy went to work for Uncle Sam. There was regret at this parting, as much regret as a man can have in bidding goodbye to a machine made of inanimate metals, but far from inanimate itself....a sure and steady steed, quick to respond to every pressure, every gesture of its rider. There were Lockheed Hudson bombers over the French coast, Lockheeds patrolling the North Sea, Lockheeds at Hawaii and in the Philippines, and I know that wherever ours went, it would hold its head up and fly fast and sure and deliver the goods.

Gene Beattie left us to go with American Airlines after we turned the Lockheed over to an army officer at Rochester Municipal Airport on August 20. We used the single-motored Stinson for a month, and then got a Spartan, a low-winged, all-metal job with my old favorite, a 450-horsepower Wasp motor, only 10 miles slower than the Lockheed, but less roomy and comfortable.

It was difficult to get new planes at that time, but Larry Bell, head of Bell Aircraft, makers of the deadly fighting ship Aircobra, came to our rescue and sold Gannett his own Spartan. He was a flying man, turning out great airplanes in astounding quantities, but he was too busy to fly. The War Department took over the Spartan a few months after we got it, leaving us again with the faithful Stinson Reliant.

That, too, is now in government service, leased by the U.S. for use in civilian pilot training at Municipal Airport, Rochester, where we have been busy filling government contracts. Necessary restrictions in civilian flying, designed to guard against flights by fifth columnists, saboteurs, espionage agents and others who would abuse the privileges of the skyways to the nation's disadvantage, have changed the whole civilian flying picture in the United States. No taking off and flying the length and breadth of the land at will now. Flight plans have to be filed in advance and clearance obtained. Broadcasting of weather reports is out. So now in teaching civilians how to fly under the government program, I am back flying by ground contact only, back in the 1920s, almost back in the old airmail days. But I feel lucky to be flying at all. Better a pusher biplane than nothing.

I'll be off the Navy's reserve list as soon as our government contracts have been fulfilled. I want to wear my wings over my heart again....on the Navy Blue this time instead of the Army's khaki as I did at Hazelhurst in 1917 and 1918. If they give me a desk, I'll go batty. I want a plane... a two-motored plane. For I'm a flying man.

There's a place in this war for every man who ever took hold of a stick, as long as his health is reasonably good. There's certainly a place for every living veteran of the airways.

There was a place for Frankie Cordova until he hit that mountain in Africa. The news items on Frankie Cordova's death were brief. The Associated Press sent one out from Garden City. It read: "Mrs. Evelyn Cordova, wife of Frankie Cordova, 38 year old commercial pilot, said yesterday she had received word that her husband had been killed in Africa, April 12, in an airplane crash. She said that he had been ferrying bombers to England and Africa for Pan American Airways but that she had no details of the accident." There was little else. That was the story of Frankie Cordova's end, briefly told. But there is more.

He was a speed flyer, a transport flyer, at home at the stick of a racer or an airliner, a seasoned veteran at 38. We all knew him, admired his skill, felt the pang that comes with learning of a friend's death. Cordova started ferrying bombers, soon after that method of getting big American fighting ships to the front lines of the fighting, was instituted. All through the summer of 1941, he flew the North Atlantic, through drenching storm and blazing sun, through wall-thick fog and windy maelstrom, through gloom and night. He flew bombers over and was flown back with other pilots by transport. He would land on this side, and then take another bomber across to England. Once when he was forced down in the ocean, he was rescued to fly more bombers.

For some months before his death, he had been ferrying bombers across the southern sky route of the Atlantic....across the sea to Africa. He made the trip many times, spent little time at home, because he always seemed to be taking off again. On one trip to Africa, Cordova landed a bomber at its destination and was informed he would have to keep on going, that it had been decided to use the bomber elsewhere. So he took off again, for Singapore.

Frankie landed the bomber in Singapore after a flight across half the world. Singapore was doomed. The brown men of Nippon were closing in. Civilians were being evacuated, but not fast enough. The British were sending out what materials could not be destroyed. Doom was in the air, and into that atmosphere of doom Frankie Cordova sailed with his bomber, landed it, delivered it, and then began asking how he could get out.

There were more bombers to be ferried from the United States. He had a job to do. The Japanese were coming on relentlessly. Loss of Singapore was only a matter of a short time. No ship that sailed from the port was fast enough for Frankie. Time flew and he wanted to fly out, too. But only one plane was ready to fly with Frank Cordova.

The British wanted this plane out of Singapore. It was a giant Short Flying Boat, a mammoth thing, useful as a transport but not much use in Singapore. They didn't want the Japanese to have it. There was only one pilot to fly it, and that pilot was Cordova. They put the question to him....would he fly it out? It would mean he could escape to ferry more bombers, and it would mean saving the flying boat.

Frankie said he'd fly it. He had never flown a Short before. Flying such an airboat requires a different technique. But he flew it. He took off without mishap and brought it from the danger zone, landed it safely and delivered it far away from Singapore. Then he came back home to get another bomber.

When the final crash came, Frankie was on the job. What happened when he hit the African mountain will never be known. But if the crash could have been avoided,

Frankie would have brought the ship out safely, and himself in it. He had done his duty, that Frankie Cordova, like veterans learn to do it.

I have retold his story to show what I mean about the veteran flying man's place in these flaming times. How old is Doolittle? Forty five? Spencer Punnett, our old Rochester friend, with the RCAF three years now, learned to fly in 1920 at old Curtiss Field, Long Island. General Chennault was a World War flyer. He gave a veteran's cunning to the Flying Tigers over Burma. Col. Edward Peck Curtis of Rochester, chief of staff for Lieut. Gen. Carl Spaetz in the North African theater of war, downed five German planes in the First World War.

There are others whose feats are still unsung, who have flown for the love of flying and the love of freedom… RCAF bomber ferry pilots such as Carl Hickerman, the Arizona school teacher; Ogden Brower, to whom New York's airports were as familiar as his own front lawn; Freddie Cain, the Oklahoma barnstormer; G. Myron Matteson of Arkansas and Harold Hassenflow of Iowa.

Who knows better the value of veterans than the Army Air Force's Ferrying Command? For who are better qualified to fly for that vital division of our armed forces than the men who have made a specialty of cross-country flying, the airline pilots? Many of these veterans of the sky, fairly young in years perhaps, but old in the ways of airplanes, have averaged 1,000 hours a year flying experience, mail and passengers. Under the Ferry Command, theirs is the task of moving vital supplies and men to the front lines. It is a task for which their experience and training have fully equipped them. Experience gained in thousands of hours in the air, of flying blind on instruments, of meeting strict schedules, of keeping multi-motored planes roaring through the night, through gloom and fog, and keeping them on time is invaluable to the Ferry Command. They can handle the job and do it well.

The young man's place is in flying fighter ships and other light, swift-darting craft in the front line skirmishes. It would be foolish to say that many veterans more than 30 years old could last 10 minutes in a dog fight. Aviation has developed to such a peak that fights to the death in the sub-stratosphere are the rule, rather than the exception. Only young reflexes, young bodies can take that kind of punishment.

But we aviation oldsters like to think we have our place, too. And there are dozens of our long-time colleagues, graduates of the World War Jenny days, who have found their places in this war and are winning everlasting glory. No hardy airways veteran needs a crystal ball to forecast the future of aviation. That future is limitless. Using as a scale of progress the strides that science has made in the last 15 years, one might easily foretell the shape of aerial things to come.

Not long ago I heard someone cry outside my hangar office, "Here comes an auto-gyro!" I went back to work, for I had seen countless autogyros. But shouts kept pouring into my room, and there was excitement on the field, so I succumbed to the lure and went to see for myself. Shades of Wilbur Kimball and his 20-propeller helicopter, but it wasn't an autogyro at all! It was a Sikorsky helicopter, the first successful ship of its kind. It landed straight down, like an elevator, and as easily. It could rise straight up and pivot, hang five feet over the ground, sit down without a bounce and without rolling an inch. "Now I've seen everything!" I said to myself. But I knew I hadn't.

Sikorsky had done what Kimball was trying to do back in Morris Park on that November day in 1908. He had succeeded where countless experimenters have failed in all the years between. Sikorsky's ship is something like a glimpse into the future... the peaceful future to be won and made secure by our fighting planes and fighting men in the skyways.

The helicopter may be the answer to the public's enthusiasm for the sky, that eagerness to fly which has grown in this, the airplane's own century, until it hardly knows bounds. It may be the means by which every man, if he so desires, can make his backyard an airport, right next to his garage. For as the automobile developed with gigantic strides in design and construction after the First World War, so the airplane will come into its own after this war. There can be no question of this.

If the ordinary man of tomorrow is going to fulfill his ambition to fly, he will need a plane as nearly foolproof as the ingenuity of science can make it. The answer to this is the helicopter. If aerial transportation and commerce are to develop along the routes being hacked out for them in sky battles and the gigantic battle of supplies today, then the answer lies not in the helicopter, but in the certain development of huge flying boats and land transports.

The Army's B-19, 82 tons of it; the Navy's flying boat, Mars, developed and built by Glenn Martin's marvelous craftsmen, and Lockheed's new super-transport are but forerunners of a vast fleet of skyliners, capable of carrying tremendous cargoes of merchandise and large numbers of passengers to any and every corner of the world.

The mass production of big cargo planes for war purposes is now under way. There is no reason why this should cease when the final battle of the war is won. Who to man this commercial sky fleet, who to pilot the average's man's helicopter? There can be no question of this, either.

For we are training our civilian and commercial pilots, engineers and airways executives of tomorrow in every Army, Navy and Marine flying base in our land. We are guaranteeing them a great potential career, helping them to build the foundations of a thrilling and prosperous future. In our airplane factories, skilled craftsmen are learning new and better ways of construction; inventing geniuses are finding new facts, winning new experimental battles, developing new metals, better motors, new designs, and learning daily the tremendous possibilities of plastic in airplane construction.

Even as the battles rage hourly over the fighting fronts, the struggle of skills is waged in laboratories and shops, over test fields and in wind tunnels. When peace comes, these tremendous forces…the forces of trained energy now upon the science of aviation….cannot cease action and lie dormant. It is inevitable that they carry on. In so doing, they will shape the destiny of aviation, and carry it to boundless heights.

We know now that we may never be able to live alone as a nation again, that our well being and the well being of countless other national units will depend upon free and steady intercourse between and among the nations of the world.

Upon the airplane, as the swiftest means of transportation likely to be devised, will rest a large share of the burden of binding nations by unbreakable ties of friendship and commerce. It will span the oceans, seas and continents, and bring our neighbors nearer to us.

If this was the dream of the Wright Brothers, the vision of Glenn Curtiss, the hope of far-seeing Glenn Martin and countless others in those first and second decades of our amazing century, then the grief, the heartache and the tragedy of those who made the first brave flutterings into the new world of the sky will not have been suffered in vain.

The future of aviation rises as an indestructible monument to those who gave their lives, their fortune and their health, that other men might fly more safely, might span greater distances.

And every good flyer who has ever taken a stick, from John B. Moisant, the young Chicago architect, to Jimmy Doolittle, the bomber of Tokyo, has placed a new stone upon that monument.

Addendum

On August 23, 1974, Russell Holderman was the recipient of Honorary Doctor of Aeronautical Science Degree from Embry Riddle Aeronautical University.

This honor was awarded in recognition of his outstanding career in aviation. It was in 1910, just seven years after the history making twelve second flight of Orville Wright, the first recorded powered flight of an airplane, that Russ Holderman made his first unsuccessful attempt to defy gravity. Three years later in 1913, he completed his first solo flight in a Curtiss pusher biplane. In 1913, Russell Holderman was the youngest pilot in the U.S.A. In 1973, at retirement, Russ Holderman (ATR 227) was the oldest ATR pilot in the country. His motto was, "I don't want to be the most spectacular pilot, just the oldest." His lengthy career, however, was spectacular. He was a stalwart in aviation through sixty years. He served his country, in aviation, through the World Wars, he taught many hundreds of men and women to fly; and achieved success in his chosen field. Stunt pilot, barnstormer, World War I flying instructor, airmail pilot, airport manager, flying school president, Lieutenant-Commander U.S. Naval Reserve, Chief Pilot for the Gannett Newspapers, Past President of the Early Birds, and 1972 inductee of the OX-5 Club Aviation Hall of Fame – a true pioneer.

On April 22, 1976, Embry Riddle Aeronautical University honored Russell Holderman by dedicating a building to him.

Russell Holderman felt strongly about passing on his interest and enthusiasm for aviation, and much of his flying career was devoted to the teaching of aviation and flying to many hundreds of young people.

Presentation of Honorary Doctor of Aeronautical Science degree,
Embry Riddle Aeronautical University, August 23, 1974

There was a young Bronx boy named Russ,
As a bricklayer, he was a "bust".
 So, at last, in despair
 He turned to the air,
And left all his friends in the dust.

As a pilot, he flew without fears,
Respected and loved by his peers.
 His home was the sky;
 He lived just to fly.
His career lasted through sixty years.

He married a Princess, named Dot,
And together they climbed to the top.
 Her presence each day
 Made his work seem like play;
Now, with Dot's help, he's a Doc.

Embry-Riddle, that school of the air
Has so honored Russ; and it seems only fair
 That a man great as he
 A doctor should be;
Dr. Russ H. you've earned this degree.

Legend says Icarus was first in flight,
Then came Bleriot, Farman, and the brothers Wright,
 Rickenbacker, Hall,
 And Albert Ball;
But our own Dr. Russ is the greatest of all.

Daytona Beach, Fla.
August 23, 1974

Written by John Wilbur Holderman and presented to his
brother, Russell Holderman, on this day

Commencement

Program

April 23, 1976

EMBRY RIDDLE AERONAUTICAL UNIVERSITY
Regional Airport
DAYTONA BEACH, FLORIDA 32015

As part of its Golden Anniversary celebration, Embry-Riddle is proud to name three of its campus buildings for outstanding men who are devoted to aviation and have demonstrated their great belief in Embry-Riddle Aeronautical University, the world's leading aviation university.

On Thursday, April 22, the Joseph Goldstein Building and the Russell Holderman Building were dedicated at the Gill Robb Wilson Flight Technology Center.

Immediately following the commencement exercises, the George R. Wallace Building will be dedicated at the Academic Complex.

DR. GEORGE R. WALLACE

Dr. George R. Wallace, of Fitchburg, Massachusetts and Miami Beach, is a member of the National Advisory Council of Embry-Riddle Aeronautical University and holds an honorary Doctor of Aeronautical Engineering Degree from the University.

In December, 1974, he donated $100,000 for the creation of the George R. Wallace Research Center, which uses the campus facilities, staff, faculty and students in its work. Research in the areas of flight safety and training are of special interest to this outstanding industrialist and philanthropist, who built his family business — Fitchburg Paper Company — into a multimillion dollar enterprise through his own personal research efforts.

DR. JOSEPH I. GOLDSTEIN

Dr. Joseph I. Goldstein, Prince Frederick, Maryland, is president and chairman of the Board of Star Enterprises Ltd. and chairman of the Board of Anderson-Stokes Inc., both of Washington. An active aviator, he uses helicopters and an airplane extensively in his business operations, which cover several states.

He is chairman of the Development Committee of the Board of Trustees of Embry-Riddle Aeronautical University and holds an honorary Doctor of Aviation Management from the University.

DR. RUSSELL F. HOLDERMAN

Dr. Russell F. Holderman, one of the world's most honored aviators, made his first solo flight in 1913 and retired in 1973 as the oldest active ATR (Air Transport Rated) pilot in the United States.

He has taught military pilots in both World War I and II, flown and held executive positions with the U. S. Post Office flying service, operated his own passenger flight service, managed an airport, sold airplanes, flown on errands of mercy and won air races. He holds an honorary Doctor of Aeronautical Science from Embry-Riddle Aeronautical University and has been a generous donor of his time and resources on behalf of the University.

DR. RUSSELL F. HOLDERMAN

AVIATION PIONEER WHOSE CAREER, SPANNING 60 YEARS OF
FLYING, INSTRUCTION AND MANAGEMENT BEFORE HE
RETIRED AS THE OLDEST ACTIVE ATR PILOT IN THE U.S., IS
AN INSPIRATION TO STUDENTS AT EMBRY-RIDDLE AERONAUTICAL
UNIVERSITY.

Embry Riddle President, Jack Hunt, and John Wilbur Holderman

COLLECTED PHOTOGRAPHS

Signed photograph of Eddie Stinson, George Haldeman, Jimmie Doolittle,
and Russell Holderman,
LeRoy, 1929

Russell Holderman and Jimmie Doolittle, 1972

Amelia Earhart, January 1929, LeRoy, NY

Rochester Times-Union, Saturday, May 9, 1953
"As Chief Pilot for Gannett Newspapers, Russell Holderman celebrated 40 years in the air. Pictured in his office at the Rochester Airport, he displays the stick and string gadget used to measure air speed in the early days of flying."

THE GANNETTEER

A Monthly Magazine of and for Employes of 22 Gannett Newspapers, 5 Radio Stations; 25th Year, from the Central News Office, 517 Times-Union Building, Rochester 14, N. Y.

July • 1953

RUSSELL F. HOLDERMAN
A SPIRITED AVIATION PIONEER

THIS PLAQUE IS DEDICATED IN TRIBUTE TO HIS 40 YEARS AS A PILOT AND IN RECOGNITION OF HIS CONTRIBUTION TO THE ADVANCEMENT AND PUBLIC ACCEPTANCE OF AIR TRANSPORTATION.

EARLY BIRD: WORLD WAR I FLIGHT INSTRUCTOR: AIR MAIL FLIER: BARNSTORMER: NAVAL RESERVE PILOT AND CHIEF PILOT, THE GANNETT NEWSPAPERS.

JUNE 21, 1953
THIS 50TH YEAR OF AVIATION.

THE HOLDERMAN STORY:

A Dream—A Flight—A Career

By HARRY SCHMECK

Rochester Times-Union Staff Writer

H E WAS 18 years old and weighed 110 pounds.

An "aeroplane" was a contraption that looked like a box kite and "might" fly, if conditions were perfect.

Aviation was 10 years old.

That's the way things were when RUSSELL F. HOLDERMAN, now Gannett Newspapers chief pilot, made his first solo flight.

It was just 40 years ago — early May of 1913 — at Mineola, L. I.

The veteran Rochester airman today is one of that dwindling pioneer band who grew up with aviation.

Living in the Bronx in 1908 he had been a starry-eyed on-looker at the first "aerial exhibition and tournament" of the Aeronautical Society of America. None of the power planes brought there that day got off the ground even though the weather was beautiful, but to 13-year-old Holderman it was all magic.

Holderman was in the very first generation of model airplane builders. Later he built his own full-size glider —which never flew. He broke his collarbone and two ribs after a crash from 40 feet in another glider. This was an early Chanute "hang-type" glider. The "pilot" hung by his arms from the box-kite type frame and controlled the craft's movements by shifting body position.

A FTER learning to fly in 1913, he had to give up flying for four years. His parents considered it too dangerous. They bought him a motorcycle and he took up racing and stunt riding.

World War 1 brought him back to aviation—the way of life he has followed ever since.

Holderman served as an Army fly-ing instructor at the same field on which he first flew. After the war he joined that small band of courageous pilots who first flew the U.S. Air Mail.

Holderman served the air mail as pilot, chief flying mechanic and finally New York terminal manager. In 1920, he bought and rebuilt an old Curtiss Jenny, a World War training plane of the same type he had flown in the service. Shortly afterward he quit the government air mail service and went into business with his new plane, tak-ing passengers on short rides and giving flying instruction.

W HEN he married Dorothy Harris in June 1921, newspapers reported that the young couple were going on the "world's first honeymoon by air-plane." His wife later became one of the world's top woman glider pilots.

The Holdermans flew, sold real estate and airplanes in Florida in the famous land boom there in the '20s. It was there that Holderman took baseball's famous John J. McGraw on his first airplane ride.

In 1928 they moved to Le Roy at the behest of the millionaire Donald Woodward, who sponsored Holder-man in establishing the D.W. Airport there. By the following Spring the D.W. had expanded its facilities to 14 airplanes and its staff to six in-structors.

HOLDERMAN'S newspaper career started in 1934 when he sold Frank Gannett his first airplane and agreed to pilot it on a part-time basis. Hol-derman gave up the Le Roy airport in 1936 and became a full-time news-paper pilot.

With photographers and reporters from *The Times-Union* and *The Democrat and Chronicle*, Holderman has helped report some of the biggest news stories in the East by air.

He has visited almost every city in the Group, repeatedly.

He has covered floods, fires, air-plane crashes, wrecks. He flew to New England to bring out photo-graphs of the disastrous 1937 hurri-cane. Later he escorted 'Wrong Way' Corrigan across the skies of New York State after Corrigan's famous transoceanic flight in a small plane.

He has piloted Gannett airplanes on errands of mercy, delivering medical supplies and bringing the desperately ill to hospitals.

In 1940 he took time off to enter a New York to Miami passenger plane race and entered another 25-mile pylon race while he was in Florida. Holderman brought back to Rochester $2,500 in prize money and a gold trophy. He lost the first race by 36 seconds and won the second.

In World War 2 he flew light, un-armed airplanes along the Atlantic Coast on submarine hunts with the Civil Air Patrol. He has held a com-mission as lieutenant-commander in the U.S. Naval Reserve since the mid-30s.

Today Holderman is one of the few surviving members of the Early Birds, an organization of pilots who soloed before 1916. He is probably the only one to hold a Civil Aeronautics Authority instrument rating.

This Spring and Summer, Sperry Gyroscope Company is honoring Hol-derman on his 40th year of flying by using his photograph in advertise-ments in leading aviation and business magazines.

Now beginning his 41st year of fly-ing, the veteran aviator has no thought of quitting the air. To him, America's destiny is in the skies. While he is able, Holderman will stay a part of that destiny.

His motto, he says, is "I don't want to be the most spectacular pilot, just the oldest."

OX5 NEWS

Published by and for Members of the OX5 Club of America

Subscription Price: $1.00 per year

FEBRUARY 1971   Volume 13 — Number 1

RUSSELL F. HOLDERMAN

RUSSELL F. HOLDERMAN

A quick glance at the material in the Personal File of Russell Holderman, our member No. 175, establishes the fact that here is a really great "Aviation Pioneer." There are newspaper clippings and pictures by the dozen, and several magazine articles that are fully illustrated.

The flying bug bit Russ when he was a high school boy in the Bronx in 1912. He got his first big flying thrill when he saw Wilbur Wright fly up the Hudson River. A neighbor, Fred Schneider, really started him on his career. He built his own plane and would take Russ to Mineola where he ran a flying school. He gave Russ his first lessons, and in 1913 Russ made his first solo flight.

When America entered World War I, Russ promptly enlisted and asked for an assignment as pilot. He was turned down for underweight, but was appointed an instructor at Mineola where he taught many other men to fly.

After the war, Russ enrolled with the U.S. Post Office Flying Service, starting as a mechanic, moving up to pilot, and later becoming manager of the New York Terminal. When the government discontinued flying the mail, Holderman left the service and purchased an old plane which he overhauled and operated his own passenger flight service around Long Island. In the winter he flew to Miami where he carried on a flight business and where he met Donald Woodward, who was to play such an important part in his future.

Holderman's wife, Dorothy, also a flying enthusiast and a sales agent for airplanes, met Woodward, who finally agreed to buy a plane if she could get him a pilot. That was easy — she sold Woodward a package deal — a plane and her husband.

This was a big turning point in Russ's career because it brought him into the Rochester area and put him in touch with Frank E. Gannett. Woodward brought Holderman back to his home in LeRoy in 1928 and made him manager and chief pilot of the Donald Woodward Airport. Russ had taken on the agency for Stinson planes and in 1934 sold one to Mr. Gannett who agreed to purchase it if Holderman would fly it. Holderman took the job on a part time basis until 1936 when he gave up his LeRoy job and became a full-time Gannett flier. In the years since that date, he has had many memorable trips, errands of mercy, hazardous newspaper flights to crashes and wrecks, and one race from New York to Miami which he lost by 36 seconds. He won a second feature race, along with $2,500 and a gold trophy.

Prior to World War II, Russ enlisted in the Naval Reserve and during that conflict he ran a school for Navy pilots in Rochester, thereby serving his country in both wars.

Of the many plaques and trophies that attest to the fame of Holderman there are two that are his prized possessions. One is the Legion of Merit Plaque presented to him at one of the first pilgrimages of the OX5 Club members to the Glenn Curtiss Museum at Hammondsport in 1964, and the other is a plaque presented to him in 1963 by the Early Birds, marking the 50th anniversary of his solo flight. Russ served as President of the Early Birds, an honor that he looks back on as one of the highlights of his career.

Russ was elected to the National Board of Governors of the OX5 Club at the last election, to serve for a three year term. This is not the first time Russ was so elected. He served as a National Governor when the OX5 Club was first organized and also served as Vice President. In addition to his National Board activities, he is a member of the Committee for the OX5 Club of America Aviation Hall of Fame.

Profile of a Man Who is Still Up in the Air

By Arthur P. Kelly

"In less than eight more years I'll finish my first half century of flying," says Russell F. Holderman, Rochester's No. 1 aviator. "That is," he adds, "unless I get hit by a truck or slip on an icy sidewalk!"

"Russ" anticipates no flying accidents to cut short his career but he does worry about other hazards.

Only a few weeks ago, at a gathering of Air Mail Pioneers on Long Island, Grover Loening, an oldtime flier, told the group that the most marvelous achievement in all fields of transportation was the development of aviation from flights in freight crates to trans-ocean journeys in luxury liners via the safest of all travel methods — aviation. Holderman agrees emphatically with this appraisal.

First Big Thrill

"Russ" Holderman was born in Buffalo in 1895 but his family moved from there to the Bronx when he was only six months old. He grew up in that New York area where he attended grade and high schools. He was more interested in flying than in studies, however, and left high school for a job with a man who was building his own plane and who taught him to fly. "Russ" got his first big flying thrill when he saw Wilbur Wright fly up the Hudson River from the Battery. His own first flying experience came through a glider, but that was simply hopping off the top of a hill and soaring a few feet to the bottom.

The man who really started Holderman on his career was Fred Schneider, who lived in the neighborhood and who built his own plane which he overhauled and operated in an empty store. He gave Holderman scraps of wood which they used to build model planes. Schneider took Holderman with him to Mineola on Long Island, where he ran a flying school and gave "Russ" his first lessons. That was in early 1913 and two years later Holderman became a mechanic at the field and thereby got a thorough training in aeronautical science. The boy made his first solo flight in May 1913 and his employer wanted to take him on a tour of the country, making exhibition flights as the world's youngest aviator. Holderman's parents objected and because he was not yet 18 years old, he had to forgo that experience. He did "sneak" in a few flights at Mineola, however.

When America entered World War I in 1917 Holderman promptly enlisted and asked for an assignment as pilot. He was turned down for underweight but was appointed an instructor at Mineola where he taught many other men to fly. During the war he made many flights around the country in the promotion of Liberty Loan campaign.

Operated Own Service

After the war Holderman enrolled with the U.S. Postoffice Flying Service, starting as a mechanic, moving up to pilot and later becoming manager of the New York Terminal.

When the government discontinued flying the mail Holderman left that service and purchased an old plane which he overhauled and operated his own passenger flight service around Long Island. In the winter he flew to Miami, where he carried on a flight business and where he met Donald Woodward, who was to play such an important part in his future.

Holderman's wife, Dorothy, also a flying enthusiast and a sales agent for airplanes, met Woodward and she finally got him to agree to buy a plane if she would also get him a pilot. That was easy for Mrs. Holderman. She sold Woodward a package deal — a plane and her husband.

This was a big turning point in Holderman's career because it brought him into this area and eventually put him in touch with Frank E. Gannett. Woodward brought Holderman back to his home in LeRoy in 1928 and made him manager and chief pilot of the Donald Woodward Airport, then the finest small airport in the country. There "Russ" was in charge of 14 planes and six instructors and he remained in LeRoy until 1936. He had taken on the agency for Stinson planes and in 1934 sold one to Mr. Gannett who agreed to purchase it if Holderman would fly it. Holderman took the job on a part-time basis until 1936 when he gave up his LeRoy job and became a full-time Gannett flier. In the years since that date he has had many memorable trips — errands of mercy, hazardous newspaper flights to crashes and wrecks and one race from New York to Miami which he lost by 36 seconds. He won a second feature race, along with $2,500 and a gold trophy.

Ran 'School For Pilots'

Prior to World War II Holderman enlisted in the Naval Reserve and during that conflict he ran a school for navy pilots here in Rochester, thereby serving his country in both wars.

One of Holderman's proudest records is his place among the Early Birds of aviation — men who flew planes before December 1916. "Russ" is one of only three Early Birds who are still active fliers and are some eight of these now operating in this territory and the number will grow. Executive planes, according to Holderman, now fly more miles annually in this country than all the commercial airlines.

His fortieth anniversary in the air was observed two years ago by the presentation of an honor award by Fred Lee, head of the U. S. Civil Aeronautic Authority, the first such award ever given. Now he has only eight years to go to hit the fiftieth anniversary, and, as he states in the opening paragraph of this article, he is sure that through the help of the Lord and avoidance of street traffic perils, he will make it.

Holderman has flown about three million miles in his career to date. The highest he has ever flown, strangely enough, was in one of the antiquated crates he flew during World War I and in which he soared to 24,500 feet.

Holderman has never had any particular desire to be a daring exhibitionist. "I don't want to be the most daring or the best pilot," he says, "I just want to be the oldest."

"Russ" sees a steadily increasing use of "executive" planes — airships used by industry and business.

Praise For Airport

Holderman is particularly enthusiastic over the new Monroe County Airport. "It is without doubt the finest in this country for any city of comparative size," he asserts. He gives Frank Gannett credit for much of the development of aviation in this area, not only through his own business but for his efforts to promote the enlargement of the Rochester airport and the fine new administration building which was dedicated two years ago and on which occasion a special bronze tablet honoring Holderman's achievements was set permanently into the wall.

Today "Russ" Holderman has his headquarters at the old airport on the Scottsville Road, where he still actively carries out whatever flying assignments the Gannett newspapers may hand him. He had a new thrill a few weeks ago when he flew his first jet from Rochester to Westchester.

"Fifteen years ago," says "Russ" reflectively, "if somebody had told me that planes would be flying regular schedules across the ocean at 400 miles per hour I would have smiled at such idle dreaming. Now I'm ready to believe that air travel can accomplish anything — even a flight to the moon. There is no field of transportation which has achieved so much in such a short span of years and its future is limitless. I'm thrilled to have had some small part in it."

BILLY GRAHAM
November 2, 1957

Mr. Russ Holderman
Pilot for Gannett Newspapers
Rochester Airport
Rochester, New York

Dear Russ:

Just a note to thank you for the
wonderful trip from Rochester to
Newark last Tuesday.

You are a terrific pilot and a
wonderful guy.

Cordially yours,

Billy

BG:L

August 30, 1957

Dear Russ:

      This is just a note to thank you for your letter of August 13 enclosing the pictures which were taken after our flight from Washington to Rochester.

      I have copies of them which Carl Hallauer sent to me and it was a pleasure to autograph them for you.

      I certainly enjoyed my weekend and hope that we will have another chance to have a game of golf before too long.

      With kindest personal regards,

      Sincerely,

      Richard Nixon

Lieutenant Commander Russell Holderman
Municipal Airport
Rochester, New York

Russel Holderman, pilot (right front) taking baseball immortal, John McGraw (left front) on Mr. McGraw's first flight, 1925. San Leon Studios, Sarasota, FL

Russell and Dot Holderman, Roscoe Turner (New York to Los Angeles record holder, 1930), Jacqueline Cochran (war-time head of the WASPs and first woman to break the sonic barrier, 1953), and Frank Gannett

Russ Holderman, Highland Benefactor Was Courageous Aviator, 'Early Bird'

Russell F. Holderman became a friend of Highland Hospital through his friendship with Dr. John R. Williams, Sr. over 40 years ago. (Dr. Williams established the first clinical laboratory in a private hospital at Highland and served on the staff here for over 30 years. He was also the first physician in the United States to administer insulin to a diabetic patient.) Mr. Holderman remained a friend of Highland and last year established a residuary trust of $100,000 to be used for construction of a new John R. Williams, Sr. Health Sciences Library.

Russ Holderman was a special man. His accomplishments were so great that when a Democrat and Chronicle writer attempted in 1947 to write a story about him, he had to divide it into three parts, running on consecutive Sundays as a special feature on "Half a Lifetime in the Clouds!"

Fred Rollins, Associate Curator of History at the Rochester Museum and Science Center, delivered a eulogy for Mr. Holderman at his funeral on May 28th. Rollins has had the privilege of re-living some of Mr. Holderman's experiences with him through gathering material for the Oral History Program for the Museum and could therefore share the uniqueness of the man:

"I only knew Russ Holderman in the twilight of his life, through our Oral History Program of tape recording prominent contributors to Rochester's past. Even so, I felt I had gotten to know Russ very well. As we talked about the highlights of his fascinating career, his great vitality and enjoyment of life itself stood out clearly despite the poor health of his later years. I really felt as if I was there as he recounted the many milestones and achievements throughout his life.

"In addition to his vitality and zest for life, other characteristics struck me about this great man. One was his tremendous drive and determination which he maintained throughout his life, and another was his kindness and warmth. Hand in hand with these was his pride in being an Early Bird - a group of America's true pioneers who had their maiden solo flight before World War I. Last but not least, Russ was also a man of great courage.

"A number of incidents and events stand out in my mind when I think of Russ - events that revealed what a great man he truly was. First and foremost was his initial solo airplane flight in 1913 at the young age of 18, a feat of great courage accomplished less than a decade after the Wright brothers flew at Kitty Hawk in 1903. When Russ recounted to me that May day before World War I, his eyes brightened and he became very excited. I re-lived with him his taxiing on the runway, the "grass cutting", as it was called, and his trousers flapping in the wind as his plane first left the ground. For Russ, flying was a special kind of freedom. That first flight was, indeed, for him, 30 seconds in the air, and 30 seconds in Heaven! Shortly thereafter, Russ become the youngest pilot in America despite his parents' misgivings. In fact, it was not long thereafter that Russ's parents bought him a motorcycle - in a vain attempt to ground him.

"Just three years before his first solo flight, Russ attended the famous Morris Park Air Meet in New York in 1910. Although none of the planes got off the ground that day, Russ saw Orville Wright there and looked up at him, to use his words, "as if he were a God". Kindled within Russ at that time was the drive and determination to fly - which would ultimately become his life's work.

"In 1917, with America's entrance into World War I, Russ wanted very badly to join the Army. He was, however, underweight and was rejected for military service. he did not let this daunt him, however, and on his third try, weighted down with peanuts, bananas, heavy cream, and a gallon of water, he was sworn into the Army. Thus throughout the war, Russ was able to pursue his love of flying by being an Army flight instructor.

"After the War, Russ's courage and determination were again evident, as he become one of a small band of pioneer Air Mail pilots. Those were indeed difficult days for the pilots who flew mail most of the time by the seat of their pants. Crashes were commonplace at Newark's tiny Heller Airfield - although Russ never had an accident. Russ was always very concerned for safety in flying - and never flew in bad weather. As a result, in all his years of flight and millions of miles in the sky, he only suffered injury once - and that was during his early glider days before World War I. I remember vividly his telling me about those early Air Mail days and the narrow field at Newark - just as if it happened yesterday.

"At every interview session, Russ made sure to mention his wife Dorothy, or Dot, a great flier in her own right. Dot become his inspiration, his advisor, his companion. In June 1921, Russ and Dot took off for the first ever recorded honeymoon in the air. Dot was to become one of the top women glider pilots and eventually established a sustained glider flight record. Russ said of Dot that, "If she hadn't become my wife, I would probably not have ended up flying. My mother had always told me that I needed someone to take me by the hand. In all these years, Dorothy has done that. I have left some of the most difficult decisions of my dangerous business up to her, and she has never failed me." In 1920, Russ's Jenny sprouted the name of Dorothy - a women that played a very important role in Russ's life for 60 years.

"But the most poignant moment of our interviewing sessions came when we discussed Frank Gannett. Russ was chief pilot for the Gannett Company from 1934 until his retirement. This meant covering many dramatic news events such as the New England hurricane of 1937, or searching and finding a missing airplane in the Adirondacks in the Winter of 1935. But Russ became the most animated when we discussed Frank Gannett and his bid for the Republican Presidential Nomination in 1940. Here, Russ exhibited a fierce and proud loyalty to the man who was his boss for a quarter of a century.

"Although, as he told me, he knew Gannett wasn't going to win, he stood by him and never mentioned his misgivings about the race. From January to June 1940, Russ flew his boss 55,000 miles around the country in a vain attempt to secure the nomination. He called Gannett "one of the greatest guys I ever met...the nicest, most honest man in the world". Gannett, he said, measured wealth in the true friends he had, which was also true of Russ himself.

"Yes, Russ was indeed one of our outstanding aviation pioneers, and a friend of many of the other great aviation figures such as Charles Lindbergh, Amelia Earhart and Eddie Rickenbacher. He was an Early Bird, World War I flight instructor, Air Mail pilot, naval reserve pilot, chief pilot for the Gannett Newspapers, head of the Flying School at LeRoy and seller of Real Estate by air in Florida.

"He also made many contributions to the advancement and public acceptance of air transportation. In addition, he has received many honors, including an honorary doctorate in Aeronautical Science from Embry Riddle Aeronautical University in Daytona Beach, Florida, selection for the Aviation Hall of Fame, the Legion of Merit from the OX-5 Aviation Pioneers, an Early Bird plaque, and was named a fellow of the Rochester Museum in 1943.

"But beyond these achievements, Russ was a man of vitality, spirit, courage, drive, and determination, as well as a man of kindness, warmth, loyalty, pride and vision."

Lt. Commander Russell Holderman, U.S.N.R.
began flying in 1913. Army aviator during
World War—Now Chief Pilot, Gannett Newspaper planes.

FOR SCIENTIFIC, COMFORTABLE GLARE PROTECTIO

"I consider RAY-BANS the ideal lenses
for flying. They not only increase visibility and sharpen the horizon, but give
100% protection against eye strain.
I am glad to recommend RAY-BANS."

BAUSCH & LOMB

Ray-Ban

ANTI-GLARE
SUN GOGGLES

MADE TO U.S. AIR SERVICE STANDARDS

Time-Saver FOR EXECUTIVES

Fast-Thinker FOR PILOTS

■ Sperry's Zero Reader* Flight Director is a "fast-thinking" calculator that saves valuable time for busy executives and relieves pilots of complex mental calculations. That's why more and more progressive corporations — large and small — are equipping their Executive Aircraft with this versatile instrument.

■ The Flight Director not only is used for en route flying but makes the difficult task of manual approaches on Instrument Landing Systems a routine procedure. Thus, business men are assured of keeping appointments even in rough weather.

■ The Flight Director utilizes attitude, altitude, heading and radio path signals and combines this information on a simple, two-element indicator. The pilot simply flies "zero," using the same instrument whether he is leisurely cruising or making landing approaches. This simplified manual control reduces pilot fatigue and permits the pilot to devote more time to other duties.

■ Sperry's Zero Reader Flight Director is widely specified for military and passenger planes as well as for Executive Aircraft. Our nearest district office will be glad to give you complete details.

*T. M. REG., U.S. PAT. OFF.

N.B.C.
FRANK BLAIR

RUSS
WINGS CLUB

Representative companies using Sperry Zero Reader Flight Director:

AVCO MANUFACTURING CORP.
BETHLEHEM STEEL CO.
BRIGGS MANUFACTURING CO.
CELANESE CORPORATION
   OF AMERICA
ESSO SHIPPING CO.
GENERAL MILLS, INC.
GREAT LAKES CARBON CORP.
HERCULES POWDER CO.
NATIONAL DAIRY
   PRODUCTS CORP.
PHILLIPS PETROLEUM CO.
TENNESSEE GAS
   TRANSMISSION CO.
TEXAS EASTERN
   TRANSMISSION CORP.

Cmdr. Russell Holderman of the Gannett Newspapers, who is celebrating his 40th year as a pilot, is one of the enthusiastic users of the Sperry Zero Reader Flight Director.

SPERRY GYROSCOPE COMPANY
DIVISION OF THE SPERRY CORPORATION

GREAT NECK, NEW YORK · CLEVELAND · NEW ORLEANS · BROOKLYN · LOS ANGELES · SEATTLE · SAN FRANCISCO
IN CANADA · SPERRY GYROSCOPE COMPANY OF CANADA, LIMITED, MONTREAL, QUEBEC

Executive Aircraft
Fly with Sperry Equipment
1922

ground which feeds the guiding signals into the gyropilot has a radius of about 50 miles from the airport, and has a glide path that is clear of all obstacles. The system is now used by all major airports in this country.

Rus Holderman is one of the many old-time pilots who are enthusiastic supporters of such new devices as the Gyrosyn Compass, A-12 Gyropilot and Zero Reader. By the end of this month, he will have flown for 37 years, having soloed for the first time in 1913. He says that his first "instrument" was a piece of string with a plumb bob on the end of it. When Holderman first began to assemble the piano-wired "crates" he used to fly in back in the early days-- he is a member of the Early Birds, an organization of aviation pioneers -- he made the classic remark that "when the plane was finished they would put a bird in it, and if the bird flew out, they knew they had forgotten one of the wires."

A-12 GYROPILOT PRAISED
BY RUSSELL HOLDERMAN

Gannett Newspapers recently printed a feature article quoting Rus Holderman, their chief pilot, on the subject of the automatic pilot. Gannett's executive plane, a lockheed Lodestar, has an A-12 Gyropilot, and an order has just been received for a Zero Reader for the same plane. In his article Holderman called attention to a CAA DC-3 which has made 1,200 automatic approaches (using the A-12 with Automatic Approach Control) without a miss. He added that since its installation in the Gannett executive plane last summer, he had made 50 approaches under poor visibility and low ceilings without difficulty with the A-12. The instrument landing system on the

Pilot Russell Holderman with Gannett Newspapers' Lockheed Lodestar. This plane is equipped with an A-12 Gyropilot with Automatic Approach Control, and is to be fitted also with a Zero Reader.

"THE NEXT THING TO FLYING IS DRIVING AN OLDS HYDRA-MATIC!"

Says Lieut.-Commander **RUSSELL HOLDERMAN,** U. S. N. R.

Lieut.-Commander Russell Holderman, U.S.N.R., of Rochester, is pictured at the wheel of his new 1941 Oldsmobile Hydra-Matic Club Cabriolet. In the background is the Gannett Newspapers Plane which he pilots. Holderman, who has covered over two million miles in his 29 years of flying, praises his "no clutch, no shift" Olds Hydra-Matic® "Sky High." He says: "It's The Next Thing To Flying."

*Hydra-Matic Drive optional at extra cost on all Oldsmobile models.

Try A "Flying Ride" Yourself...See Your Olds Dealer

In a photo dating from the 1940s, Holderman sits in cockpit
... "I never wanted to be the best, just the oldest" airplane pilot, he said.

Only the air holds Holderman up as he sails along in glider
... photo was taken in 1939. Flying "felt like being freed," the pilot said

Russell Holderman dead at 86; 'never stopped flying'

By DENA BUNIS
D&C Staff Writer

Russell Holderman's pilot license, number 227, was signed by Orville Wright in 1925, 13 years after he had made his first flight in a glider.

Holderman, whose career spanned from the infancy of aviation to the corporate jet, died yesterday of cancer at his Brighton home. He was 86.

"I never wanted to be the best, just the oldest" pilot, Holderman once said.

"It felt wonderful," Holderman said of a 1913 flight he made in a powered Curtiss biplane. The flight lasted a few minutes and covered 200 yards.

"It felt like I had had lead shoes and like I was kicking them away, kicking the earth away. It was like being freed," he said.

As the early gliders and biplanes gave way to propellers and jets, Holderman's career included stints as a stunt pilot, early air mail pilot, World War I and World War II flying instructor, flying school and airport manager in Le Roy and chief pilot for Gannett Co. for 26 years.

Turn to HOLDERMAN, Page 3B

Russell Holderman as a boy
... he made his first flight at 17

From Page 1B

"I don't think he ever really stopped flying. He may not have been at the controls in recent years but I don't think I ever saw him when he wasn't talking flying. Like a little kid he would drool over the new planes," said Jack Gallagher, Gannett's chief pilot.

Holderman dropped out of high school in the Bronx so he could fly. He said he "wasn't interested in geometry and all that."

After learning to fly, Holderman gave it up because his parents considered it too dangerous. They bought him a motorcycle and he began racing and stunt riding.

He went back to aviation as an instructor during World War I and never left.

After marrying his wife Dorothy in 1921, he flew and sold real estate and airplanes in Florida during the land boom there.

In 1928 he moved to Le Roy at the request of millionaire Jello magnate Donald Woodward who asked Holderman to establish an airport there.

While working at the Le Roy airport, Holderman met Frank Gannett, founder of Gannett Co. Inc. He sold Gannett his first plane in 1934 and piloted it on a part-time basis. Two years later he left the Le Roy airport and worked full time for Gannett until he retired in 1959.

"He was my father's greatest friend," said Sally Gannett McAdam, daughter of Frank Gannett.

"My father would never have gone in an airplane

if it hadn't been for Russ. He was the safest pilot I have ever known. He never flew in bad weather, never took chances," Mrs. McAdam said.

Paul Miller, chairman of the executive committee of Gannett Co. Inc., said, "He remained a loyal and trusted friend. A colorful figure, he was well known and active in national aviation circles."

Holderman was a member of the Early Birds, pilots who soloed before Dec. 17, 1916. His name is inscribed on a bronze plaque with other pioneer aviators that hangs in the Smithsonian Institution.

In 1970, he was named to the Aviation Hall of Fame.

In 1940 he won the Curtiss Trophy for averaging 198 miles an hour in the then-annual 25-mile air race in Miami. He held a world's loop record for a glider and received the Legion of Merit award from the OX-5 Aviation Pioneers.

Holderman received an honorary doctorate in aeronautical science from the Embry-Riddle Aeronautical University in Daytona Beach, Fla. in 1974.

While a stunt pilot, he flew a plane for a man who would switch from an automobile to the plane, grasping onto the wing skid, a metal loop near the tip of the wing.

The man then walked along the wings. At the show, they'd pass the hat for their earnings.

But Holderman, a friend of such pioneers as Eddie Rickenbacker and Charles Lindbergh, was not a true daredevil.

In 1928, a year after Charles Lindbergh's dramatic flight, he was offered $25,000 to fly the Atlantic. But, he said, "I couldn't see the percentage."

Gallagher called Holderman one of the leaders of corporate aviation.

"He had a desire to put corporate aviation on the map," Gallagher said, adding Holderman never had any interest in being a commercial pilot.

After his retirement from Gannett, Holderman operated the Holderman Air Service, buying and selling airplanes. He also was a consultant to Page Airways.

His only injury during his flying career — which totaled 260,000 hours in the air when he retired — came in one of his early glider flights.

Holderman said he cracked up when he came down too steeply in the glider. He broke his collarbone and three ribs.

He credited a man named Fred Schneider for giving him the chance to solo in a motor-driven plane in 1913. He'd met Schneider when he was building model planes.

"This man Schneider decided to teach me to fly. I used to help him gas up the plane. I got so professional at taxiing up to the runway, he decided to let me solo. He did, and I was the youngest pilot in America," Holderman said in 1974.

Holderman's Brighton home is filled with flying memorabilia including a chair from one of Amelia Earhart's planes and pictures of him with presidents, celebrities and famous flyers.

Dorothy Holderman, ex-glider pilot

Dorothy C. Holderman, who once held the women's world record for sustained glider flight, died Monday night, according to a family friend.

Mrs. Holderman, 81, was an active glider pilot in the 1930s but in recent years had suffered from ill health, said Edmund Case, a friend of the family. The cause of death was not available.

Her husband, Russell Holderman, who had been flying since 1912 and was the chief pilot for Gannett Co. Inc. for 26 years, died May 25.

Mrs. Holderman set her first record Aug. 12, 1931, in a 46-minute flight near Elmira. Her flight surpassed the former record by 20 minutes and qualified her for a Class B glider license for flights of more than 10 minutes.

In the next five years, Mrs. Holderman continued to improve her gliding ability and on June 29, 1934, she shattered her own record by staying aloft four hours and 21 minutes.

But she relinquished the record July 13, 1935, when Mrs. Richard C. du Pont of Wilmington, Del., flew her glider five hours and 31 minutes. On the same day, Mrs. Holderman glided for five hours and three minutes.

In a July 1938 newspaper article, Mrs. Holderman described becoming a glider pilot.

"I went out to the field to get my picture taken and became a glider pilot instead," she

obituaries

wrote. "They had to argue me into it quite some, but I can say now that I'm glad they won. I've had a thousand thrills and a thousand enjoyments. I've soared for records — and made them too — and I've soared just for the sweeping, swooping excitement of it. I've been so scared I actually couldn't see, and I've had so much fun that I couldn't talk about it."

Case said the Holdermans had no children. Mrs. Holderman is survived by a niece and a nephew in California.